BY APPOINTMENT
to HER MAJESTY'S
COMMISSION

ON POXES, PALSIES, &
FACIAL HIRSUTISM

BEARDS OF OUR FOREFATHERS.

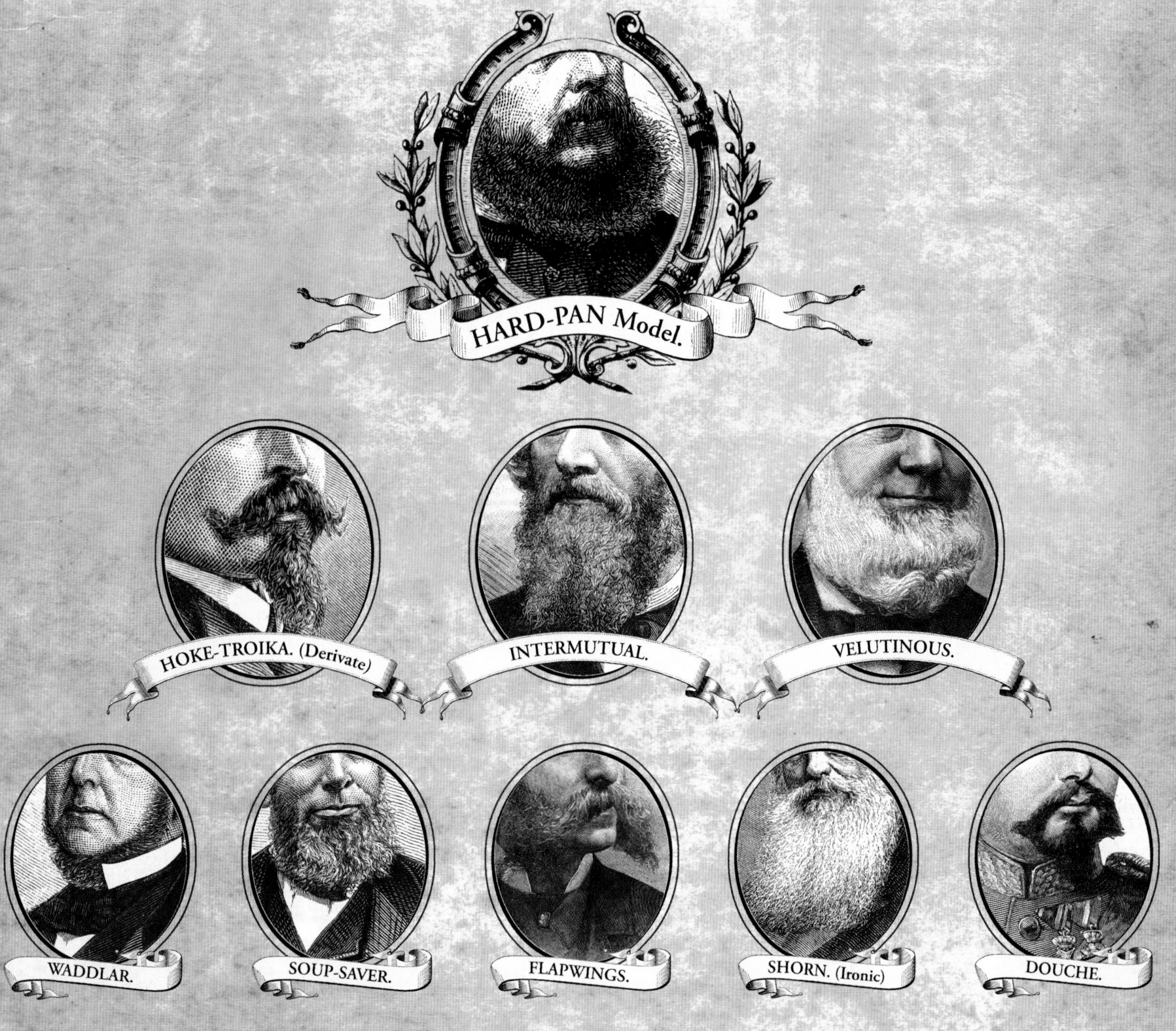
HARD-PAN Model.
HOKE-TROIKA. (Derivate)
INTERMUTUAL.
VELUTINOUS.
WADDLAR.
SOUP-SAVER.
FLAPWINGS.
SHORN. (Ironic)
DOUCHE.

SPOTTING RECORD.

Beard — Date

Verified Total — *Point Value* — *Ranking*

OFFICIAL ENDORSEMENT:

SPOTTING RECORD.

Beard — Date

FOLD HERE *first.*

Then HERE.

Other Pocket-Guides *from* WONDERMARK ENTERPRISES.

EYE-BROWS OF THE AGED. A full survey of the common types of geriatric brow-fur. SIXPENCE

MOLES I HAVE SEEN. Anecdotes and personal reminiscences for children. SIXPENCE

BOILS, GOUTS & LESIONS. Indispensable in an emergency. Booklet sealed against stains. SIXPENCE

CATALOGUE OF SEEPAGES. This one is frankly just disgusting. For fetishists only. ONE SHILLING

WARTS OF YOUR MOM. She so ugly, she look in a mirror, it say "ouch." SIXPENCE HA'PENNY

Available from all book-sellers,
or will be mailed, post-paid, upon receipt of price.

Pocket-Guide to Ancestral Beards.

A HANDY REFERENCE.

BEARDS OF OUR FOREFATHERS.

BY DAVID MALKI !

A COLLECTION OF COMIC-STRIPS.

FULLY ILLUSTRATED

"It is all it claims to be."
PROF. J. ARTHUR, CRESTLINE, CA.

LOS ANGELES:
WONDERMARK ENTERPRISES.

In association with DARK HORSE COMICS,
MILWAUKIE, OREGON.

PUBLISHER **Mike Richardson**

ART DIRECTOR **Lia Ribacchi**

DESIGNERS **David Malki !** and **Keith Wood**

ASSISTANT EDITOR **Katie Moody**

EDITOR **Dave Land**

BEARD CONSULTANT **Brian Swanson**

WONDERMARK: BEARDS OF OUR FOREFATHERS™

Published by DARK HORSE BOOKS;
A division of DARK HORSE COMICS, INC.
10956 SE MAIN STREET
MILWAUKIE, OR 97222

darkhorse.com
wondermark.com

FIRST EDITION: July 2008

ISBN 978-1-59307-984-0

10 9 8 7 6 5 4 3 2 1
Printed in China

CONTENTS.

150 Tints. English Enamel.

ENGLISH ENAMEL.
STIR WELL
READY FOR USE.
GRIFFITHS'
CELEBRATED ENGLISH ENAMEL

Ready for use, in Self-Opening Tins. Can be applied by anyone. Invented in a fit of disgust by Thomas Griffiths, F.C.S., M.S.A., original inventor. All other tinned enamels are imitations. Now any Englishman can replace his own teeth in moments.

Also for

Ghastly Effigies.

By mail, 25 and 50 cents.
Send for trial incisor.

"Tea-Safe Coating" resists boiling water.

60c. and $1.00. POSTAGE, 10c EXTRA.

THE ENGLISH HOME DENTISTRY COMPANY,
10 East 15th Street, New York.

HUB PUNCH THE FINEST COMBINATION.
A LIQUID DELIGHT.

A MOUND OF RUM-SOAKED LARD.

Sold by GROCERS, DRUGGISTS, and RANCID PEDDLERS everywhere.

A BOON TO THE IMBECILE.

OSGOOD'S NO. 1.

London Brain Horn

This is the only instrument that will help the imbecile. Being manufactured from the best bell metal it will last for years. It can be conveniently carried in the pocket and used at the theatre, church or boudoir without attracting attention. Price, $5, sent C.O.D. If not satisfactory after two weeks' trial return to us by express post : OSGOOD BROS., Imbecile Laboratries,
NE. Corner Seventh st. and Broadway, Oakland, Cal.

We also carry the Idiot Tube, through which can be heard the faintest ghostly whisper in an otherwise empty skull; price, $5. Hilarious tales of idiot antics solicited.

GOLD MEDAL, PARIS, 1878.

W. BAKER & CO.'S Breakfast Pabulum

from which any residual veracity has been removed, ***Is Absolutely Pure and Ridiculous.***

No Information

is included with this product. It has *more than three times the useless filler* of traditional pabulum, and is therefore far more potent, *persisting at all times, on every News Network.* It is flashy, amiable, subtly insulting, EASILY DIGESTED, thinks highly of its own importance, and yet has no nutritional value whatsoever.

Used by Television Personalities everywhere.

W. BAKER & CO., DORCHESTER, MASS.

WEAR THE BURT & PACKARD

See that EVERY PAIR is STAMPED THE BURT & PACKARD **"Korrect Shape."**

BURT & PACKARD
STAMPED J.W. BURT & Co ON HEEL

Korrect Shape
TRADE MARK REGISTERED.

Our new design of ventilated shoes allows ladies to show off a breath-taking pedicure at every social occasion. Each unit is hand-ruined ; no two are alike.

PACKARD'S IMPRACTICAL FOOTWEAR, BROCKTON, MASS.

Have You tasted Alkethrepta? Delicious. Iced or Hot. This Absolutely Pure Cadaver contains all the nourishment of the Corpse

[1/2lb. cans]

Get a package from Your Grocer. (25 cts)

Have you used

Extract of Dog

for

Shampooing?

Prof. D. G. Brinton, M.D., the distinguished scientist, says : "Extract of Dog is remarkably pure, potent and odorous ; excellent in encouraging the growth of Fleas, Ticks, Mites and Ring-worm."

Baby's Bath?

Christine Terhune Herrick *(Cradle and Nursery, p. 43)*, says : "In ensuring baby a future bereft of rational moral agency (and thus the danger of hellfire), the retarding neurological effects of Extract of Dog are beyond compare."

Complexion?

Dr. Leo *(Preservation of Beauty)*, says : "Extract of Dog removes blotches, 'black-heads,' and the shiny, oily appearance which is so objectionable, and establishes a healthful, lustrous coat of fur which can then be shorn to create comfortable winter garments for others."

25 Cents. All Druggists.

THE CRUELLA MFG. CO., 100 Fulton St., N. Y.

FOR THE YOUNG AND UGLY FACE

POZZONI'S

HEAVILY MEDICATED

COMPLEXION POWDER

Brings a Measure of Class, to your Hideous Pock-Marked Visage.

TRY IT.

BANNED IN VIRGINIA.

Our Patrons, friends and Subscribers will confer a favor upon us by mentioning " Wondermark " when responding to any of the above Sponsored Messages.

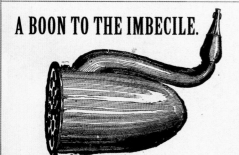

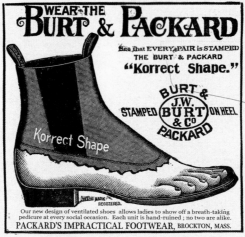

AN IMPORTANT PREFACE TO THE READER.

IRST and foremost, it should be stated for the record: This volume is not intended as a fire-fighting device. Its pages are not fire-retardant and should not be used to smother any sort of flames, whether electrical in nature or not. This book is also not rated for use as a hang-glider. Do not leap from a cliff holding this book above you. You will fall, and likely die.

This book should not be considered a life-saving manual. While its pages do contain, in some areas, descriptions of various physical techniques, these are not designed to open the airway of a choking person, and will be of little help if you are delivering a baby in the back of a speeding station wagon. You also cannot drink this book in a desert emergency. (It should be noted that the book's hard covers *may* be of limited utility as snowshoes, but this is an "off-label" use at best.)

Wild Internet rumors have generated unreal expectations. It must be reiterated: This is simply a book, made of paper and ink. It cannot rescue puppies, refine ethanol, or cure cancer. It is printed in China, so it may in fact *cause* cancer.

That all being said, there is one persistent rumor that is absolutely, 100% true.

This book *can* quell the aching loneliness deep within every one of us.

As you peruse this book, watch for the emblem to the right. Wherever you see it, simply hold that page up to the light, and read the secret message that appears in the center. You will feel a sense of calm wash over you at once.

A-HA! You've turned the page! Did you feel it? Was it invigorating?

You've taken an important first step into the larger world of Wondermark. In the following pages you will discover as fine a collection of japes, drollery, questionable assertions and straight-faced poppycock as has ever been published. Should you already be familiar with Wondermark, you need no further introduction; you may skip the following paragraphs and proceed directly to the section headed "A KEY TO SUPPLEMENTARY FEATURES."

But what of *you,* gentle soul, still tentatively reading in a brightly-lit bookstore aisle? Your feet may be weary; to either side may be the garish covers of this year's current best-sellers, *If You Buy This Book I'll Claim You Can Be Rich* and *I Agree: People Unlike Us Are Bad.* What does *this* slim volume offer that you can't find in *those* famous titles?

One word: Paget's disease of the nipple. It's not an easy thing to promise, but you won't be disappointed. In fact, it's already too late—we've coated the pages.

But perhaps you're *not* in a bookstore? Perhaps it's Christmas morning, and you've torn open the wrapping to discover *this,* instead of what you *really* wanted. Don't cry; it's not all that bad, and besides it's unbecoming. You really are lovely, you know, and don't let anyone else tell you differently.

You're going to like this book. It's right up your alley.

And if you *don't?* Well, plenty of other people *have,* so...maybe the problem isn't with the *book.* Just throwing that out there.

A KEY TO SUPPLEMENTARY FEATURES.

You will find the following symbols throughout the pages to come. Each spotlights some content that may be valuable to the reader. The "secret message" emblem, introduced on the previous page, will not be repeated here, because you might hold *this* page up to the light, and you'd just get some gibberish backwards-text from the previous page, which would frankly ruin the effect.

I DON'T GET IT

Designates an explanatory sidebar for those who may have trouble comprehending some item on the page.

"This was taken entirely out of context."

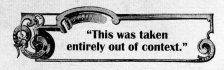

Heralds an additional perspective on the item, either from an affected party or outside commentator.

For a red wine spill, blot with club soda.

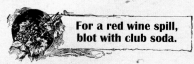

Indicates a handy tip that may be useful in a variety of common situations.

YOU ARE PROBABLY NOT
QUITE AS WRETCHED AS
YOU FEAR YOU MAY BE.

You are now prepared to read this book. Enjoy!

THE PUBLISHERS.

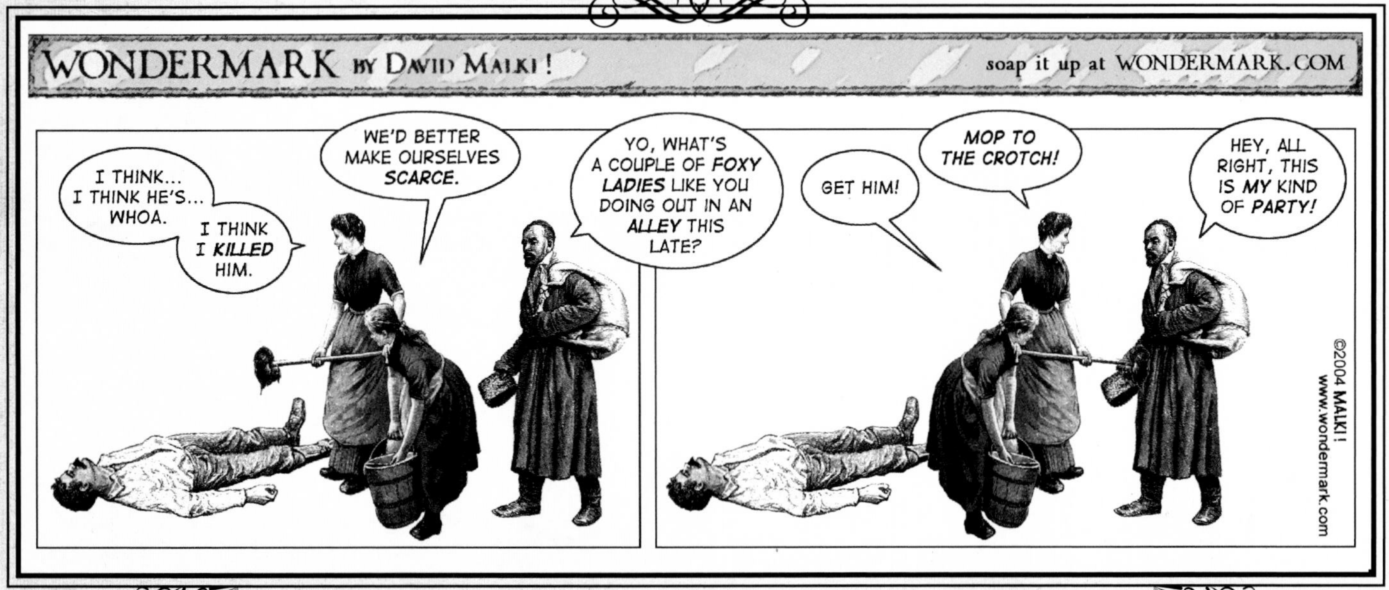
WONDERMARK by David Malki !
soap it up at WONDERMARK.COM
I THINK... I THINK HE'S... WHOA.
I THINK I *KILLED* HIM.
WE'D BETTER MAKE OURSELVES *SCARCE.*
YO, WHAT'S A COUPLE OF *FOXY LADIES* LIKE YOU DOING OUT IN AN *ALLEY* THIS LATE?
GET HIM!
MOP TO THE CROTCH!
HEY, ALL RIGHT, THIS IS *MY* KIND OF *PARTY!*
©2004 MALKI!
www.wondermark.com

considering the pick-up line, i'm not really sure what kind of party he expected it to be

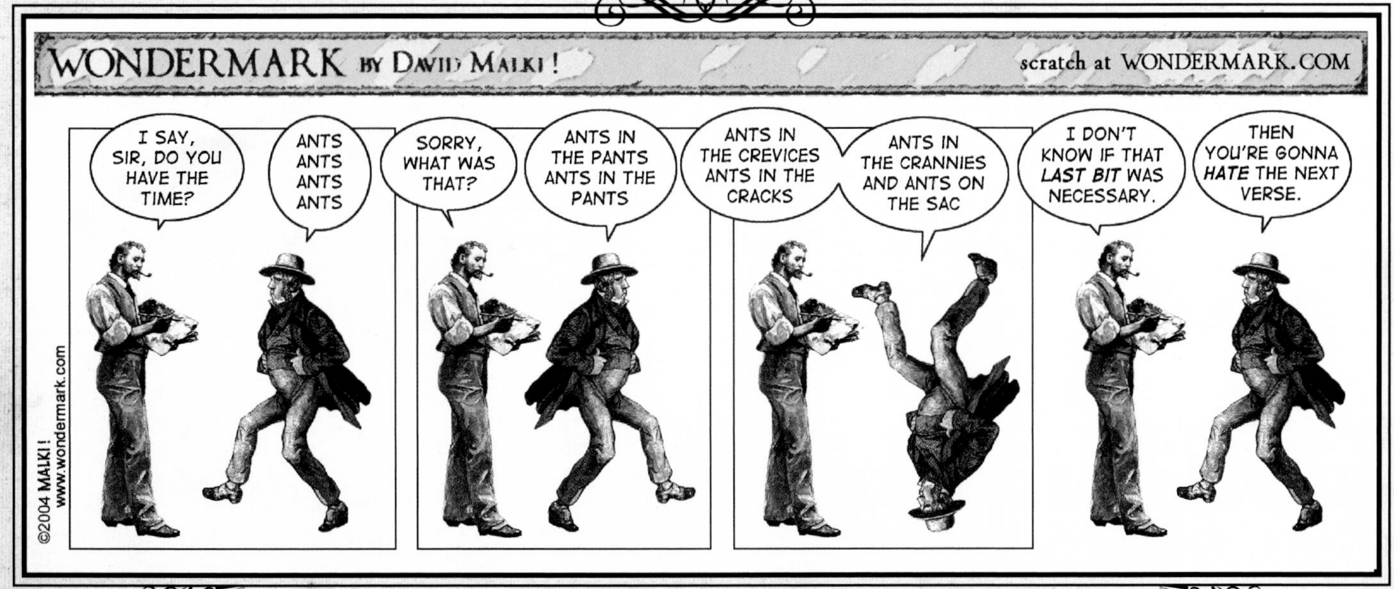
WONDERMARK by David Malki !
scratch at WONDERMARK.COM
I SAY, SIR, DO YOU HAVE THE TIME?
ANTS ANTS ANTS ANTS
SORRY, WHAT WAS THAT?
ANTS IN THE PANTS ANTS IN THE PANTS
ANTS IN THE CREVICES ANTS IN THE CRACKS
ANTS IN THE CRANNIES AND ANTS ON THE SAC
I DON'T KNOW IF THAT *LAST BIT* WAS NECESSARY.
THEN YOU'RE GONNA *HATE* THE NEXT VERSE.
©2004 MALKI!
www.wondermark.com

an infestation of insects is invariably interesting

In which Fraud is suspected

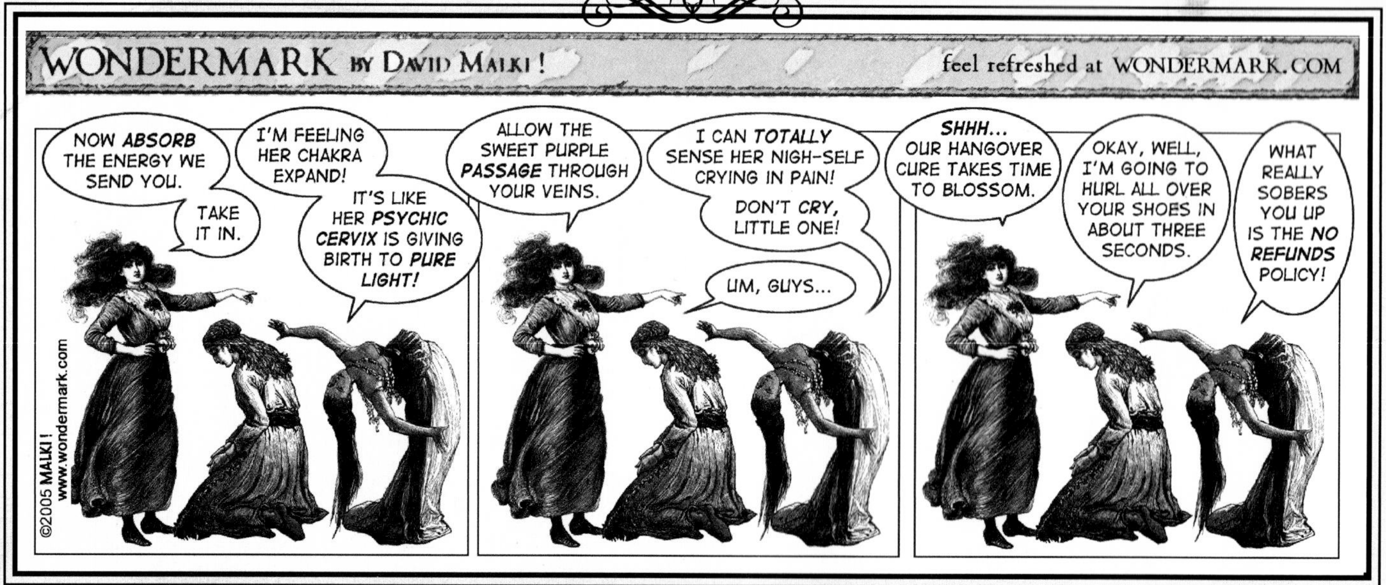
WONDERMARK by David Malki !
feel refreshed at WONDERMARK.COM
NOW ABSORB THE ENERGY WE SEND YOU.
TAKE IT IN.
I'M FEELING HER CHAKRA EXPAND!
IT'S LIKE HER PSYCHIC CERVIX IS GIVING BIRTH TO PURE LIGHT!
ALLOW THE SWEET PURPLE PASSAGE THROUGH YOUR VEINS.
I CAN TOTALLY SENSE HER NIGH-SELF CRYING IN PAIN!
DON'T CRY, LITTLE ONE!
UM, GUYS...
SHHH... OUR HANGOVER CURE TAKES TIME TO BLOSSOM.
OKAY, WELL, I'M GOING TO HURL ALL OVER YOUR SHOES IN ABOUT THREE SECONDS.
WHAT REALLY SOBERS YOU UP IS THE NO REFUNDS POLICY!
©2005 MALKI!
www.wondermark.com

your psychic cervix is, uh, located in your esophagus!
THE VOMIT IS A KEY PART OF THE PROCESS

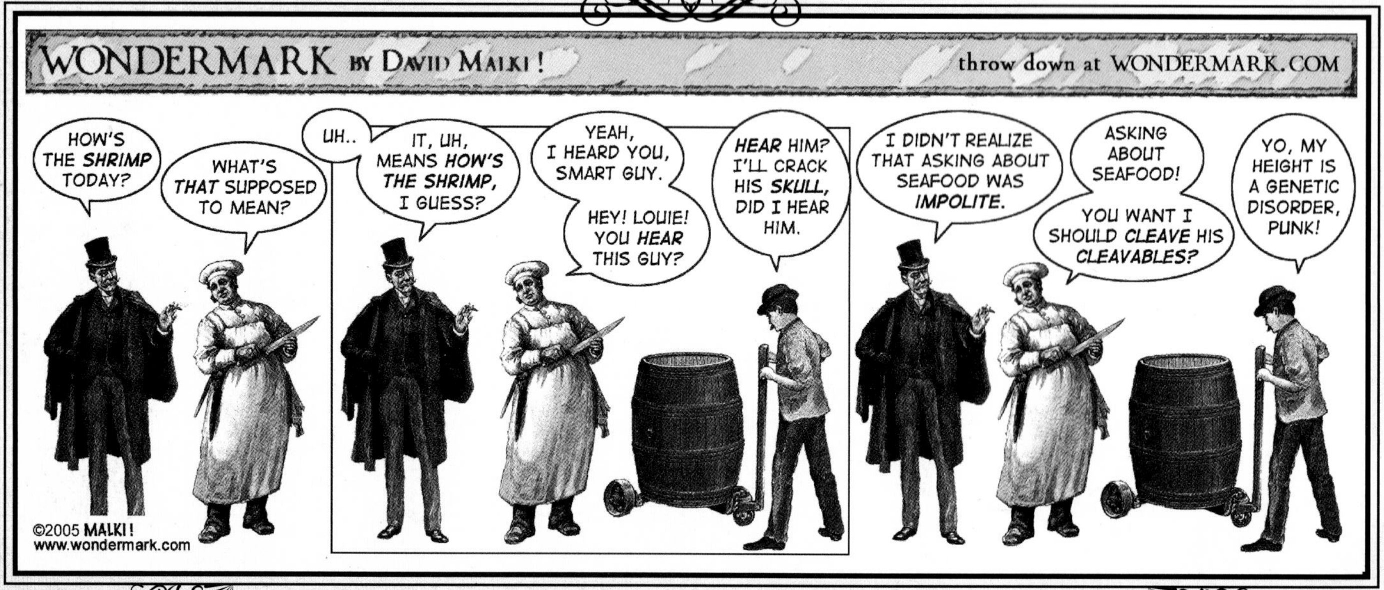
WONDERMARK by David Malki !
throw down at WONDERMARK.COM
HOW'S THE SHRIMP TODAY?
WHAT'S THAT SUPPOSED TO MEAN?
UH..
IT, UH, MEANS HOW'S THE SHRIMP, I GUESS?
YEAH, I HEARD YOU, SMART GUY.
HEY! LOUIE! YOU HEAR THIS GUY?
HEAR HIM? I'LL CRACK HIS SKULL, DID I HEAR HIM.
I DIDN'T REALIZE THAT ASKING ABOUT SEAFOOD WAS IMPOLITE.
ASKING ABOUT SEAFOOD!
YOU WANT I SHOULD CLEAVE HIS CLEAVABLES?
YO, MY HEIGHT IS A GENETIC DISORDER, PUNK!
©2005 MALKI!
www.wondermark.com

if you say 'what's in the barrel, 100 gallons of cocktail sauce?' i will cut you

In which a Slight is inadvertently made

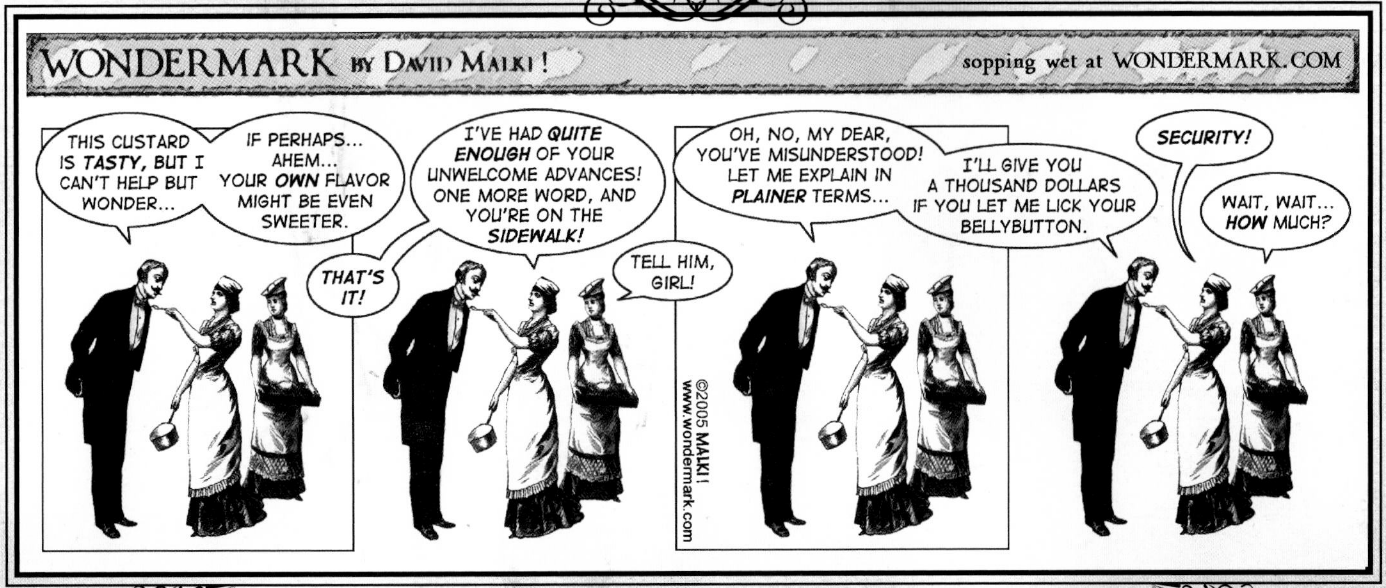
WONDERMARK by David Malki !
sopping wet at WONDERMARK.COM
THIS CUSTARD IS TASTY, BUT I CAN'T HELP BUT WONDER...
IF PERHAPS... AHEM... YOUR OWN FLAVOR MIGHT BE EVEN SWEETER.
THAT'S IT!
I'VE HAD QUITE ENOUGH OF YOUR UNWELCOME ADVANCES! ONE MORE WORD, AND YOU'RE ON THE SIDEWALK!
TELL HIM, GIRL!
©2005 MALKI! www.wondermark.com
OH, NO, MY DEAR, YOU'VE MISUNDERSTOOD! LET ME EXPLAIN IN PLAINER TERMS...
I'LL GIVE YOU A THOUSAND DOLLARS IF YOU LET ME LICK YOUR BELLYBUTTON.
SECURITY!
WAIT, WAIT... HOW MUCH?

always hear the offer out, after all it is textbook-buying season

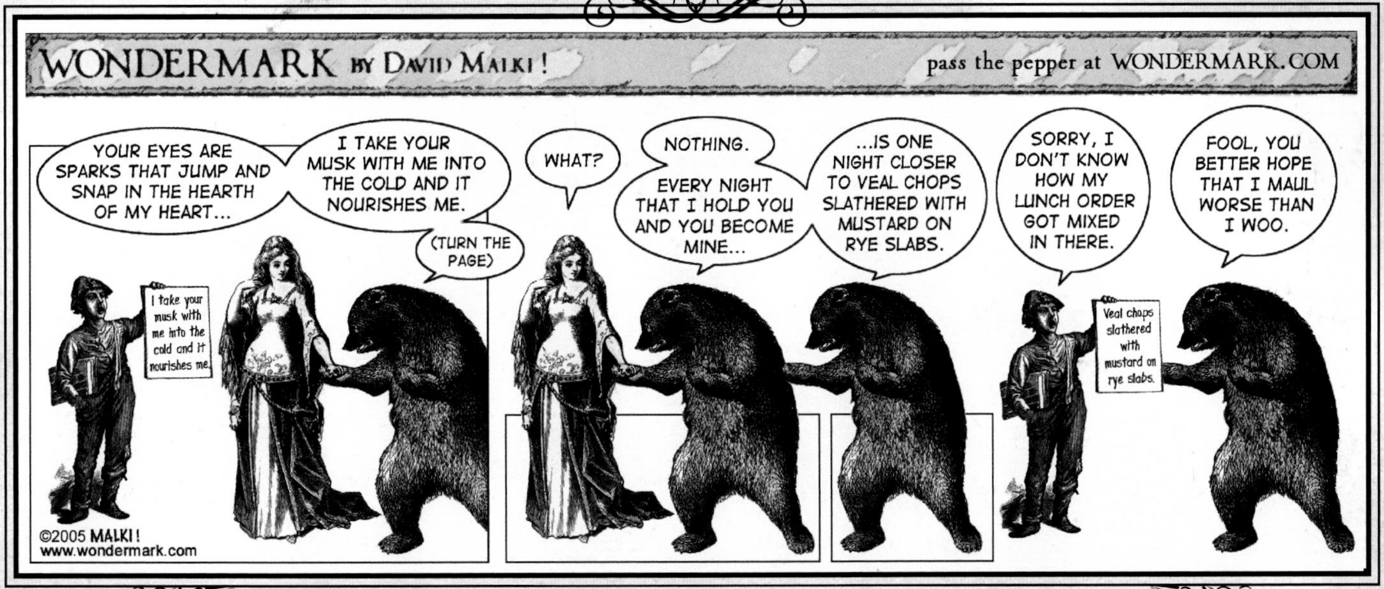
WONDERMARK by David Malki !
pass the pepper at WONDERMARK.COM
YOUR EYES ARE SPARKS THAT JUMP AND SNAP IN THE HEARTH OF MY HEART...
I TAKE YOUR MUSK WITH ME INTO THE COLD AND IT NOURISHES ME.
(TURN THE PAGE)
I take your musk with me into the cold and it nourishes me.
©2005 MALKI! www.wondermark.com
WHAT?
NOTHING.
EVERY NIGHT THAT I HOLD YOU AND YOU BECOME MINE...
...IS ONE NIGHT CLOSER TO VEAL CHOPS SLATHERED WITH MUSTARD ON RYE SLABS.
SORRY, I DON'T KNOW HOW MY LUNCH ORDER GOT MIXED IN THERE.
Veal chops slathered with mustard on rye slabs.
FOOL, YOU BETTER HOPE THAT I MAUL WORSE THAN I WOO.

i hope it's not racist to say that grizzlies are ALWAYS this temperamental

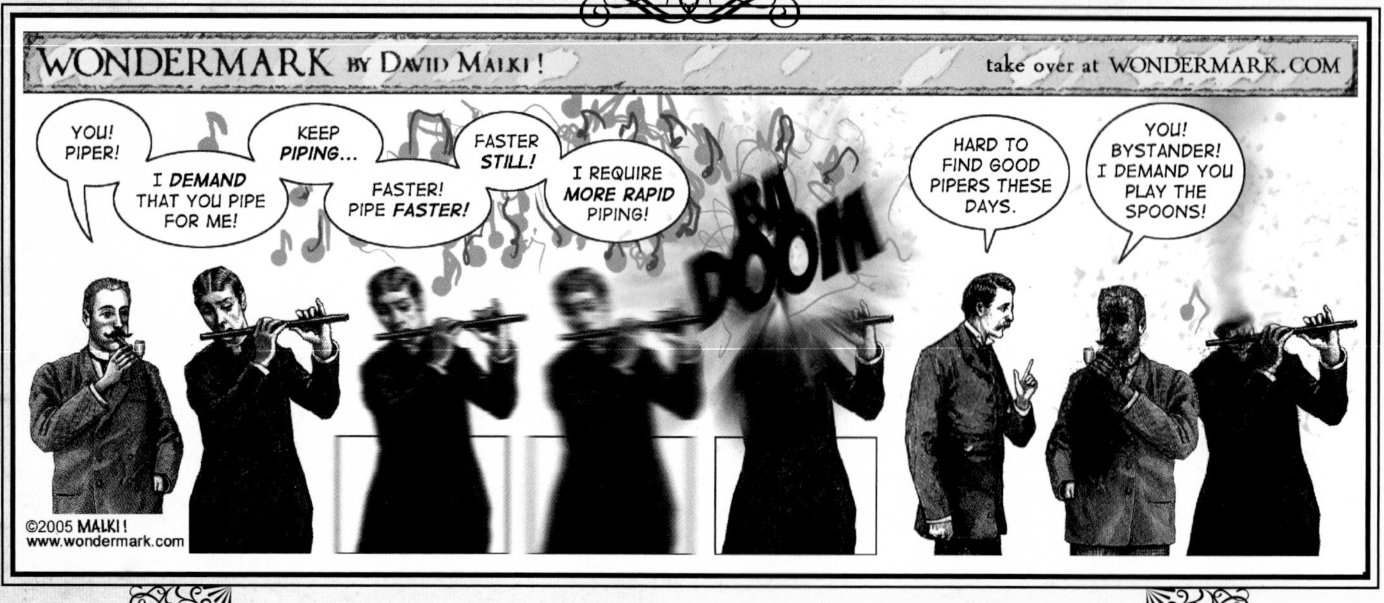
WONDERMARK BY DAVID MALKI !
take over at WONDERMARK.COM
YOU! PIPER!
I DEMAND THAT YOU PIPE FOR ME!
KEEP PIPING...
FASTER! PIPE FASTER!
FASTER STILL!
I REQUIRE MORE RAPID PIPING!
BA DOOM
HARD TO FIND GOOD PIPERS THESE DAYS.
YOU! BYSTANDER! I DEMAND YOU PLAY THE SPOONS!
©2005 MALKI!
www.wondermark.com

DEEEEEMAAAAAAAND IIIIIIITTT

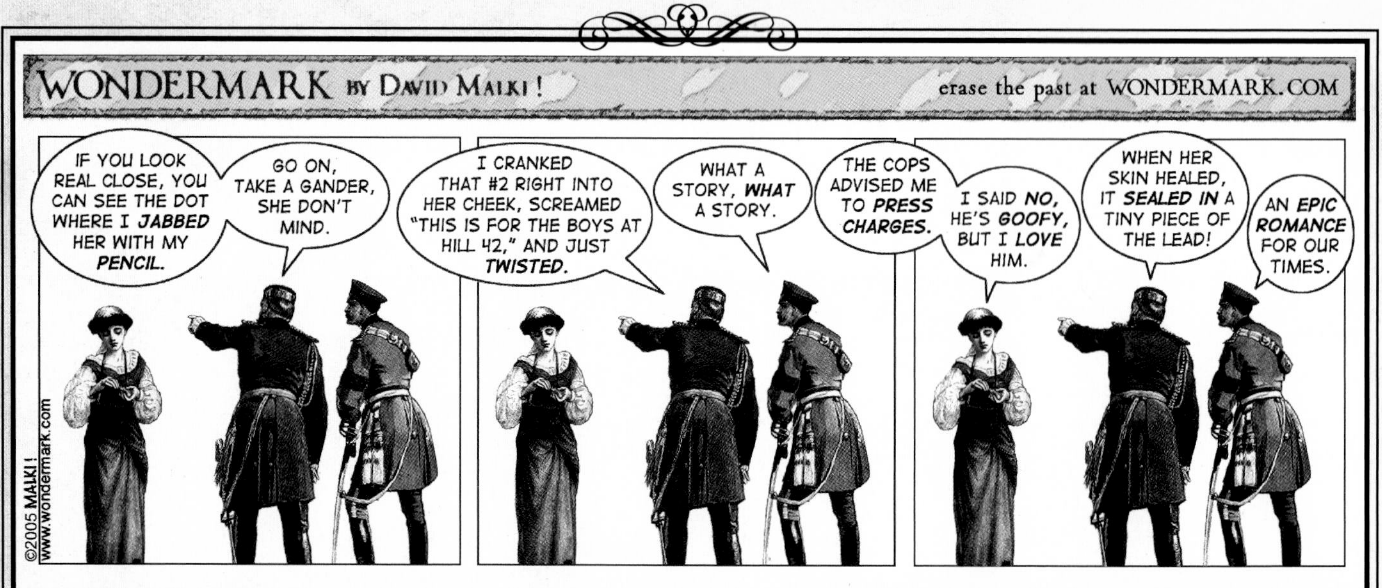
WONDERMARK BY DAVID MALKI !
erase the past at WONDERMARK.COM
IF YOU LOOK REAL CLOSE, YOU CAN SEE THE DOT WHERE I JABBED HER WITH MY PENCIL.
GO ON, TAKE A GANDER, SHE DON'T MIND.
I CRANKED THAT #2 RIGHT INTO HER CHEEK, SCREAMED "THIS IS FOR THE BOYS AT HILL 42," AND JUST TWISTED.
WHAT A STORY, WHAT A STORY.
THE COPS ADVISED ME TO PRESS CHARGES.
I SAID NO, HE'S GOOFY, BUT I LOVE HIM.
WHEN HER SKIN HEALED, IT SEALED IN A TINY PIECE OF THE LEAD!
AN EPIC ROMANCE FOR OUR TIMES.
©2005 MALKI!
www.wondermark.com

thus, the boys at hill 42 can rest, avenged.

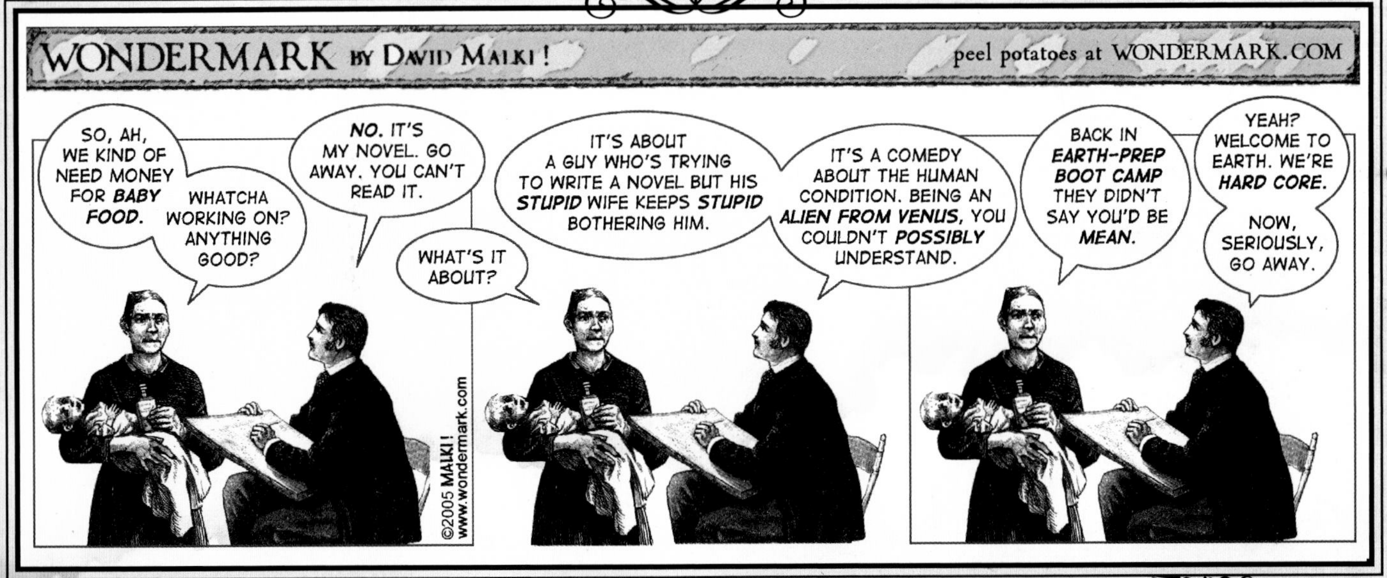
WONDERMARK BY DAVID MALKI !
peel potatoes at WONDERMARK.COM
SO, AH, WE KIND OF NEED MONEY FOR BABY FOOD.
WHATCHA WORKING ON? ANYTHING GOOD?
NO. IT'S MY NOVEL. GO AWAY. YOU CAN'T READ IT.
©2005 MALKI! www.wondermark.com
WHAT'S IT ABOUT?
IT'S ABOUT A GUY WHO'S TRYING TO WRITE A NOVEL BUT HIS STUPID WIFE KEEPS STUPID BOTHERING HIM.
IT'S A COMEDY ABOUT THE HUMAN CONDITION. BEING AN ALIEN FROM VENUS, YOU COULDN'T POSSIBLY UNDERSTAND.
BACK IN EARTH-PREP BOOT CAMP THEY DIDN'T SAY YOU'D BE MEAN.
YEAH? WELCOME TO EARTH. WE'RE HARD CORE.
NOW, SERIOUSLY, GO AWAY.

the days back in earth-prep boot camp were actually shockingly softcore

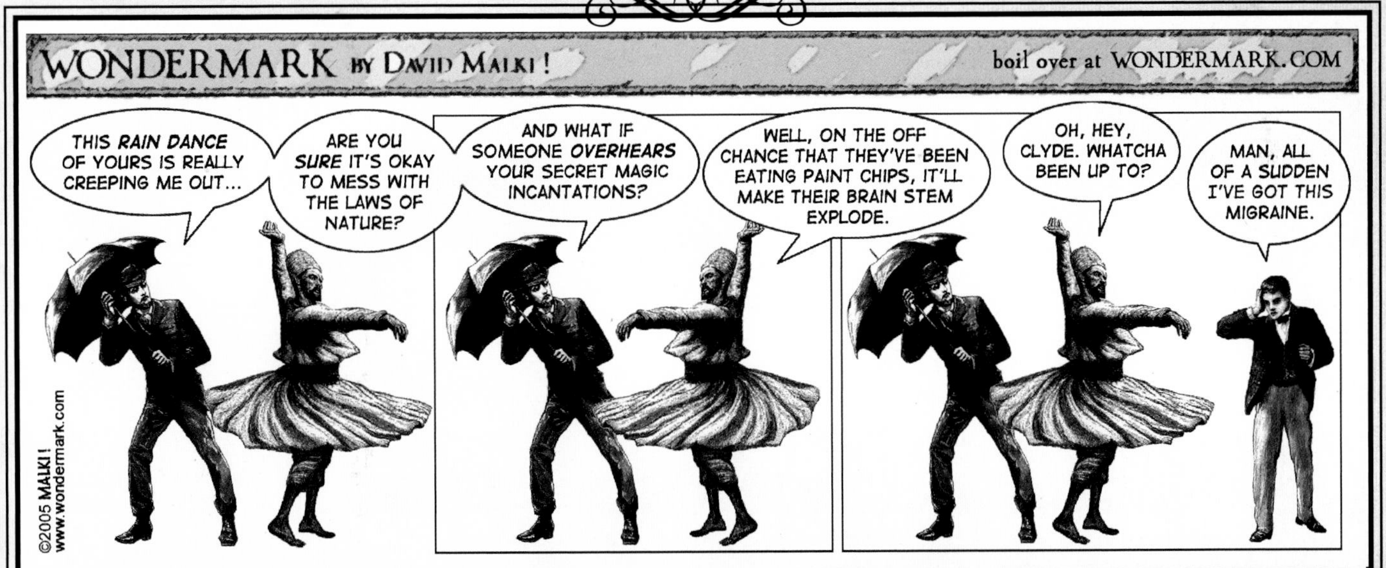
WONDERMARK BY DAVID MALKI !
boil over at WONDERMARK.COM
THIS RAIN DANCE OF YOURS IS REALLY CREEPING ME OUT...
ARE YOU SURE IT'S OKAY TO MESS WITH THE LAWS OF NATURE?
©2005 MALKI! www.wondermark.com
AND WHAT IF SOMEONE OVERHEARS YOUR SECRET MAGIC INCANTATIONS?
WELL, ON THE OFF CHANCE THAT THEY'VE BEEN EATING PAINT CHIPS, IT'LL MAKE THEIR BRAIN STEM EXPLODE.
OH, HEY, CLYDE. WHATCHA BEEN UP TO?
MAN, ALL OF A SUDDEN I'VE GOT THIS MIGRAINE.

CLYDE IT WAS A TRAP ALL ALONG

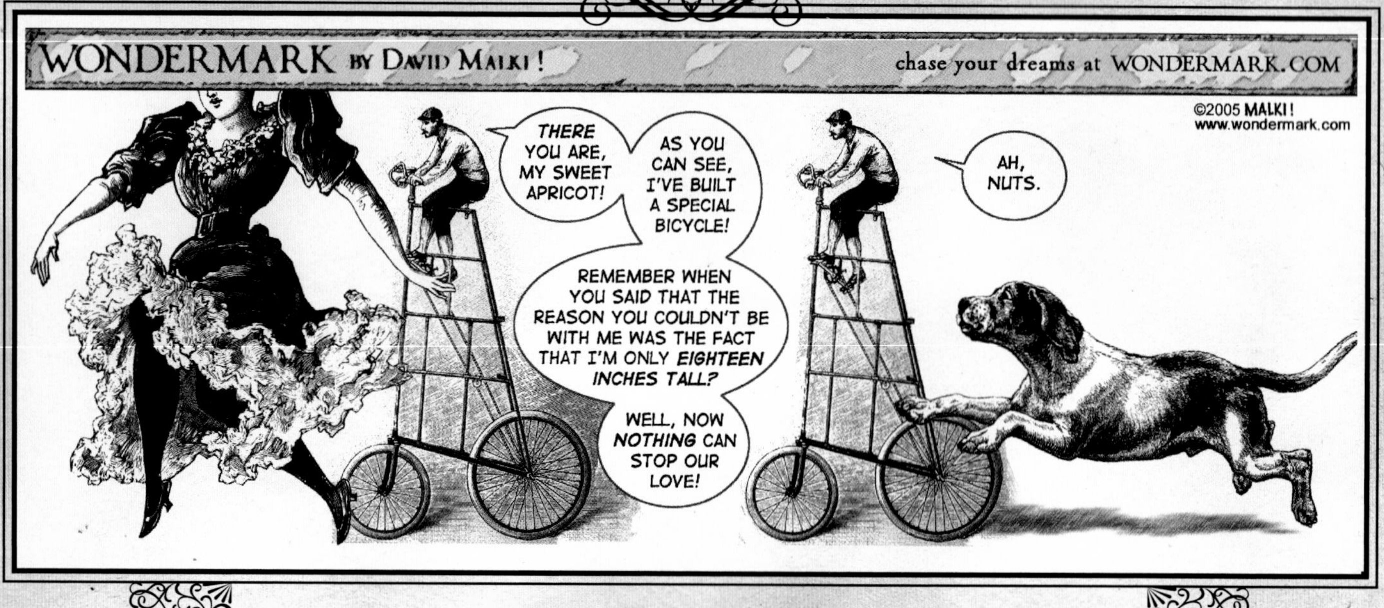
WONDERMARK by David Malki !
chase your dreams at WONDERMARK.COM
©2005 MALKI !
www.wondermark.com
THERE YOU ARE, MY SWEET APRICOT!
AS YOU CAN SEE, I'VE BUILT A SPECIAL BICYCLE!
REMEMBER WHEN YOU SAID THAT THE REASON YOU COULDN'T BE WITH ME WAS THE FACT THAT I'M ONLY EIGHTEEN INCHES TALL?
WELL, NOW NOTHING CAN STOP OUR LOVE!
AH, NUTS.

oh no! a dog! i'm horribly allergic!

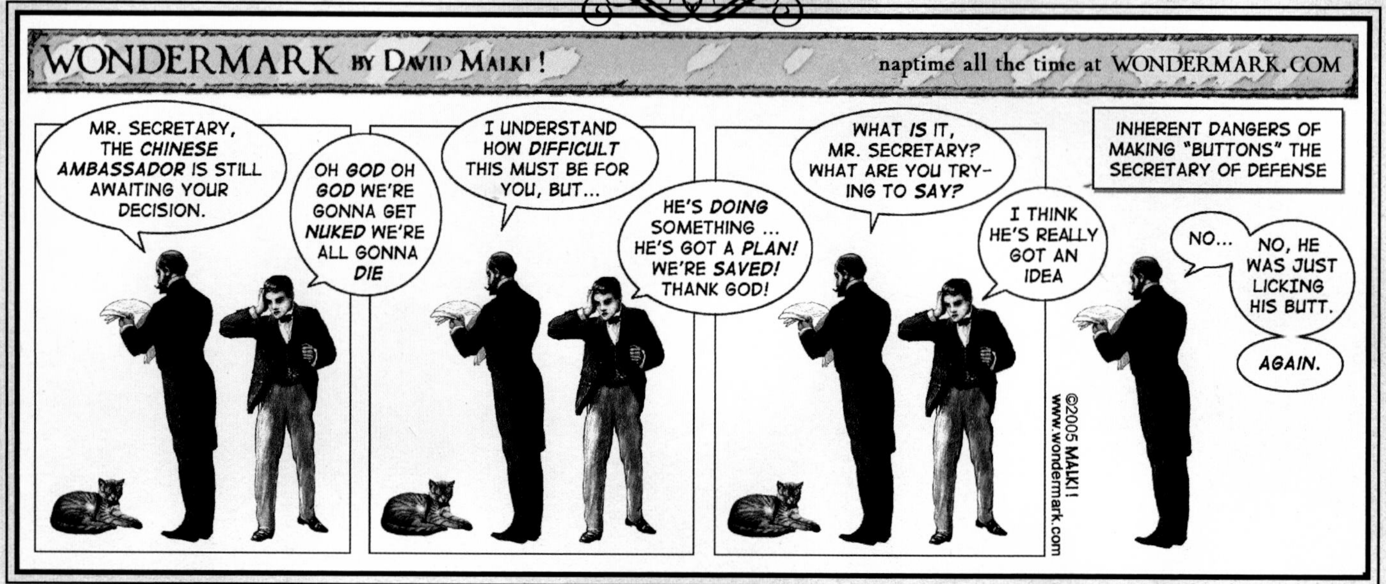
WONDERMARK by David Malki !
naptime all the time at WONDERMARK.COM
MR. SECRETARY, THE CHINESE AMBASSADOR IS STILL AWAITING YOUR DECISION.
OH GOD OH GOD WE'RE GONNA GET NUKED WE'RE ALL GONNA DIE
I UNDERSTAND HOW DIFFICULT THIS MUST BE FOR YOU, BUT...
HE'S DOING SOMETHING ... HE'S GOT A PLAN! WE'RE SAVED! THANK GOD!
WHAT IS IT, MR. SECRETARY? WHAT ARE YOU TRY-ING TO SAY?
I THINK HE'S REALLY GOT AN IDEA
©2005 MALKI !
www.wondermark.com
INHERENT DANGERS OF MAKING "BUTTONS" THE SECRETARY OF DEFENSE
NO...
NO, HE WAS JUST LICKING HIS BUTT.
AGAIN.

the critical flaw of the appointment system

WONDERMARK BY DAVID MALKI !

©2003 MALKI !

chow down at WONDERMARK.COM

SORRY ABOUT THAT.

I SHOULD THINK SO.

man, nimble

"A performance drawn as finely as any, ever."

AS AN ACTOR, Norbert the Elephant is invested with all the charms and characterized by all the defects which belong to enthusiastic genius. Before taking to the stage, Mr. the Elephant began life as a shop-boy; tried the sea, and was discouraged by a storm and shipwreck; obtained in Amsterdam a position as small clerk at an annual salary of 800 francs (equal to $160), half of which he spent upon his studies; and adopted, if he did not invent, a new method of learning languages. His remarkable performance in this comic-strip is without par in any venue; this should not be surprising, for the strip itself is a wrought work of dramatics unsurpassed in the modern era.

We recall in literature no parallel to this skillful employment of the tensions of adolescence to awaken the alternate pity and wrath of the reader or the audience. As a picture of the times, this strip is as accurate and painstaking as a history. As a study of character it is more just, and therefore more true, than the works of any of the masters now known. ABIGAIL, the central character, is admirably delineated by the fine actress Rebecca McAvoy; CALLOWAY, as portrayed by Mr. the Elephant, though occupying a subordinate position, is no less admirably conceived.

We should not dare to prophesy what measure of success may be expected to attend the production of this drama; but we should not expect the largest success for a work of art so high and pure. There is nothing sensational; the fire and blood are all behind the scenes. There is little of mere sentiment, though much of deep and earnest passion.

Yet the author has added a new laurel to his crown by this strip, for he has demonstrated that the twenty-first century is not too materialistic nor too sensational to produce a true drama of the heart.

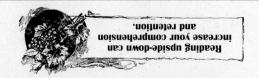

Reading upside-down can increase your comprehension and retention.

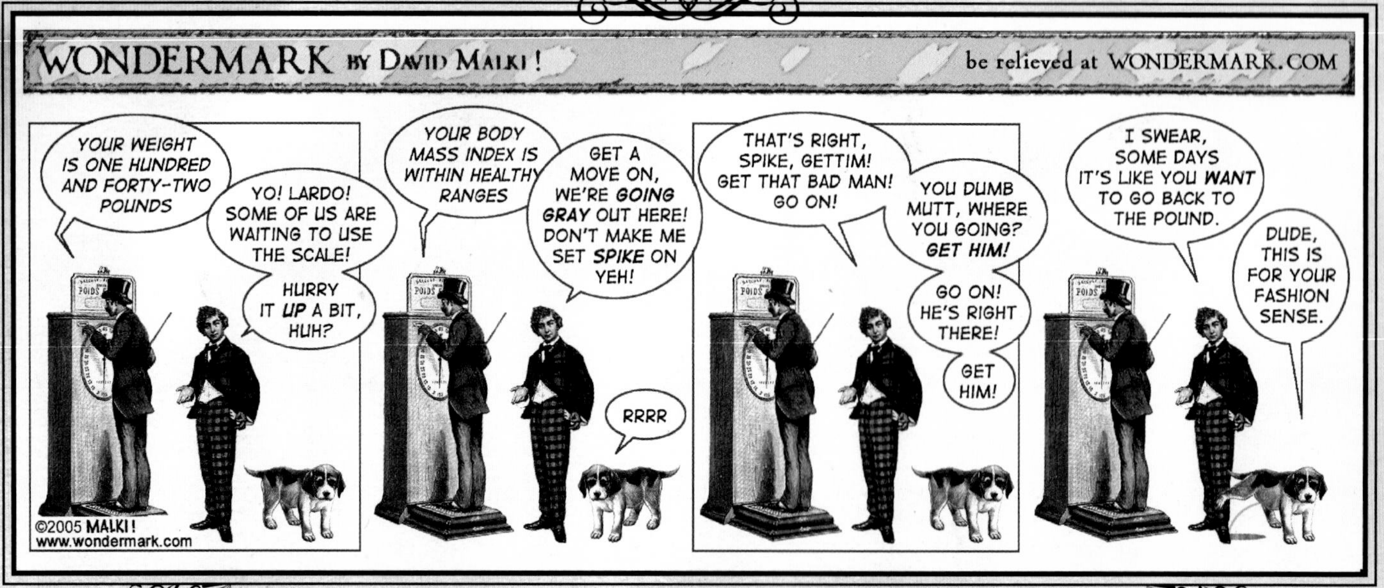
WONDERMARK BY DAVID MALKI !
be relieved at WONDERMARK.COM
YOUR WEIGHT IS ONE HUNDRED AND FORTY-TWO POUNDS
YO! LARDO! SOME OF US ARE WAITING TO USE THE SCALE!
HURRY IT UP A BIT, HUH?
©2005 MALKI ! www.wondermark.com
YOUR BODY MASS INDEX IS WITHIN HEALTHY RANGES
GET A MOVE ON, WE'RE GOING GRAY OUT HERE! DON'T MAKE ME SET SPIKE ON YEH!
RRRR
THAT'S RIGHT, SPIKE, GETTIM! GET THAT BAD MAN! GO ON!
YOU DUMB MUTT, WHERE YOU GOING? GET HIM!
GO ON! HE'S RIGHT THERE!
GET HIM!
I SWEAR, SOME DAYS IT'S LIKE YOU WANT TO GO BACK TO THE POUND.
DUDE, THIS IS FOR YOUR FASHION SENSE.

back at the pound they had a lot of PEOPLE and US WEEKLY sitting around

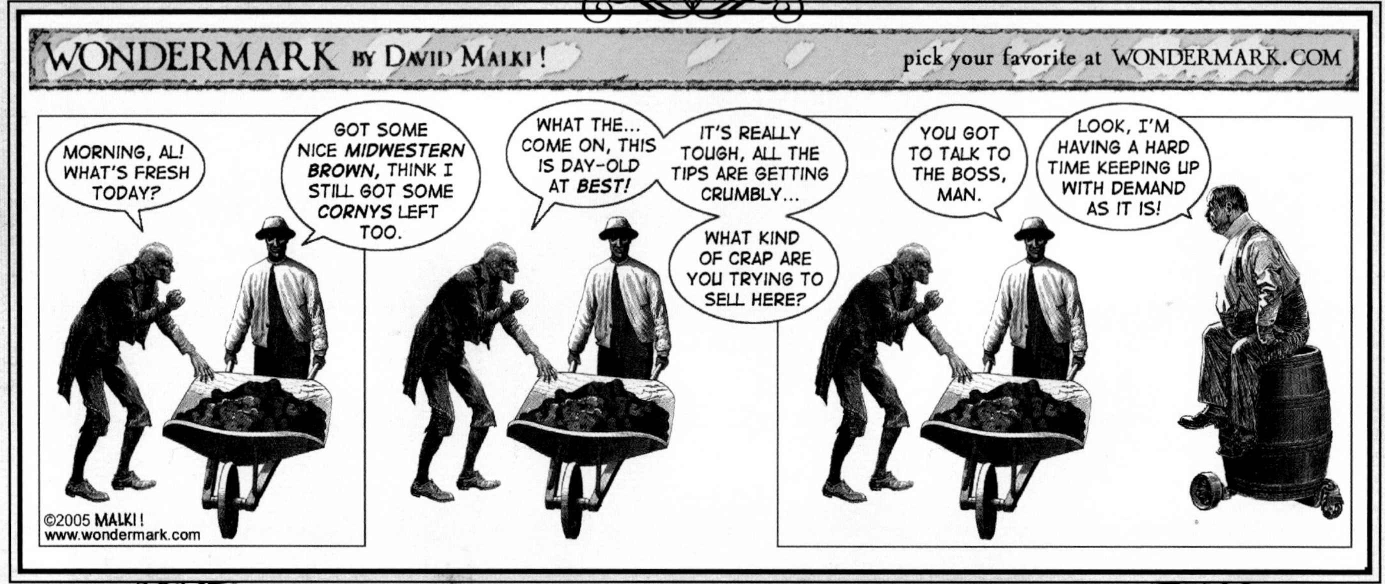
WONDERMARK BY DAVID MALKI !
pick your favorite at WONDERMARK.COM
MORNING, AL! WHAT'S FRESH TODAY?
GOT SOME NICE MIDWESTERN BROWN, THINK I STILL GOT SOME CORNYS LEFT TOO.
©2005 MALKI ! www.wondermark.com
WHAT THE... COME ON, THIS IS DAY-OLD AT BEST!
IT'S REALLY TOUGH, ALL THE TIPS ARE GETTING CRUMBLY...
WHAT KIND OF CRAP ARE YOU TRYING TO SELL HERE?
YOU GOT TO TALK TO THE BOSS, MAN.
LOOK, I'M HAVING A HARD TIME KEEPING UP WITH DEMAND AS IT IS!

the inevitable failure of poopy-side economics

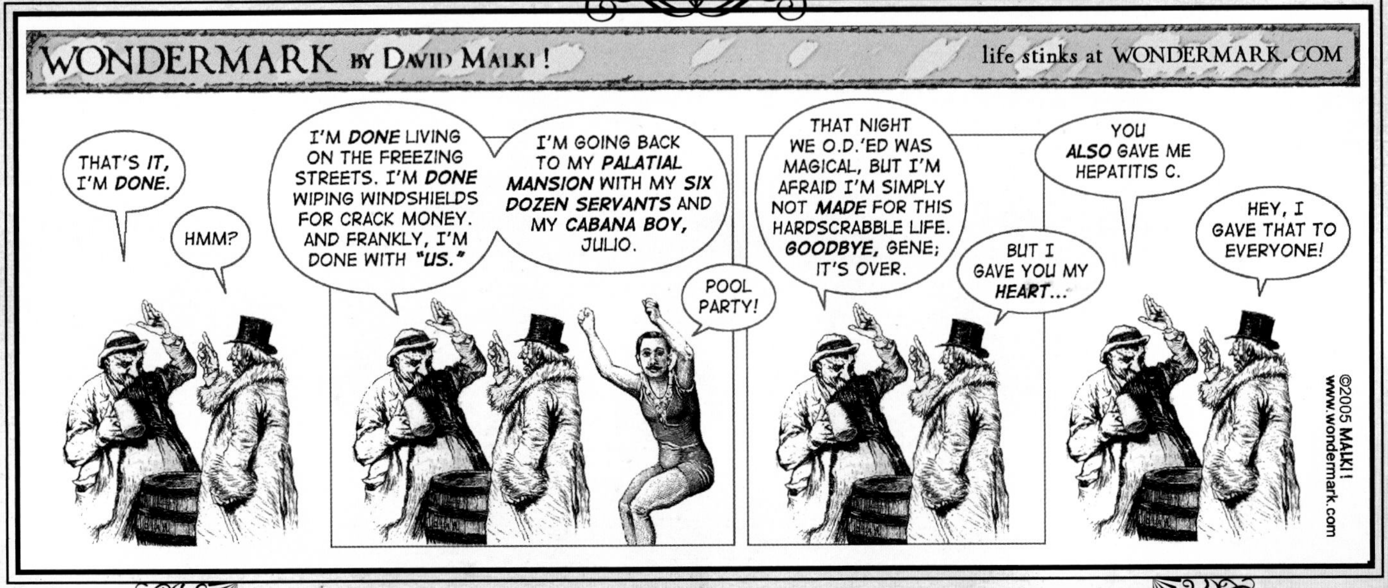

WONDERMARK BY DAVID MALKI !
life stinks at WONDERMARK.COM
THAT'S IT, I'M DONE.
HMM?
I'M DONE LIVING ON THE FREEZING STREETS. I'M DONE WIPING WINDSHIELDS FOR CRACK MONEY. AND FRANKLY, I'M DONE WITH "US."
I'M GOING BACK TO MY PALATIAL MANSION WITH MY SIX DOZEN SERVANTS AND MY CABANA BOY, JULIO.
POOL PARTY!
THAT NIGHT WE O.D.'ED WAS MAGICAL, BUT I'M AFRAID I'M SIMPLY NOT MADE FOR THIS HARDSCRABBLE LIFE. GOODBYE, GENE; IT'S OVER.
BUT I GAVE YOU MY HEART...
YOU ALSO GAVE ME HEPATITIS C.
HEY, I GAVE THAT TO EVERYONE!
©2005 MALKI! www.wondermark.com

this may not be much consolation, but if it helps, just know that julio is certified in nearly TWICE as many different types of massages as you

WONDERMARK BY DAVID MALKI !
make yourself at home at WONDERMARK.COM
HOW'S THE HOMEWORK COMING?
JAMIE?
HOW'S THE OTTER REPORT?
JAMIE -
GRAARRR!
OH, HEY, DEIMOS. THOUGHT YOU WERE JAMIE.
SHE'S IN THE FAMILY ROOM.
©2005 MALKI! www.wondermark.com

sometimes a second skin is just so much more comfy

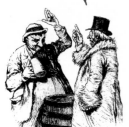

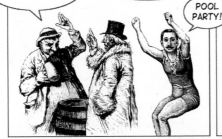

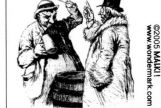

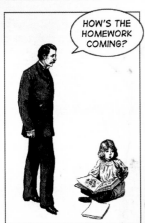

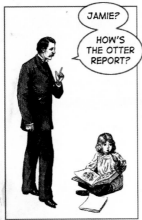

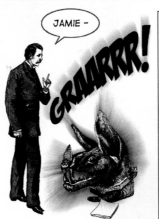

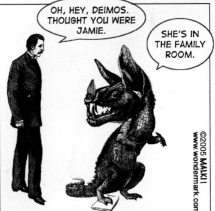

In which a Toy proves insufficient

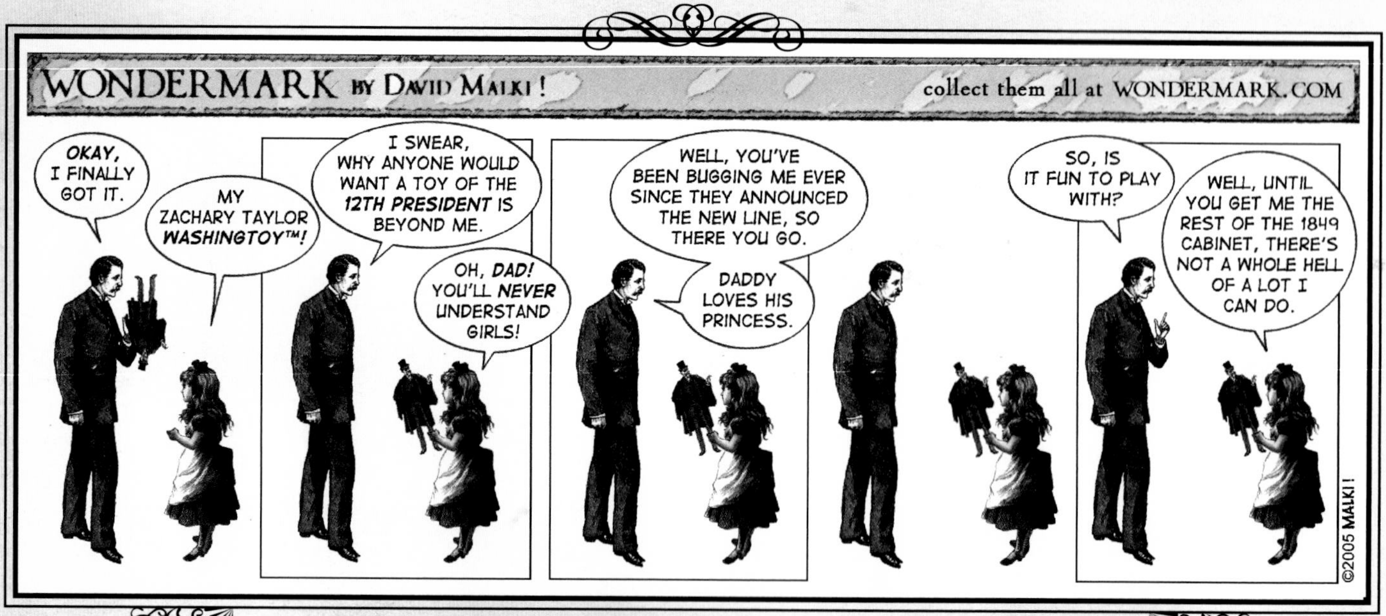
WONDERMARK by David Malki !
collect them all at WONDERMARK.COM
OKAY, I FINALLY GOT IT.
MY ZACHARY TAYLOR WASHINGTOY™!
I SWEAR, WHY ANYONE WOULD WANT A TOY OF THE 12TH PRESIDENT IS BEYOND ME.
OH, DAD! YOU'LL NEVER UNDERSTAND GIRLS!
WELL, YOU'VE BEEN BUGGING ME EVER SINCE THEY ANNOUNCED THE NEW LINE, SO THERE YOU GO.
DADDY LOVES HIS PRINCESS.
SO, IS IT FUN TO PLAY WITH?
WELL, UNTIL YOU GET ME THE REST OF THE 1849 CABINET, THERE'S NOT A WHOLE HELL OF A LOT I CAN DO.
©2005 MALKI !

officially licensed u.s. government merchandise is the best way to combat the national deficit

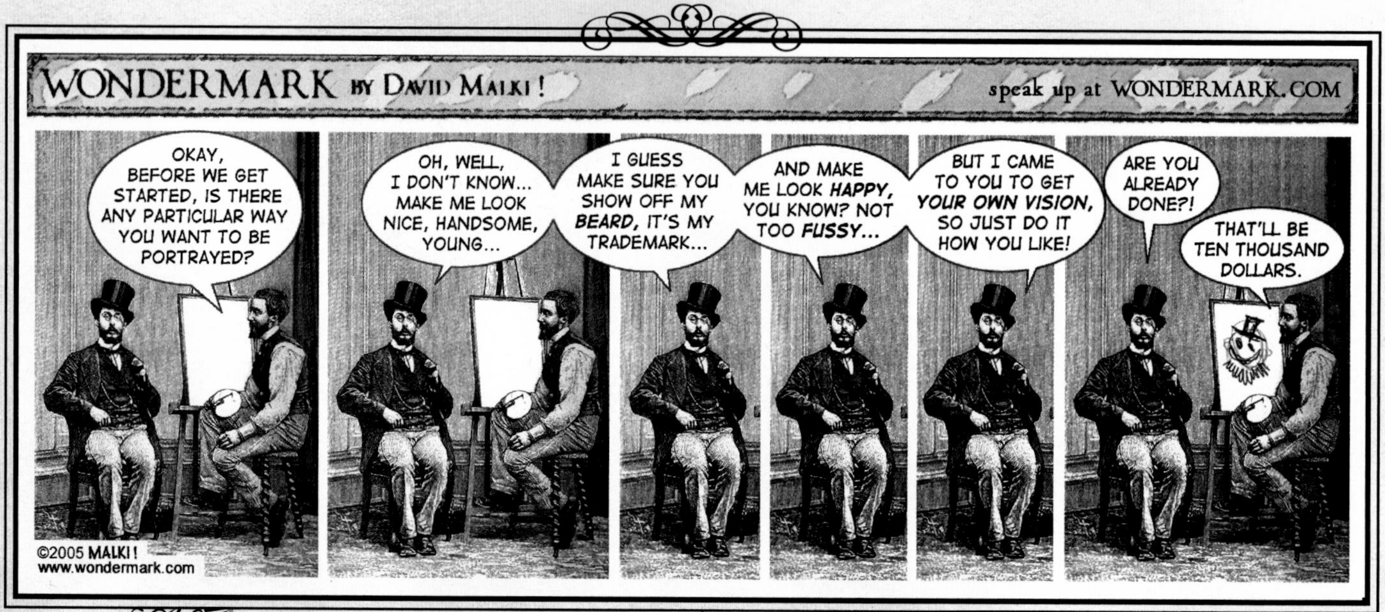
WONDERMARK by David Malki !
speak up at WONDERMARK.COM
OKAY, BEFORE WE GET STARTED, IS THERE ANY PARTICULAR WAY YOU WANT TO BE PORTRAYED?
©2005 MALKI !
www.wondermark.com
OH, WELL, I DON'T KNOW... MAKE ME LOOK NICE, HANDSOME, YOUNG...
I GUESS MAKE SURE YOU SHOW OFF MY BEARD, IT'S MY TRADEMARK...
AND MAKE ME LOOK HAPPY, YOU KNOW? NOT TOO FUSSY...
BUT I CAME TO YOU TO GET YOUR OWN VISION, SO JUST DO IT HOW YOU LIKE!
ARE YOU ALREADY DONE?!
THAT'LL BE TEN THOUSAND DOLLARS.

the dangers of leaving it to discretion

In which a Likeness is attempted

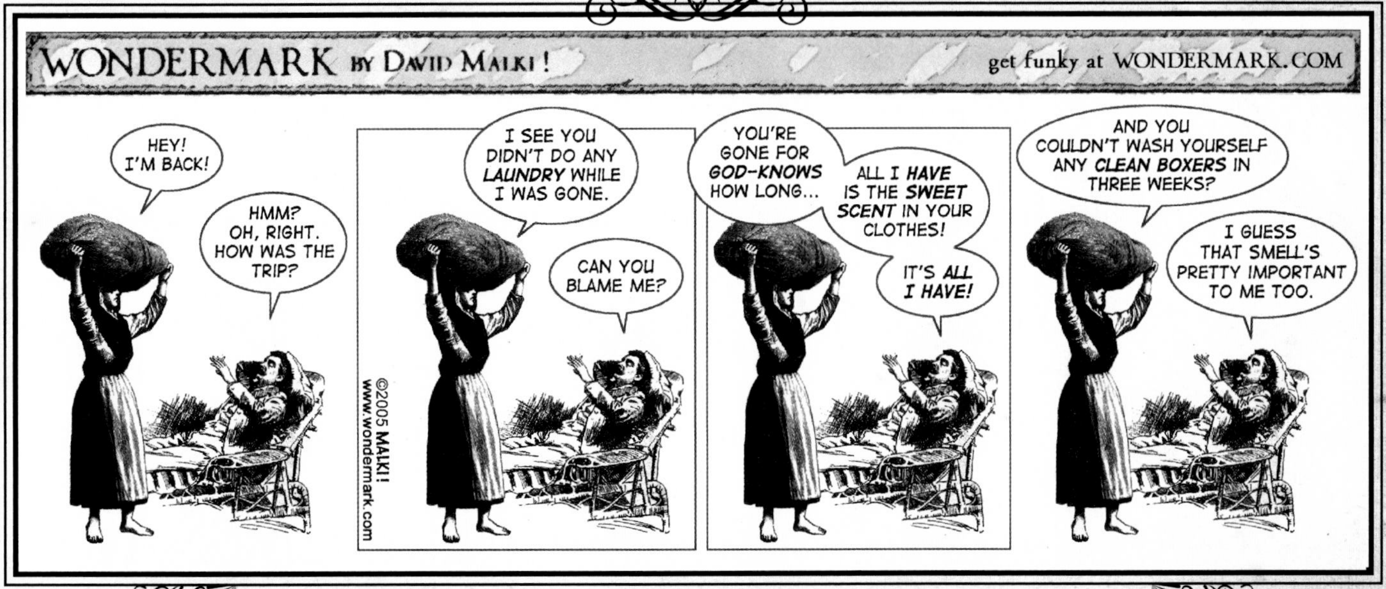
WONDERMARK BY DAVID MALKI !
get funky at WONDERMARK.COM
HEY! I'M BACK!
HMM? OH, RIGHT. HOW WAS THE TRIP?
I SEE YOU DIDN'T DO ANY LAUNDRY WHILE I WAS GONE.
CAN YOU BLAME ME?
©2005 MALKI! www.wondermark.com
YOU'RE GONE FOR GOD-KNOWS HOW LONG...
ALL I HAVE IS THE SWEET SCENT IN YOUR CLOTHES!
IT'S ALL I HAVE!
AND YOU COULDN'T WASH YOURSELF ANY CLEAN BOXERS IN THREE WEEKS?
I GUESS THAT SMELL'S PRETTY IMPORTANT TO ME TOO.

true story comics

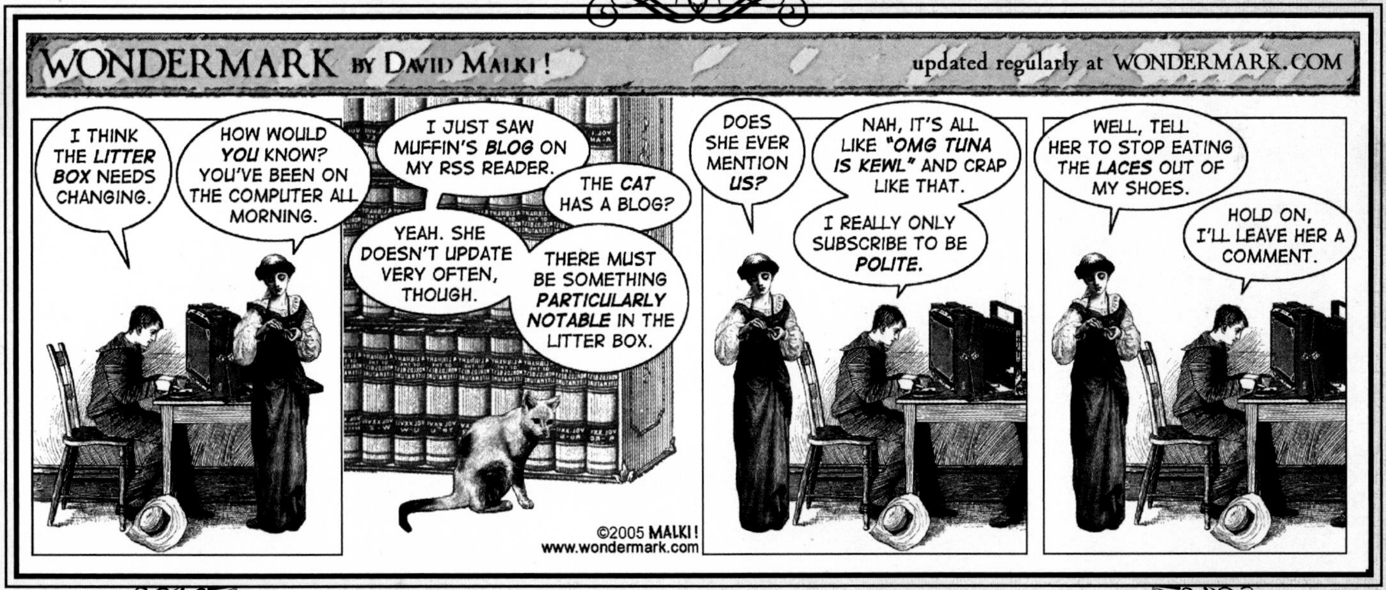
WONDERMARK BY DAVID MALKI !
updated regularly at WONDERMARK.COM
I THINK THE LITTER BOX NEEDS CHANGING.
HOW WOULD YOU KNOW? YOU'VE BEEN ON THE COMPUTER ALL MORNING.
I JUST SAW MUFFIN'S BLOG ON MY RSS READER.
THE CAT HAS A BLOG?
YEAH. SHE DOESN'T UPDATE VERY OFTEN, THOUGH.
THERE MUST BE SOMETHING PARTICULARLY NOTABLE IN THE LITTER BOX.
©2005 MALKI! www.wondermark.com
DOES SHE EVER MENTION US?
NAH, IT'S ALL LIKE "OMG TUNA IS KEWL" AND CRAP LIKE THAT.
I REALLY ONLY SUBSCRIBE TO BE POLITE.
WELL, TELL HER TO STOP EATING THE LACES OUT OF MY SHOES.
HOLD ON, I'LL LEAVE HER A COMMENT.

it's not even wordpress or blogger, it's some crap like xanga

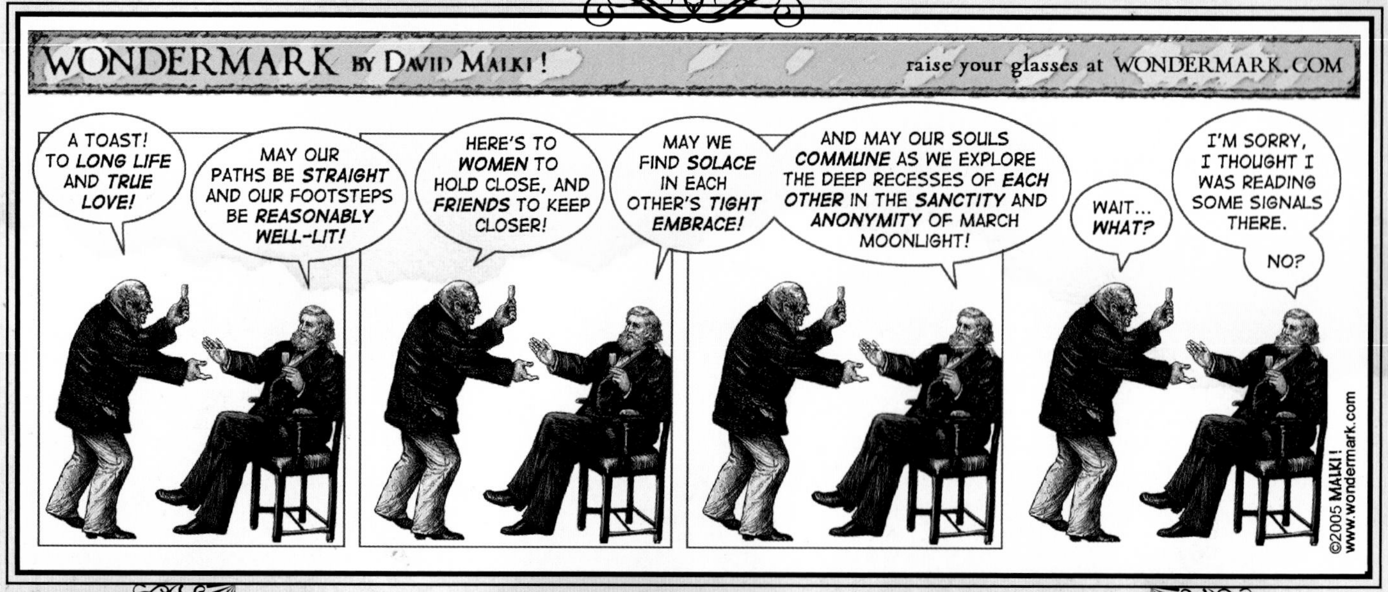
WONDERMARK BY DAVID MALKI !
raise your glasses at WONDERMARK.COM
A TOAST! TO LONG LIFE AND TRUE LOVE!
MAY OUR PATHS BE STRAIGHT AND OUR FOOTSTEPS BE REASONABLY WELL-LIT!
HERE'S TO WOMEN TO HOLD CLOSE, AND FRIENDS TO KEEP CLOSER!
MAY WE FIND SOLACE IN EACH OTHER'S TIGHT EMBRACE!
AND MAY OUR SOULS COMMUNE AS WE EXPLORE THE DEEP RECESSES OF EACH OTHER IN THE SANCTITY AND ANONYMITY OF MARCH MOONLIGHT!
WAIT... WHAT?
I'M SORRY, I THOUGHT I WAS READING SOME SIGNALS THERE.
NO?
©2005 MALKI! www.wondermark.com

90% of communication is body language. the rest is just hopeful guesses

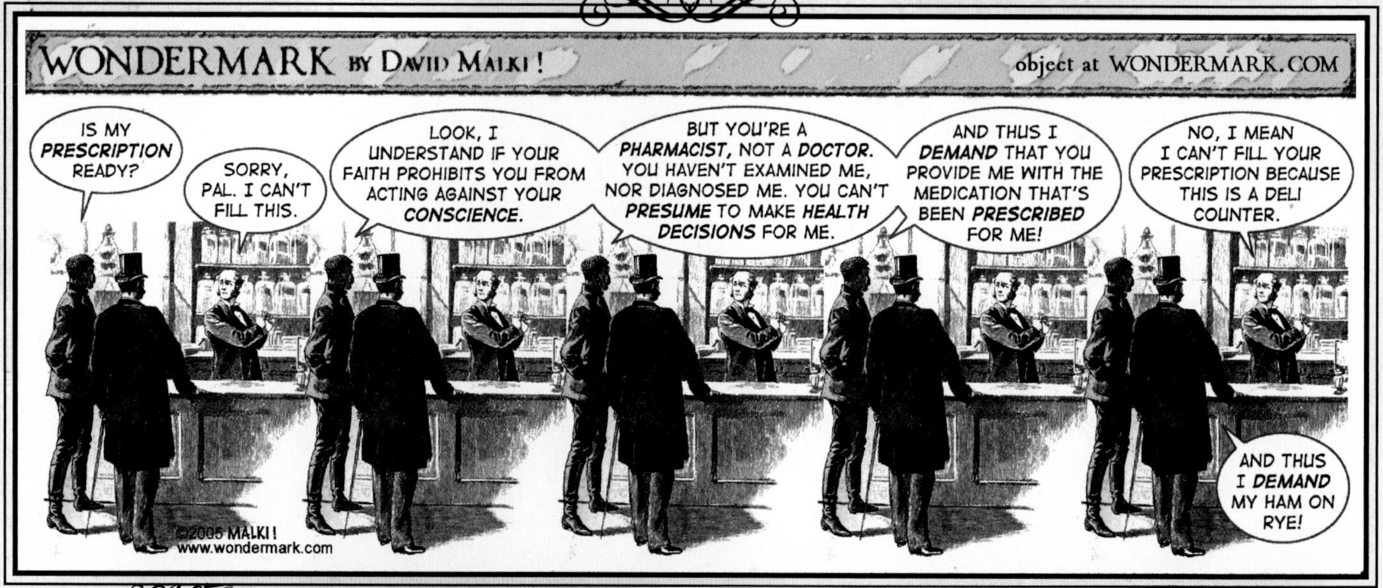
WONDERMARK BY DAVID MALKI !
object at WONDERMARK.COM
IS MY PRESCRIPTION READY?
SORRY, PAL. I CAN'T FILL THIS.
LOOK, I UNDERSTAND IF YOUR FAITH PROHIBITS YOU FROM ACTING AGAINST YOUR CONSCIENCE.
BUT YOU'RE A PHARMACIST, NOT A DOCTOR. YOU HAVEN'T EXAMINED ME, NOR DIAGNOSED ME. YOU CAN'T PRESUME TO MAKE HEALTH DECISIONS FOR ME.
AND THUS I DEMAND THAT YOU PROVIDE ME WITH THE MEDICATION THAT'S BEEN PRESCRIBED FOR ME!
NO, I MEAN I CAN'T FILL YOUR PRESCRIPTION BECAUSE THIS IS A DELI COUNTER.
AND THUS I DEMAND MY HAM ON RYE!
©2005 MALKI! www.wondermark.com

PRESCRIPTION STRENGTH ham on rye

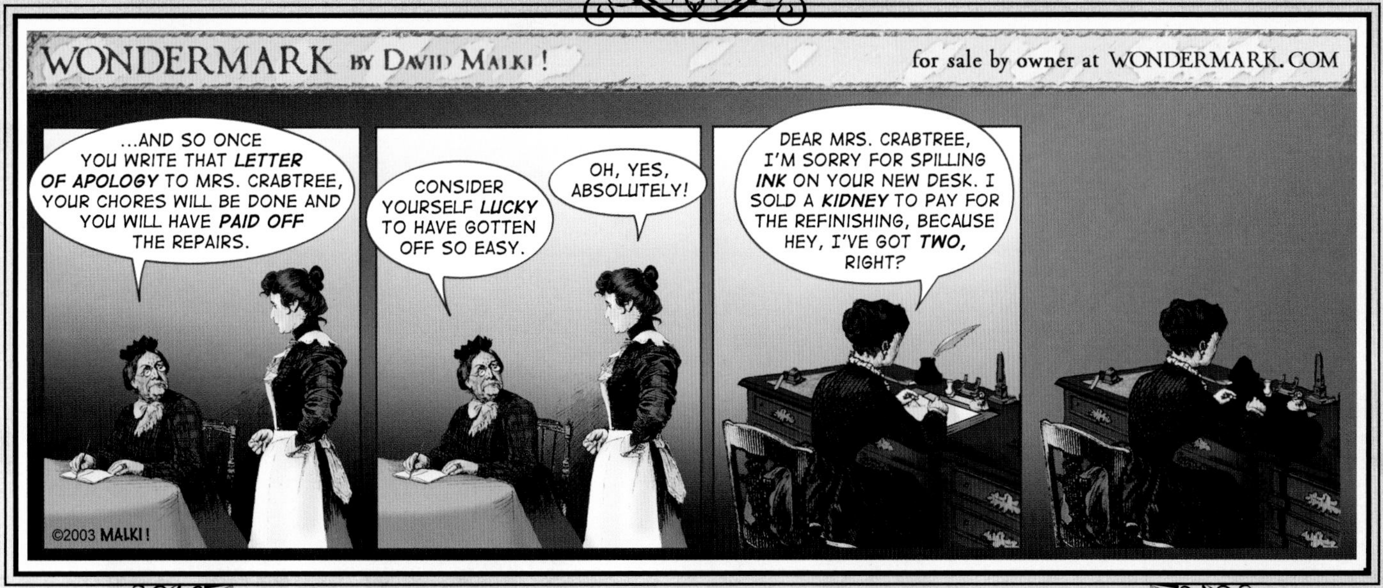
WONDERMARK BY DAVID MALKI !
for sale by owner at WONDERMARK.COM
...AND SO ONCE YOU WRITE THAT LETTER OF APOLOGY TO MRS. CRABTREE, YOUR CHORES WILL BE DONE AND YOU WILL HAVE PAID OFF THE REPAIRS.
CONSIDER YOURSELF LUCKY TO HAVE GOTTEN OFF SO EASY.
OH, YES, ABSOLUTELY!
DEAR MRS. CRABTREE, I'M SORRY FOR SPILLING INK ON YOUR NEW DESK. I SOLD A KIDNEY TO PAY FOR THE REFINISHING, BECAUSE HEY, I'VE GOT TWO, RIGHT?
©2003 MALKI !

it was...a...a squid! I HATE SQUIDS SO MUCH DON'T YOU AGREE

READER MAIL.

SIR: I am writing to express my shock and dismay at the latest episode of your comic strip. Human organ trafficking is no laughing matter. Upwards of twenty billion human organs are illegally sold every day in the United States. Often these organs are taken from immigrants or others who are coerced, and who may fear reporting the crime to authorities. I hope that future episodes of your comic will speak out against this barbaric practice.

MRS. E. EMMETT POLK, FAIRFAX, VA.

SIR: As a professional furniture-refinisher, and the owner of my own refinishing shop for the last thirty-one years, I felt I had to comment on the recent "Wondermark." Furniture refinishing has come a long way in the last decade alone, and the idea that a full refinish costs as much as one might earn from the sale of a kidney is an outdated one. Modern refinishing techniques may not be cheap, but they no longer cost "an arm and a leg."

MR. S. P. CRANFORTH, TACOMA, WA.

SIR: I used to work in a large ink-foundry, and we often experienced similar mishaps. It became such a problem industry-wide that inkers successfully lobbied Congress to pass legislation requiring that all commercially-produced ink-binders inhibit adhesion to desks, tables, etc. Nowadays, ink spilled on a desk will wipe away in an instant. I realize that your comic is not meant to be a bastion of accuracy (and it's also possible that the girl is using home-mixed or gray-market ink that does not follow the Congressional guidelines), but I thought you might like to know that the situation described is not one that could happen today.

DR. PAUL LEE, GUAM.

SIR: I am disgusted that you would characterize individuals with the surname "Crabtree" as vindictive and surly. I am not named Crabtree myself, but I am sure that those who are saddled with that awful name would take great offense.

MS. N. POOPQUICKLY, MADISON, WI.

SIR: Where can I buy a cheap used cornea? I have cash.

W. CRABTREE, ADDRESS WITHHELD.

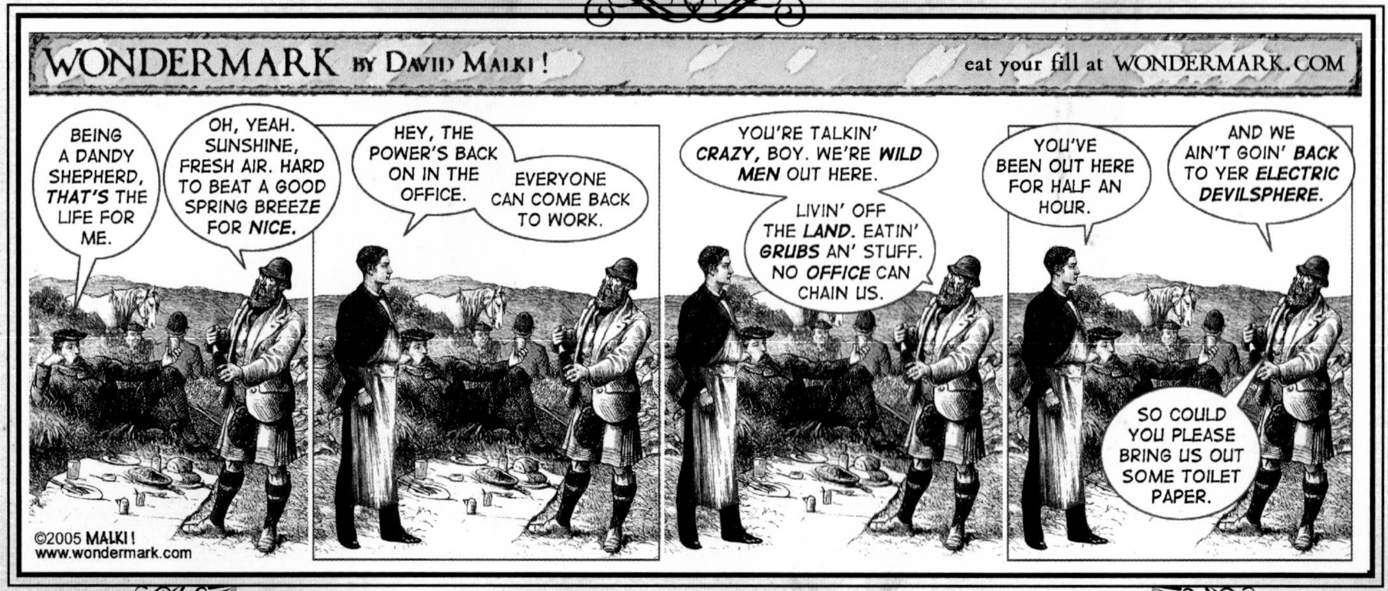
WONDERMARK BY DAVID MALKI !
eat your fill at WONDERMARK.COM
BEING A DANDY SHEPHERD, THAT'S THE LIFE FOR ME.
OH, YEAH. SUNSHINE, FRESH AIR. HARD TO BEAT A GOOD SPRING BREEZE FOR NICE.
©2005 MALKI ! www.wondermark.com
HEY, THE POWER'S BACK ON IN THE OFFICE.
EVERYONE CAN COME BACK TO WORK.
YOU'RE TALKIN' CRAZY, BOY. WE'RE WILD MEN OUT HERE.
LIVIN' OFF THE LAND. EATIN' GRUBS AN' STUFF. NO OFFICE CAN CHAIN US.
YOU'VE BEEN OUT HERE FOR HALF AN HOUR.
AND WE AIN'T GOIN' BACK TO YER ELECTRIC DEVILSPHERE.
SO COULD YOU PLEASE BRING US OUT SOME TOILET PAPER.

the power went out in L.A. today in the middle of the workday, and it made everyone so cheerful

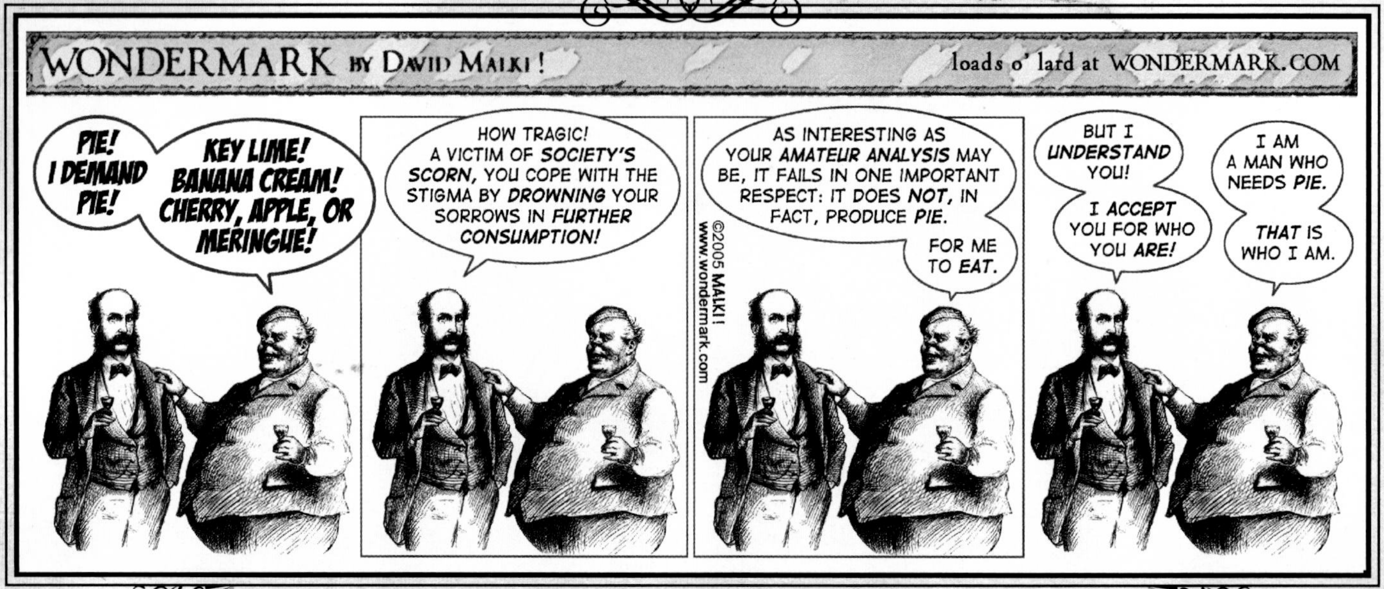
WONDERMARK BY DAVID MALKI !
loads o' lard at WONDERMARK.COM
PIE! I DEMAND PIE!
KEY LIME! BANANA CREAM! CHERRY, APPLE, OR MERINGUE!
HOW TRAGIC! A VICTIM OF SOCIETY'S SCORN, YOU COPE WITH THE STIGMA BY DROWNING YOUR SORROWS IN FURTHER CONSUMPTION!
©2005 MALKI ! www.wondermark.com
AS INTERESTING AS YOUR AMATEUR ANALYSIS MAY BE, IT FAILS IN ONE IMPORTANT RESPECT: IT DOES NOT, IN FACT, PRODUCE PIE.
FOR ME TO EAT.
BUT I UNDERSTAND YOU!
I ACCEPT YOU FOR WHO YOU ARE!
I AM A MAN WHO NEEDS PIE.
THAT IS WHO I AM.

in sophist argument, i demand pie = automatic win

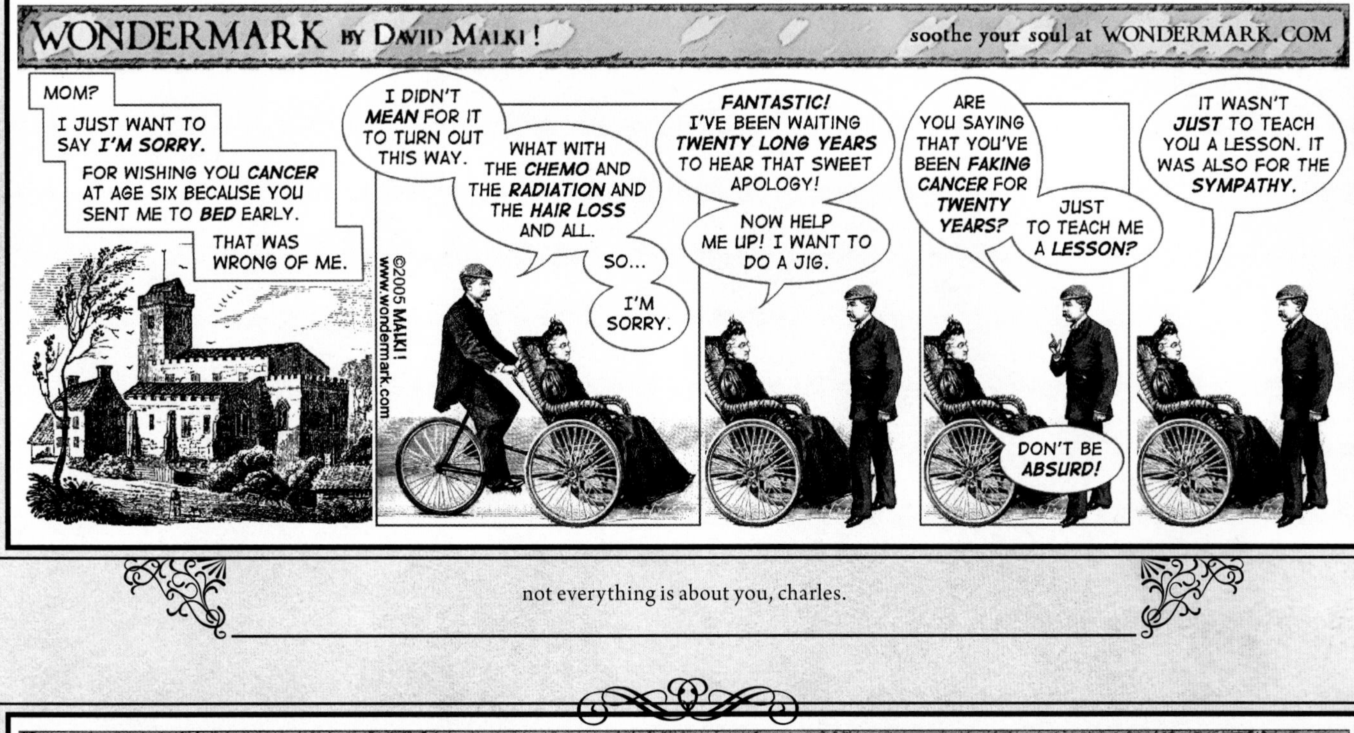
WONDERMARK BY DAVID MALKI !
soothe your soul at WONDERMARK.COM
MOM?
I JUST WANT TO SAY I'M SORRY.
FOR WISHING YOU CANCER AT AGE SIX BECAUSE YOU SENT ME TO BED EARLY.
THAT WAS WRONG OF ME.
I DIDN'T MEAN FOR IT TO TURN OUT THIS WAY.
WHAT WITH THE CHEMO AND THE RADIATION AND THE HAIR LOSS AND ALL.
SO...
I'M SORRY.
©2005 MALKI! www.wondermark.com
FANTASTIC! I'VE BEEN WAITING TWENTY LONG YEARS TO HEAR THAT SWEET APOLOGY!
NOW HELP ME UP! I WANT TO DO A JIG.
ARE YOU SAYING THAT YOU'VE BEEN FAKING CANCER FOR TWENTY YEARS?
JUST TO TEACH ME A LESSON?
DON'T BE ABSURD!
IT WASN'T JUST TO TEACH YOU A LESSON. IT WAS ALSO FOR THE SYMPATHY.

not everything is about you, charles.

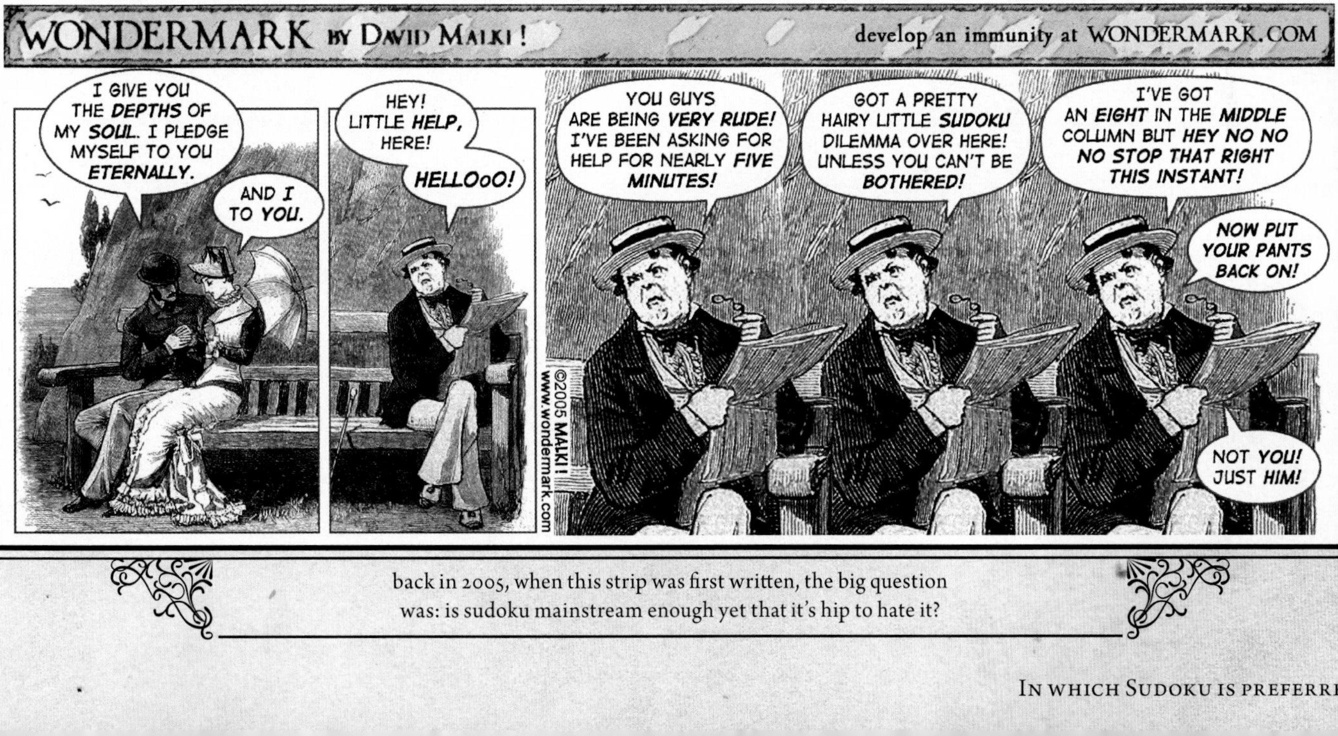
WONDERMARK BY DAVID MALKI !
develop an immunity at WONDERMARK.COM
I GIVE YOU THE DEPTHS OF MY SOUL. I PLEDGE MYSELF TO YOU ETERNALLY.
AND I TO YOU.
HEY! LITTLE HELP, HERE!
HELLOoO!
©2005 MALKI! www.wondermark.com
YOU GUYS ARE BEING VERY RUDE! I'VE BEEN ASKING FOR HELP FOR NEARLY FIVE MINUTES!
GOT A PRETTY HAIRY LITTLE SUDOKU DILEMMA OVER HERE! UNLESS YOU CAN'T BE BOTHERED!
I'VE GOT AN EIGHT IN THE MIDDLE COLUMN BUT HEY NO NO NO STOP THAT RIGHT THIS INSTANT!
NOW PUT YOUR PANTS BACK ON!
NOT YOU! JUST HIM!

back in 2005, when this strip was first written, the big question
was: is sudoku mainstream enough yet that it's hip to hate it?

In which Gracie is burned by a Jewess

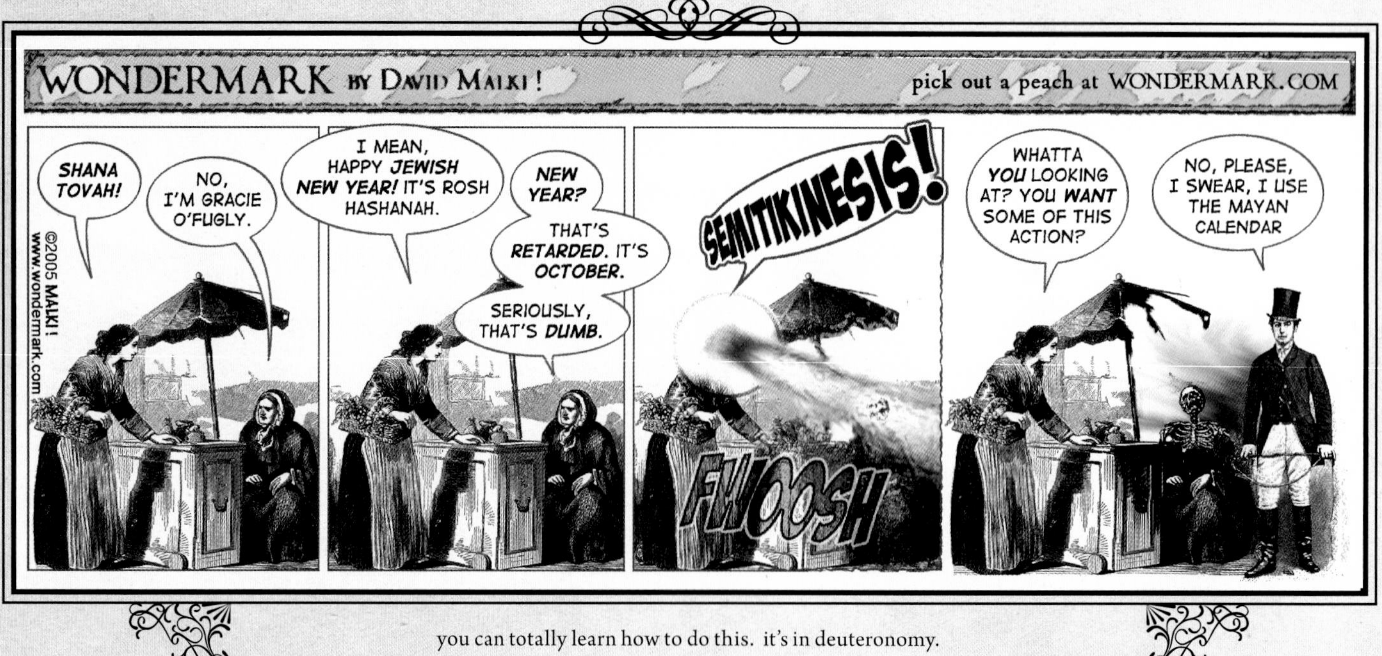
WONDERMARK BY DAVID MALKI !
pick out a peach at WONDERMARK.COM
©2005 MALKI! www.wondermark.com
SHANA TOVAH!
NO, I'M GRACIE O'FUGLY.
I MEAN, HAPPY JEWISH NEW YEAR! IT'S ROSH HASHANAH.
NEW YEAR?
THAT'S RETARDED. IT'S OCTOBER.
SERIOUSLY, THAT'S DUMB.
SEMITIKINESIS!
FWOOSH
WHATTA YOU LOOKING AT? YOU WANT SOME OF THIS ACTION?
NO, PLEASE, I SWEAR, I USE THE MAYAN CALENDAR

you can totally learn how to do this. it's in deuteronomy.

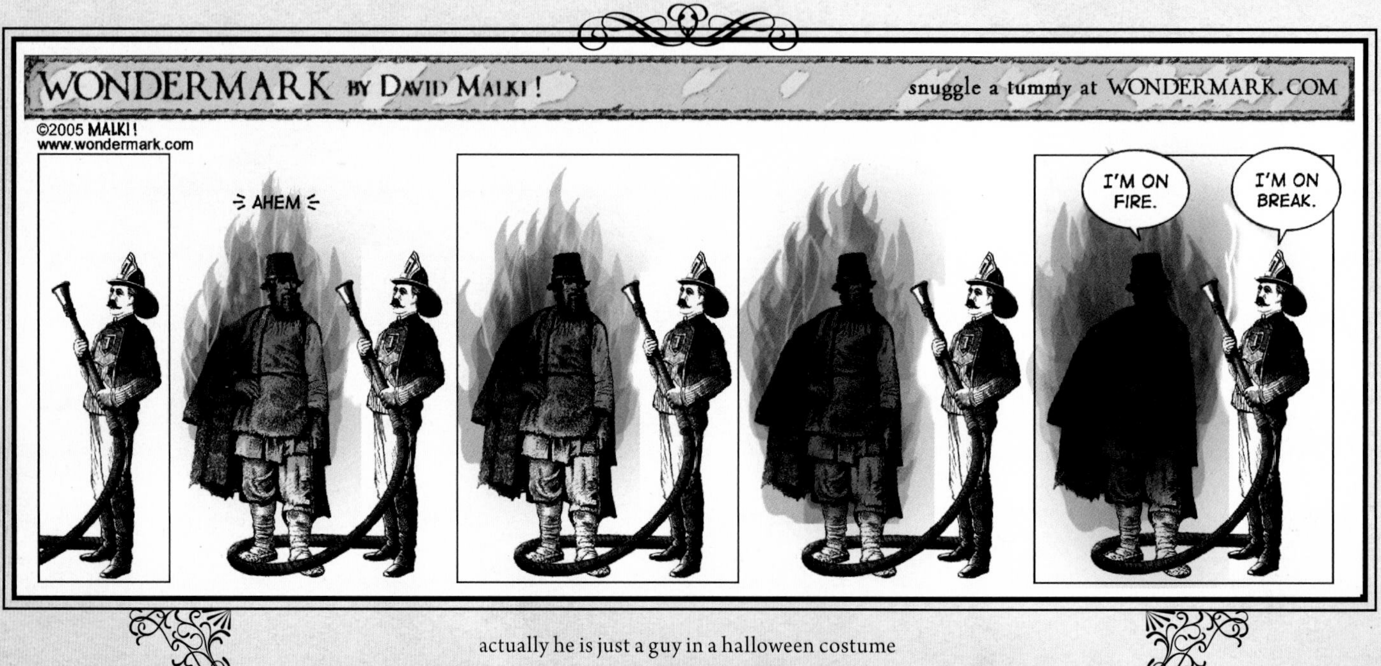
WONDERMARK BY DAVID MALKI !
snuggle a tummy at WONDERMARK.COM
©2005 MALKI!
www.wondermark.com
AHEM
I'M ON FIRE.
I'M ON BREAK.

actually he is just a guy in a halloween costume

In which Duty is shirked

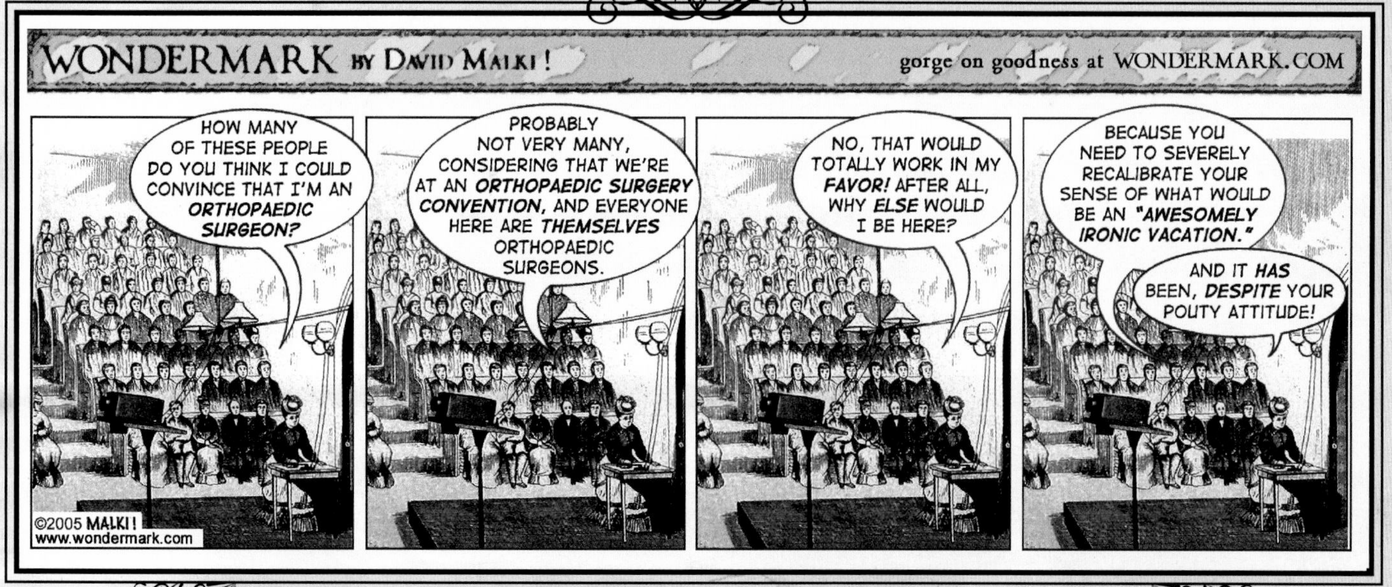
WONDERMARK by David Malki !
gorge on goodness at WONDERMARK.COM
HOW MANY OF THESE PEOPLE DO YOU THINK I COULD CONVINCE THAT I'M AN *ORTHOPAEDIC SURGEON?*
©2005 MALKI! www.wondermark.com
PROBABLY NOT VERY MANY, CONSIDERING THAT WE'RE AT AN *ORTHOPAEDIC SURGERY CONVENTION,* AND EVERYONE HERE ARE *THEMSELVES* ORTHOPAEDIC SURGEONS.
NO, THAT WOULD TOTALLY WORK IN MY *FAVOR!* AFTER ALL, WHY *ELSE* WOULD I BE HERE?
BECAUSE YOU NEED TO SEVERELY RECALIBRATE YOUR SENSE OF WHAT WOULD BE AN *"AWESOMELY IRONIC VACATION."*
AND IT *HAS* BEEN, *DESPITE* YOUR POUTY ATTITUDE!

he was all giddy while paying the registration fee

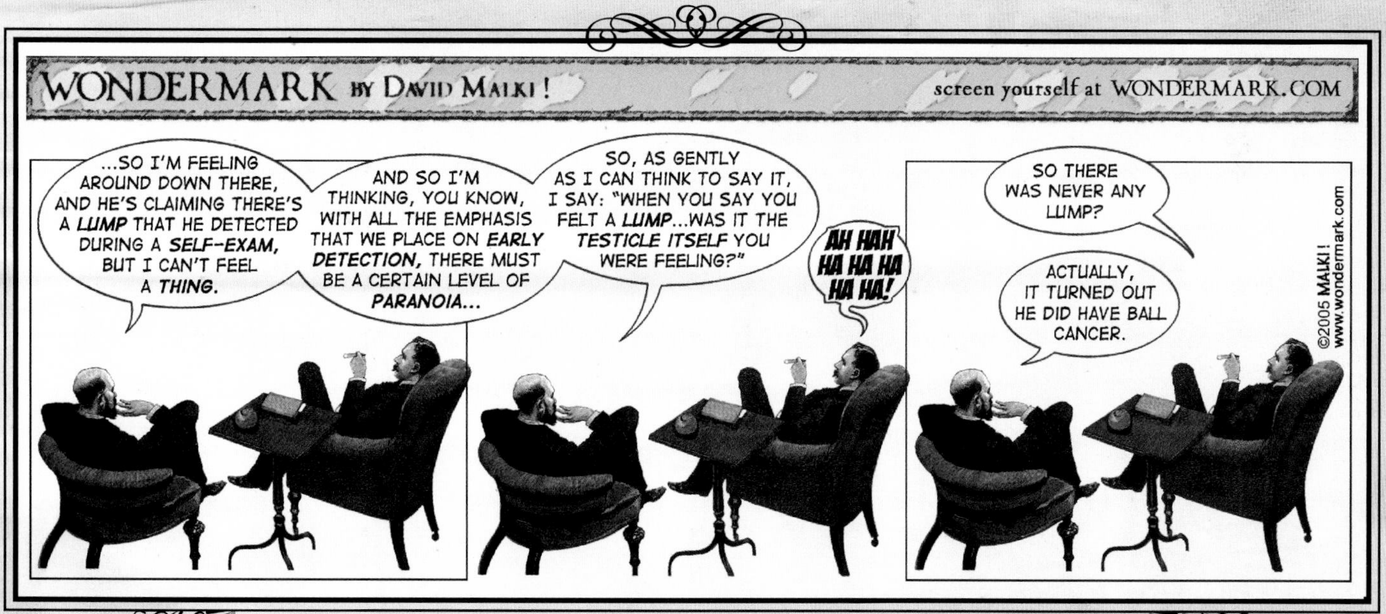
WONDERMARK by David Malki !
screen yourself at WONDERMARK.COM
...SO I'M FEELING AROUND DOWN THERE, AND HE'S CLAIMING THERE'S A *LUMP* THAT HE DETECTED DURING A *SELF-EXAM,* BUT I CAN'T FEEL A *THING.*
AND SO I'M THINKING, YOU KNOW, WITH ALL THE EMPHASIS THAT WE PLACE ON *EARLY DETECTION,* THERE MUST BE A CERTAIN LEVEL OF *PARANOIA...*
SO, AS GENTLY AS I CAN THINK TO SAY IT, I SAY: "WHEN YOU SAY YOU FELT A *LUMP*...WAS IT THE *TESTICLE ITSELF* YOU WERE FEELING?"
AH HAH HA HA HA HA HA!
SO THERE WAS NEVER ANY LUMP?
ACTUALLY, IT TURNED OUT HE DID HAVE BALL CANCER.
©2005 MALKI! www.wondermark.com

sadly, another comic based on a true story

IN WHICH CLYDE WISHES SACKING UPON HIMSELF

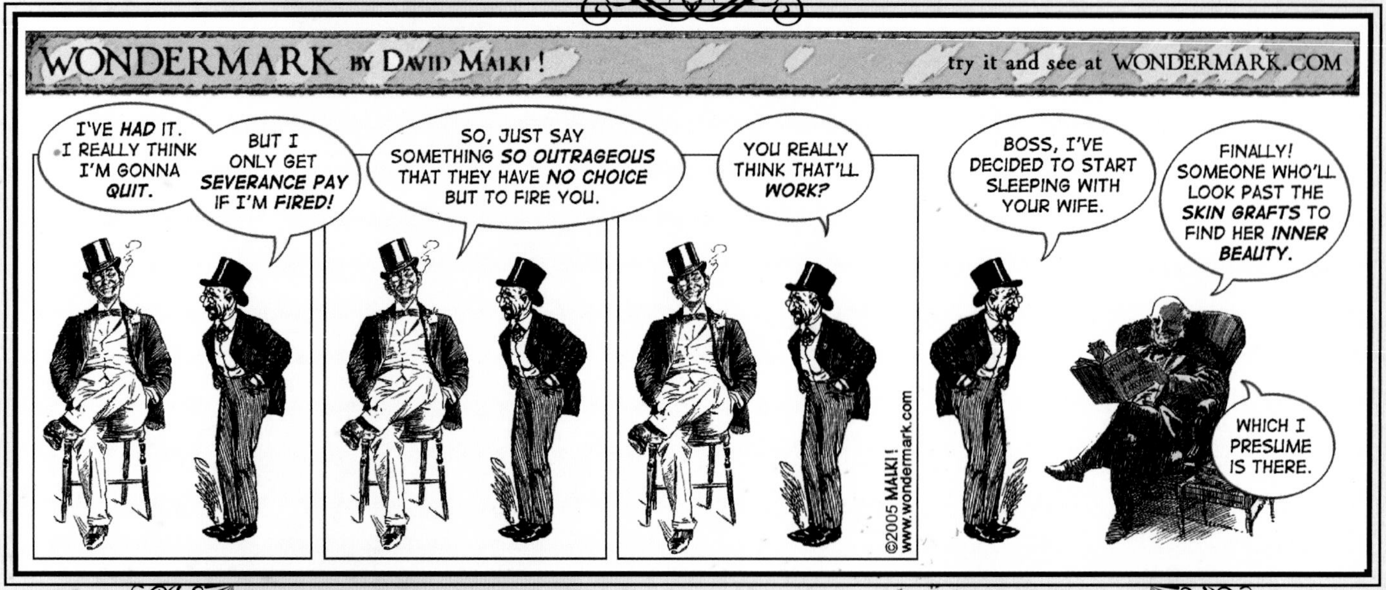
WONDERMARK BY DAVID MALKI !
try it and see at WONDERMARK.COM
I'VE HAD IT. I REALLY THINK I'M GONNA QUIT.
BUT I ONLY GET SEVERANCE PAY IF I'M FIRED!
SO, JUST SAY SOMETHING SO OUTRAGEOUS THAT THEY HAVE NO CHOICE BUT TO FIRE YOU.
YOU REALLY THINK THAT'LL WORK?
©2005 MALKI ! www.wondermark.com
BOSS, I'VE DECIDED TO START SLEEPING WITH YOUR WIFE.
FINALLY! SOMEONE WHO'LL LOOK PAST THE SKIN GRAFTS TO FIND HER INNER BEAUTY.
WHICH I PRESUME IS THERE.

historically this has been less than effective

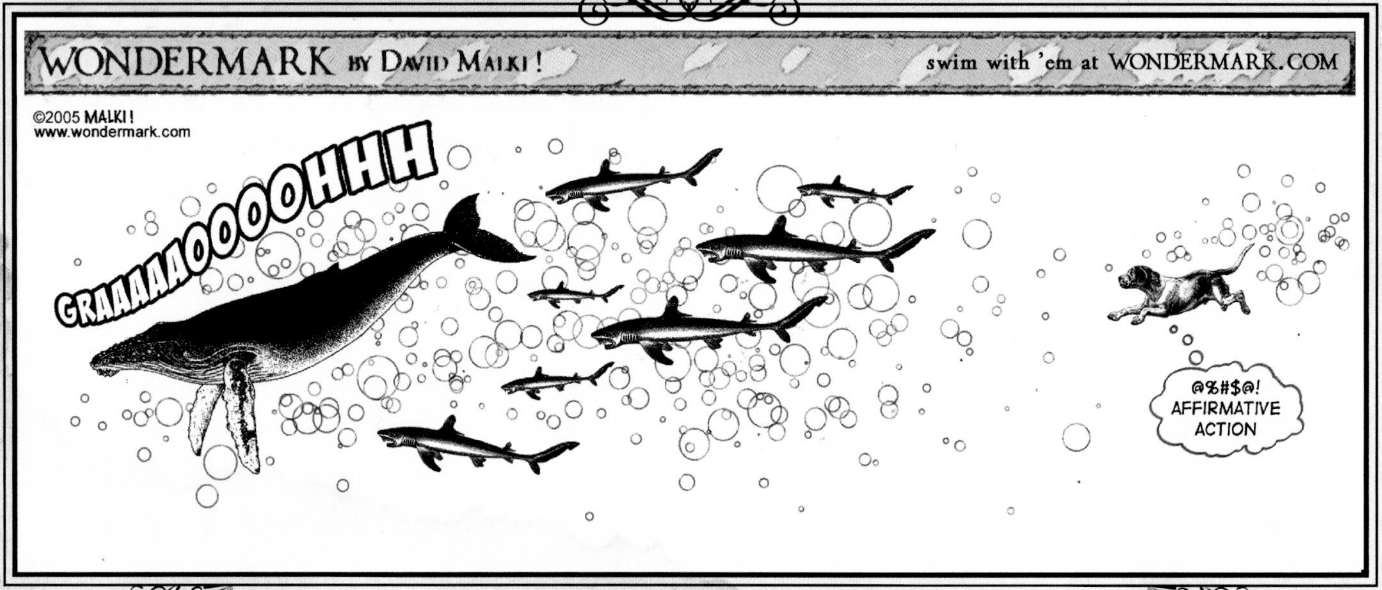
WONDERMARK BY DAVID MALKI !
swim with 'em at WONDERMARK.COM
©2005 MALKI ! www.wondermark.com
GRAAAAAOOOOOHHHH
@%#$@! AFFIRMATIVE ACTION

and he seemed so competent in the interview!

IN WHICH SHARKS ARE SWUM WITH

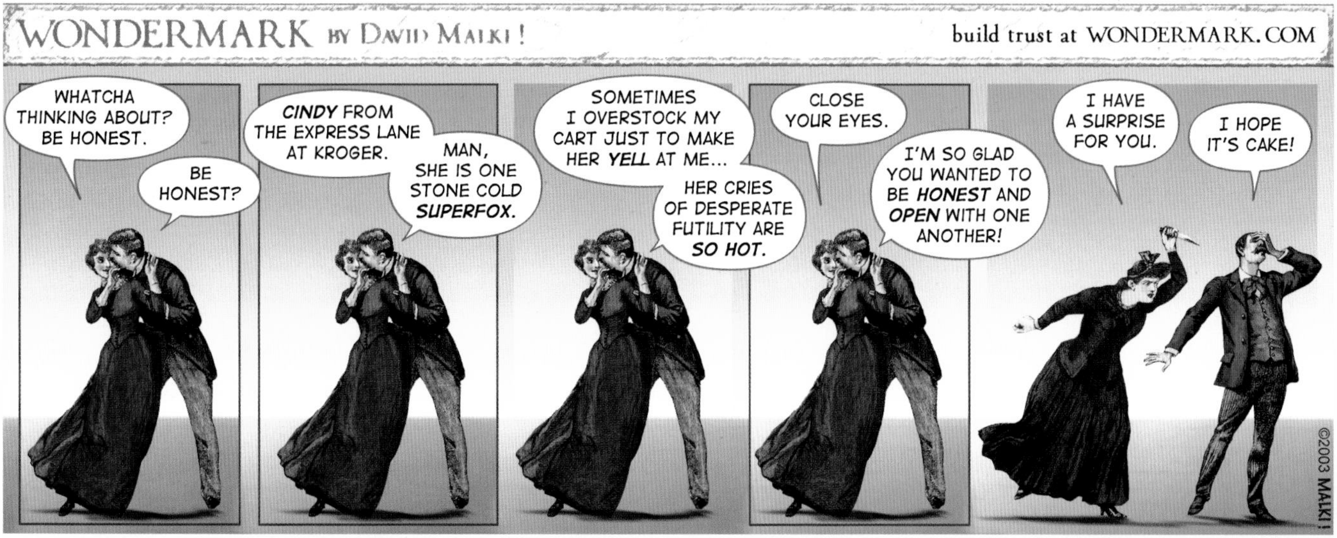
WONDERMARK by David Malki!
build trust at WONDERMARK.COM
WHATCHA THINKING ABOUT? BE HONEST.
BE HONEST?
CINDY FROM THE EXPRESS LANE AT KROGER.
MAN, SHE IS ONE STONE COLD SUPERFOX.
SOMETIMES I OVERSTOCK MY CART JUST TO MAKE HER YELL AT ME...
HER CRIES OF DESPERATE FUTILITY ARE SO HOT.
CLOSE YOUR EYES.
I'M SO GLAD YOU WANTED TO BE HONEST AND OPEN WITH ONE ANOTHER!
I HAVE A SURPRISE FOR YOU.
I HOPE IT'S CAKE!
©2003 MALKI!

the backbone of marriage is about to get a shiv shoved through it

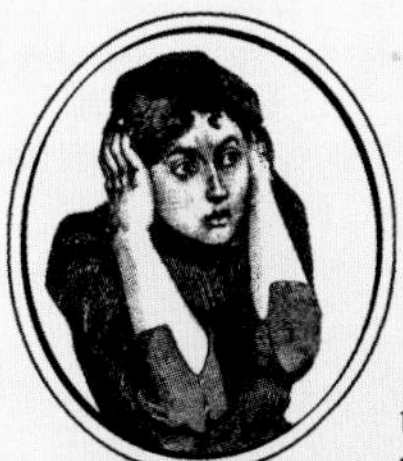

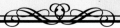

"He makes it really hard to do my job."

YEAH, I know that guy. He comes in at least twice a week, and he always buys the dumbest stuff—like twelve individual soda cans, instead of a single 12-pack that I can scan as one item. I try to tell him that twelve items disqualifies him for the express checkout, but he just smirks and says something retarded, like "Explain how."

I swear, I am *not* paid enough to deal with jerks like him. As if the clueless masses aren't bad enough—the old ladies who didn't realize that their coupons expired six months ago; the moms who let their screaming kids decimate the candy shelves; the guys buying beer at eight in the morning who "forgot" their ID at home—on top of it I have to deal with guys like *him*, who're creepy on purpose.

I mean, does he think that I'm going to go out with him? Does he really believe that my smile and friendly "hello" are anything but store policy-mandated? All I want to do is scan your crap and get you out of my lane. Anything I do beyond that is purely grease to move you along faster.

It never fails, though—someone'll claim that the price was different back on the shelf, or that this is damaged and I should discount it, or that was supposed to be on clearance. I'll have to call the manager over. Bethany *always* caves to their shrill demands, which leaves me standing there looking like an idiot for refusing. Honestly, sometimes all I want to do is just go into the bathroom and cry. The one thing I do *not* need is *his* voice intruding into my private thoughts, all smooth and trying to be sympathetic, saying "That moron doesn't deserve you" and "You are *so cute* when you're mad" and "Oh, don't these all count as one item?"

Man, it's *never* cake.

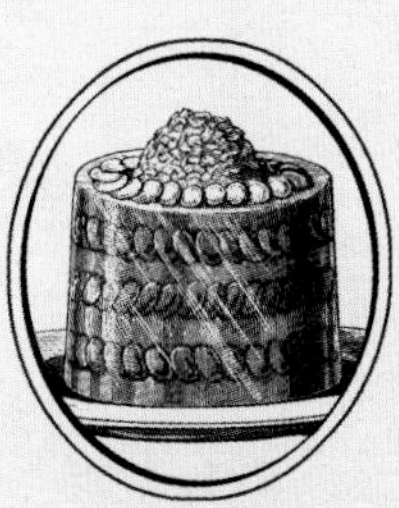

In which Awkwardness ensues

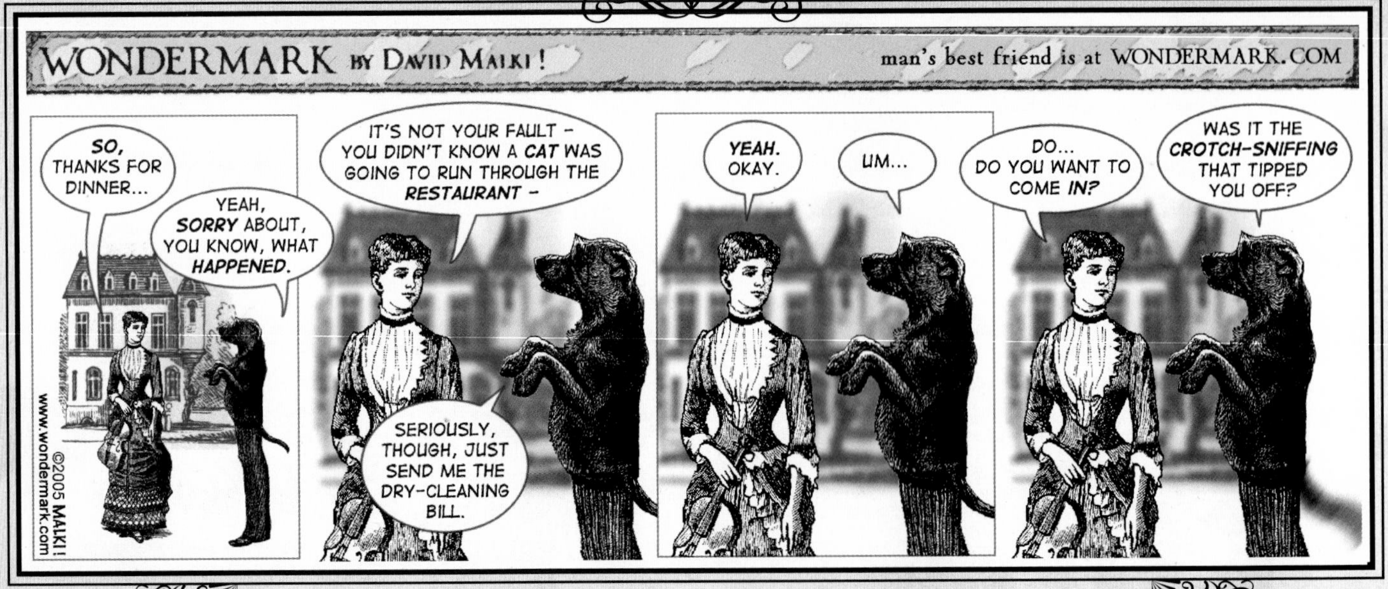
WONDERMARK BY DAVID MALKI!
man's best friend is at WONDERMARK.COM
SO, THANKS FOR DINNER...
YEAH, SORRY ABOUT, YOU KNOW, WHAT HAPPENED.
©2005 MALKI! www.wondermark.com
IT'S NOT YOUR FAULT – YOU DIDN'T KNOW A CAT WAS GOING TO RUN THROUGH THE RESTAURANT –
SERIOUSLY, THOUGH, JUST SEND ME THE DRY-CLEANING BILL.
YEAH. OKAY.
UM...
DO... DO YOU WANT TO COME IN?
WAS IT THE CROTCH-SNIFFING THAT TIPPED YOU OFF?

you don't happen to have any tables in there, do you...
because table legs also tend to, ah, set me off

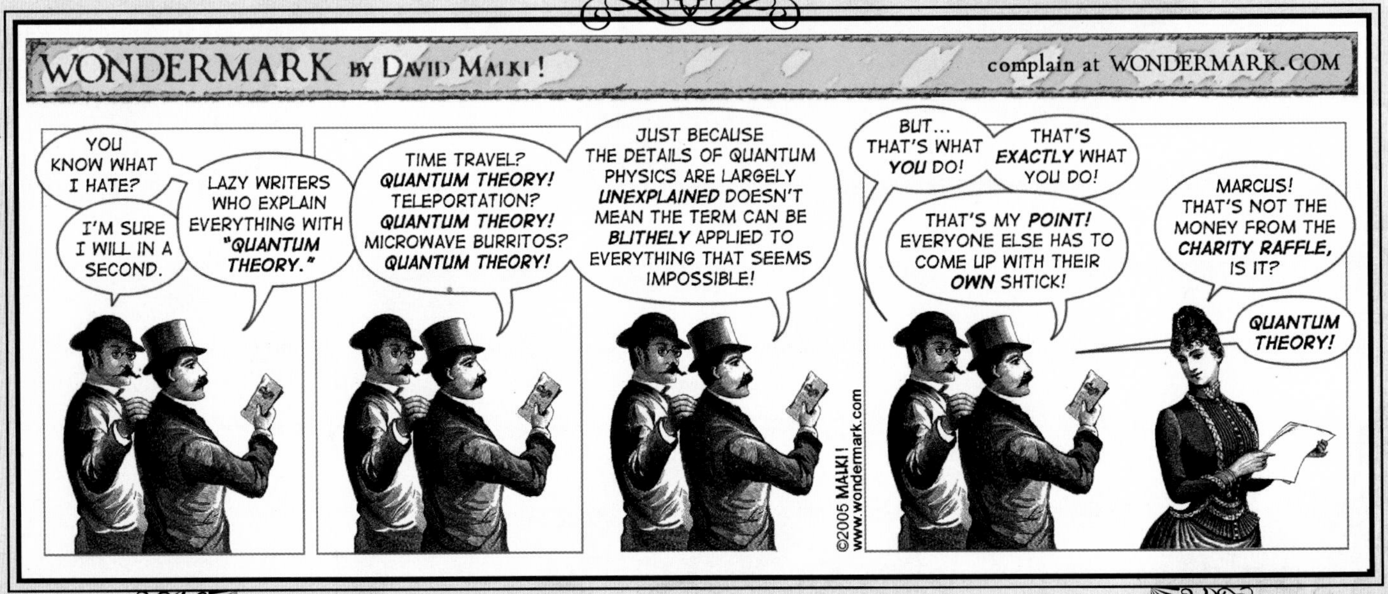
WONDERMARK BY DAVID MALKI!
complain at WONDERMARK.COM
YOU KNOW WHAT I HATE?
I'M SURE I WILL IN A SECOND.
LAZY WRITERS WHO EXPLAIN EVERYTHING WITH "QUANTUM THEORY."
TIME TRAVEL? QUANTUM THEORY! TELEPORTATION? QUANTUM THEORY! MICROWAVE BURRITOS? QUANTUM THEORY!
JUST BECAUSE THE DETAILS OF QUANTUM PHYSICS ARE LARGELY UNEXPLAINED DOESN'T MEAN THE TERM CAN BE BLITHELY APPLIED TO EVERYTHING THAT SEEMS IMPOSSIBLE!
©2005 MALKI! www.wondermark.com
BUT... THAT'S WHAT YOU DO!
THAT'S EXACTLY WHAT YOU DO!
THAT'S MY POINT! EVERYONE ELSE HAS TO COME UP WITH THEIR OWN SHTICK!
MARCUS! THAT'S NOT THE MONEY FROM THE CHARITY RAFFLE, IS IT?
QUANTUM THEORY!

someone's been reading michael crichton's 'timeline'

In which a Peeve is described

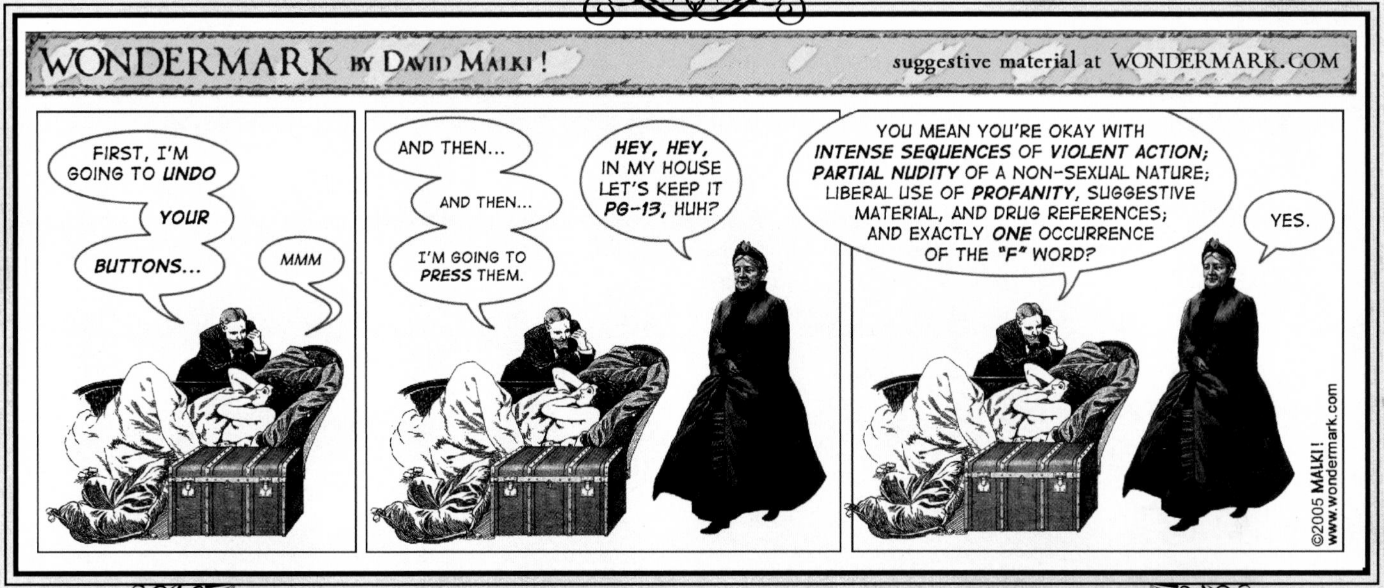
WONDERMARK BY DAVID MALKI!
suggestive material at WONDERMARK.COM
FIRST, I'M GOING TO UNDO
YOUR
BUTTONS...
MMM
AND THEN...
AND THEN...
I'M GOING TO PRESS THEM.
HEY, HEY, IN MY HOUSE LET'S KEEP IT PG-13, HUH?
YOU MEAN YOU'RE OKAY WITH INTENSE SEQUENCES OF VIOLENT ACTION; PARTIAL NUDITY OF A NON-SEXUAL NATURE; LIBERAL USE OF PROFANITY, SUGGESTIVE MATERIAL, AND DRUG REFERENCES; AND EXACTLY ONE OCCURRENCE OF THE "F" WORD?
YES.
©2005 MALKI!
www.wondermark.com

and in fact I will be satisfied with nothing less

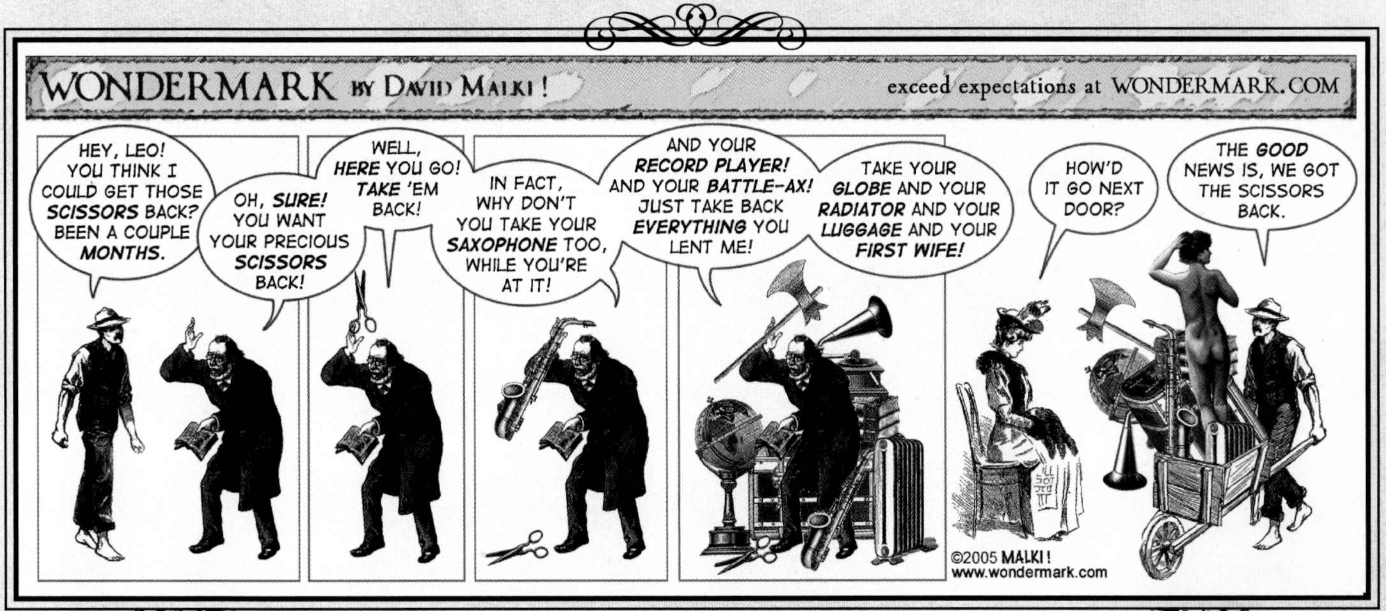
WONDERMARK BY DAVID MALKI!
exceed expectations at WONDERMARK.COM
HEY, LEO! YOU THINK I COULD GET THOSE SCISSORS BACK? BEEN A COUPLE MONTHS.
OH, SURE! YOU WANT YOUR PRECIOUS SCISSORS BACK!
WELL, HERE YOU GO! TAKE 'EM BACK!
IN FACT, WHY DON'T YOU TAKE YOUR SAXOPHONE TOO, WHILE YOU'RE AT IT!
AND YOUR RECORD PLAYER! AND YOUR BATTLE-AX! JUST TAKE BACK EVERYTHING YOU LENT ME!
TAKE YOUR GLOBE AND YOUR RADIATOR AND YOUR LUGGAGE AND YOUR FIRST WIFE!
HOW'D IT GO NEXT DOOR?
THE GOOD NEWS IS, WE GOT THE SCISSORS BACK.
©2005 MALKI!
www.wondermark.com

also the globe will be handy

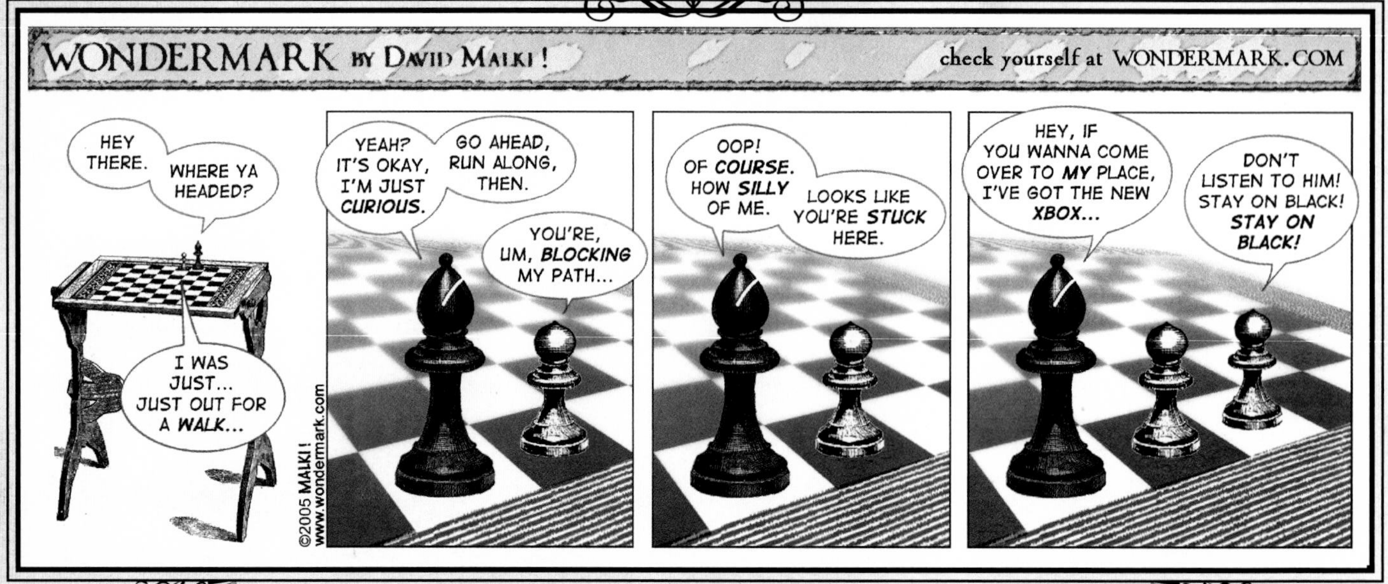
WONDERMARK by David Malki !
check yourself at WONDERMARK.COM
HEY THERE.
WHERE YA HEADED?
I WAS JUST... JUST OUT FOR A WALK...
©2005 MALKI ! www.wondermark.com
YEAH? IT'S OKAY, I'M JUST CURIOUS.
GO AHEAD, RUN ALONG, THEN.
YOU'RE, UM, BLOCKING MY PATH...
OOP! OF COURSE. HOW SILLY OF ME.
LOOKS LIKE YOU'RE STUCK HERE.
HEY, IF YOU WANNA COME OVER TO MY PLACE, I'VE GOT THE NEW XBOX...
DON'T LISTEN TO HIM! STAY ON BLACK! STAY ON BLACK!

just then a knight in shining armor came charging up, but he could only move in L-shapes so he was not terribly helpful

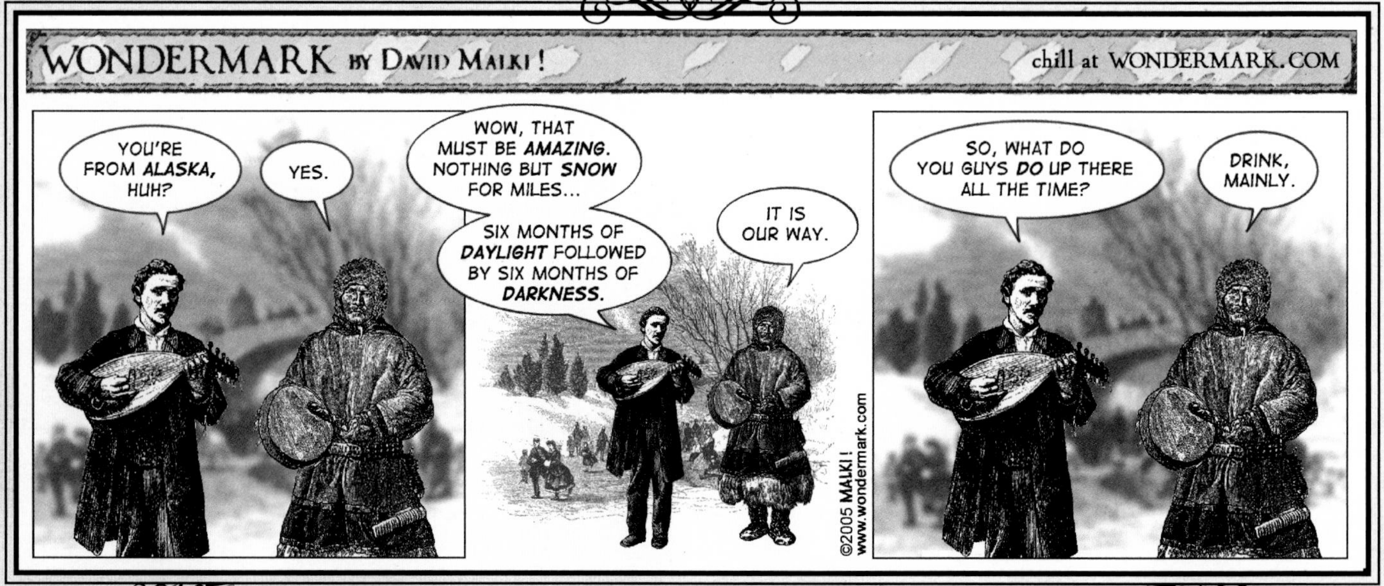
WONDERMARK by David Malki !
chill at WONDERMARK.COM
YOU'RE FROM ALASKA, HUH?
YES.
WOW, THAT MUST BE AMAZING. NOTHING BUT SNOW FOR MILES...
SIX MONTHS OF DAYLIGHT FOLLOWED BY SIX MONTHS OF DARKNESS.
IT IS OUR WAY.
©2005 MALKI ! www.wondermark.com
SO, WHAT DO YOU GUYS DO UP THERE ALL THE TIME?
DRINK, MAINLY.

real life comics #3

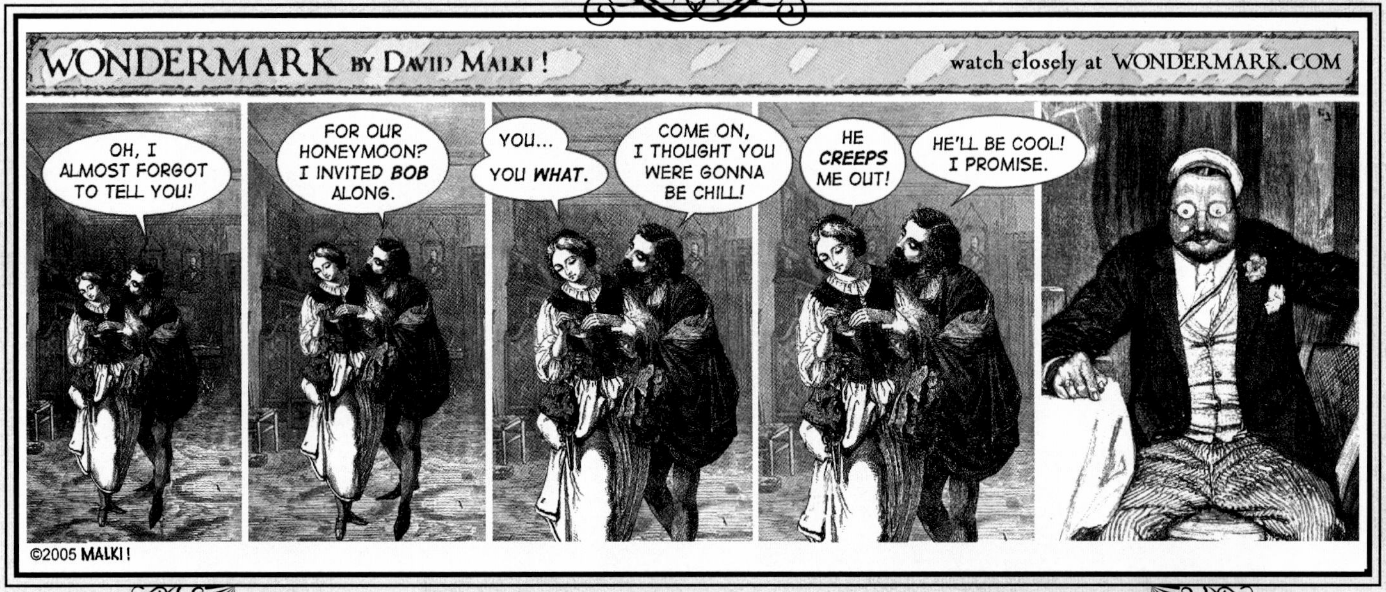
WONDERMARK BY DAVID MALKI !
watch closely at WONDERMARK.COM
OH, I ALMOST FORGOT TO TELL YOU!
FOR OUR HONEYMOON? I INVITED BOB ALONG.
YOU...
YOU WHAT.
COME ON, I THOUGHT YOU WERE GONNA BE CHILL!
HE CREEPS ME OUT!
HE'LL BE COOL! I PROMISE.
©2005 MALKI !

he's DOING it again

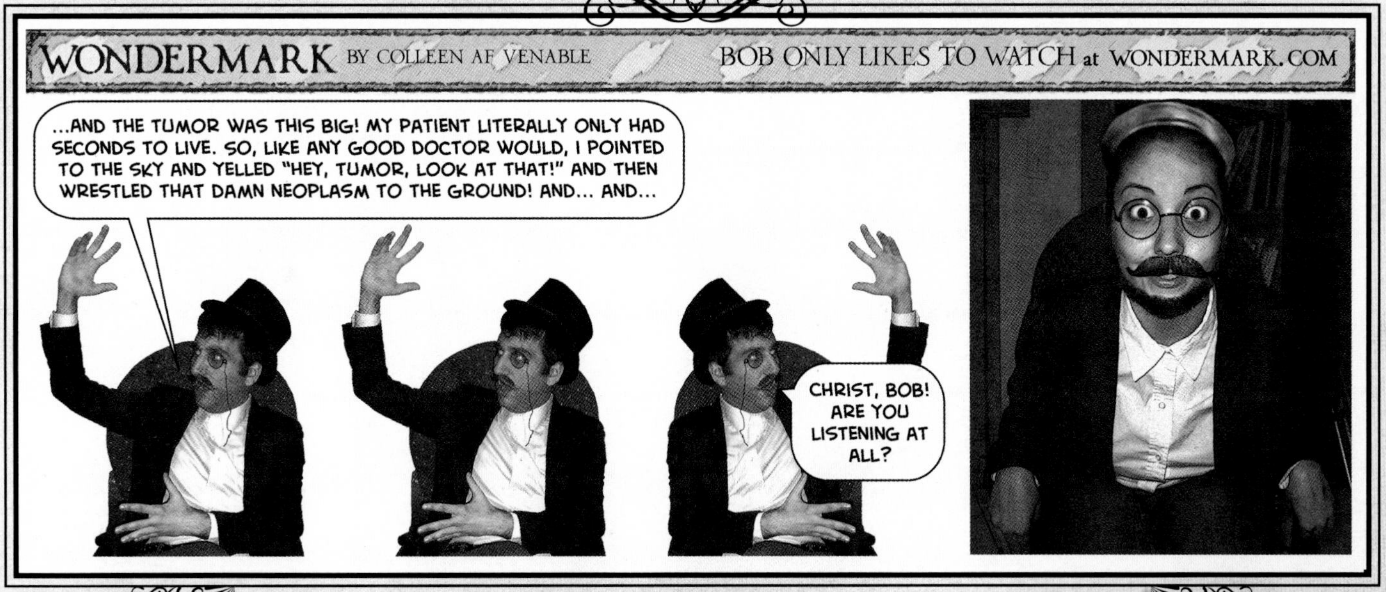
WONDERMARK BY COLLEEN AF VENABLE
BOB ONLY LIKES TO WATCH at WONDERMARK.COM
...AND THE TUMOR WAS THIS BIG! MY PATIENT LITERALLY ONLY HAD SECONDS TO LIVE. SO, LIKE ANY GOOD DOCTOR WOULD, I POINTED TO THE SKY AND YELLED "HEY, TUMOR, LOOK AT THAT!" AND THEN WRESTLED THAT DAMN NEOPLASM TO THE GROUND! AND... AND...
CHRIST, BOB! ARE YOU LISTENING AT ALL?

he's still doooooing it

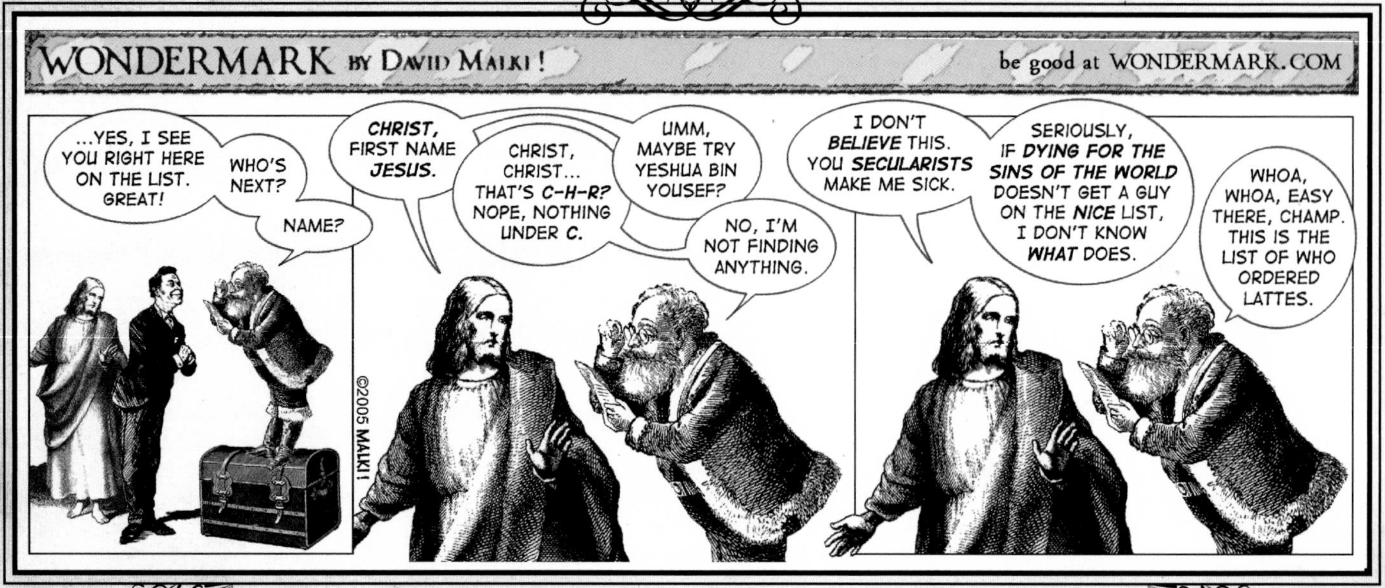
WONDERMARK by David Malki !
be good at WONDERMARK.COM
...YES, I SEE YOU RIGHT HERE ON THE LIST. GREAT!
WHO'S NEXT?
NAME?
©2005 MALKI !
CHRIST, FIRST NAME JESUS.
CHRIST, CHRIST... THAT'S C-H-R? NOPE, NOTHING UNDER C.
UMM, MAYBE TRY YESHUA BIN YOUSEF?
NO, I'M NOT FINDING ANYTHING.
I DON'T BELIEVE THIS. YOU SECULARISTS MAKE ME SICK.
SERIOUSLY, IF DYING FOR THE SINS OF THE WORLD DOESN'T GET A GUY ON THE NICE LIST, I DON'T KNOW WHAT DOES.
WHOA, WHOA, EASY THERE, CHAMP. THIS IS THE LIST OF WHO ORDERED LATTES.

don't make me call my dad

32

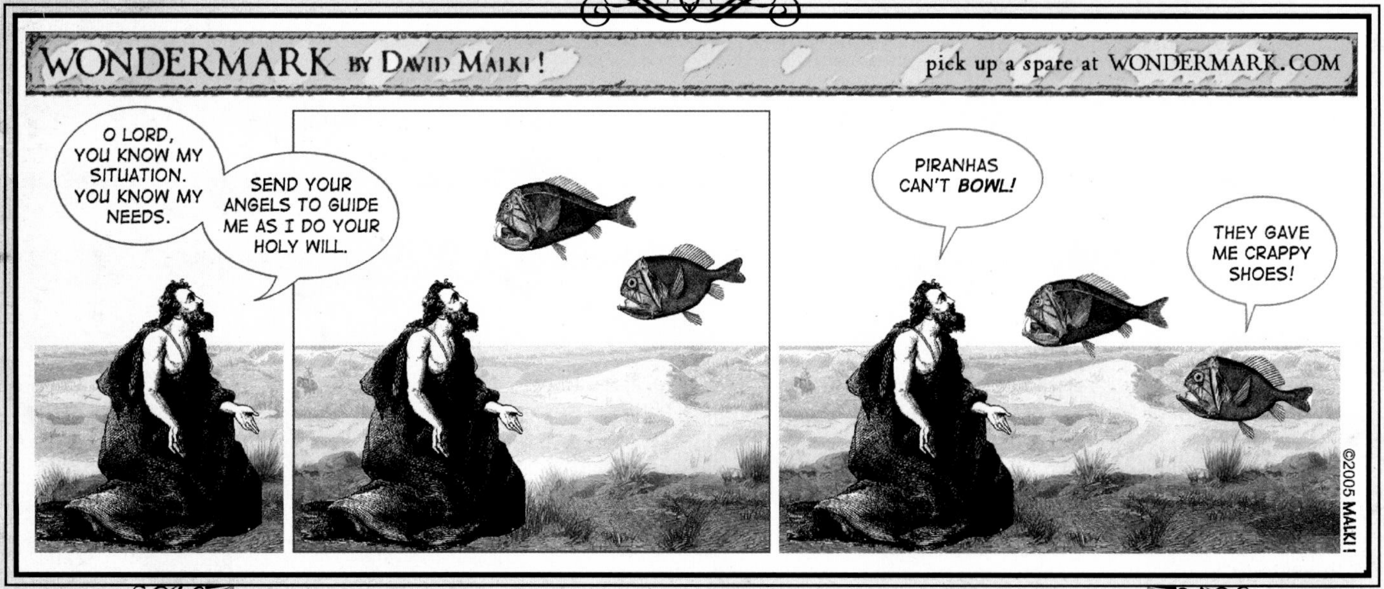
WONDERMARK by David Malki !
pick up a spare at WONDERMARK.COM
O LORD, YOU KNOW MY SITUATION. YOU KNOW MY NEEDS.
SEND YOUR ANGELS TO GUIDE ME AS I DO YOUR HOLY WILL.
PIRANHAS CAN'T BOWL!
THEY GAVE ME CRAPPY SHOES!
©2005 MALKI !

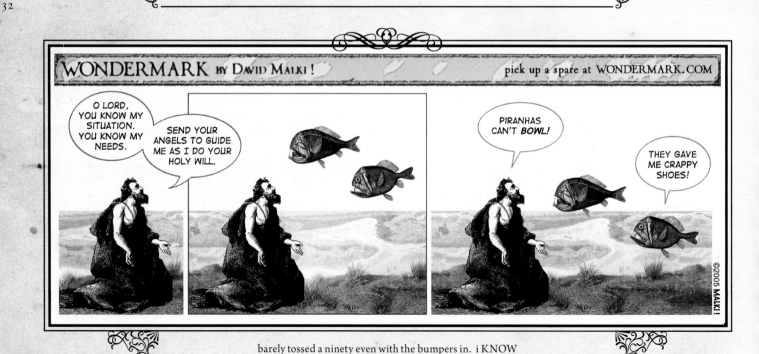

barely tossed a ninety even with the bumpers in. i KNOW

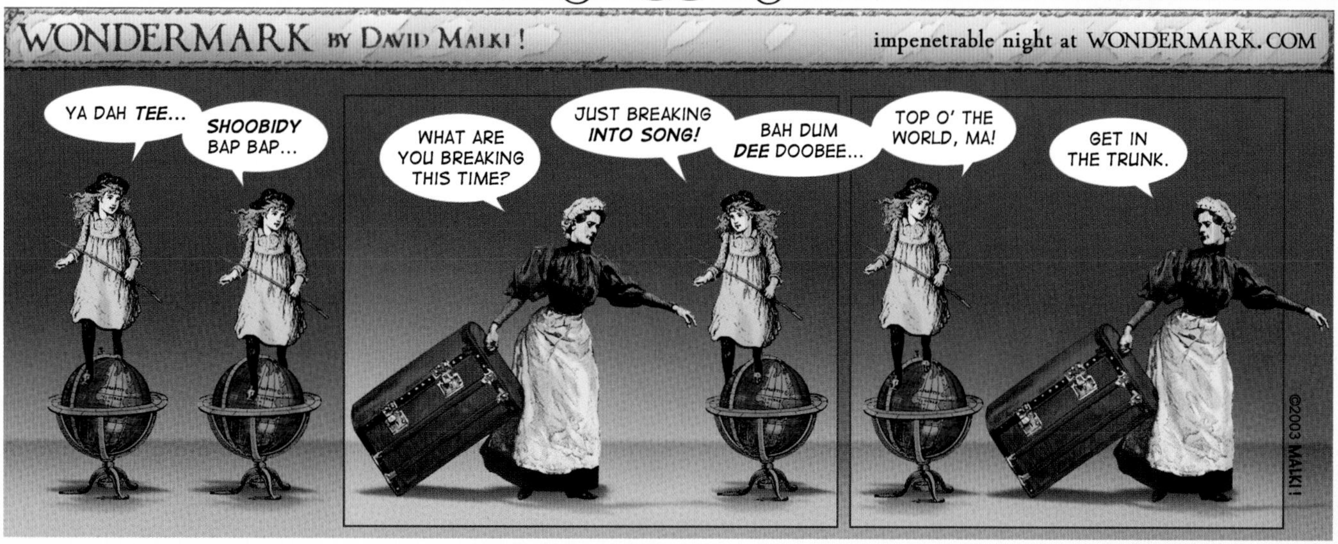
WONDERMARK BY DAVID MALKI !
impenetrable night at WONDERMARK.COM
YA DAH TEE...
SHOOBIDY BAP BAP...
WHAT ARE YOU BREAKING THIS TIME?
JUST BREAKING INTO SONG!
BAH DUM DEE DOOBEE...
TOP O' THE WORLD, MA!
GET IN THE TRUNK.
©2003 MALKI!

that's ALWAYS your answer!

Canvas Covered Trunk for $2.25.

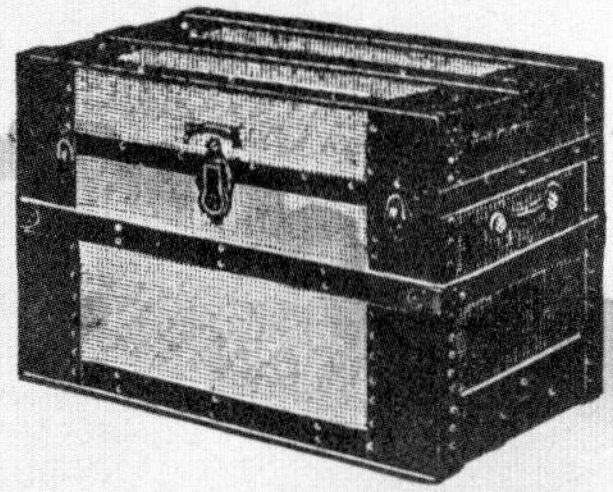

A Good Canvas Covered Trunk at a very low price. Square top, painted canvas cover, hardwood slats on top and body, protected with heavy iron clamps, heavy bottom cleats. Monitor lock and patent bolts and heavy hinges. Easily fits children up to 9 years old. As soundproof as any trunk in its price range. **The best low priced canvas covered trunk sold anywhere.**

Our Square Top Trunk, $2.75.

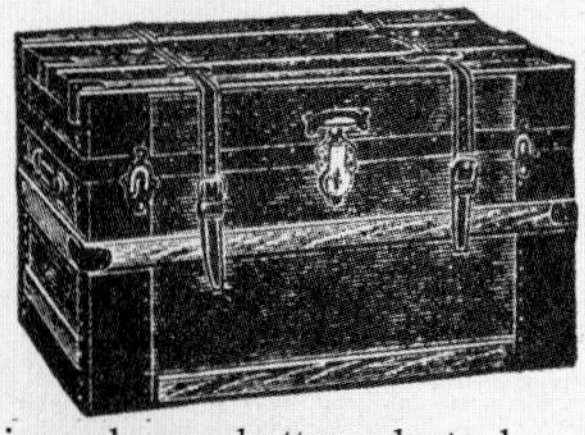

Our Special Low Priced Square Top Trunk, made with leather straps fitted for young wrists and ankles, painted, canvas covered. Hardwood slats on top and body; latch is not accessible from inside. Protected by iron clamps, bottom cleats, brass Monitor lock, buckle bar bolts, heavy hinges, with occupant food compartment separate. **Remember you can buy trunks from us as cheap as your home merchant.**

Our $3.55 Steel Bound Trunk.

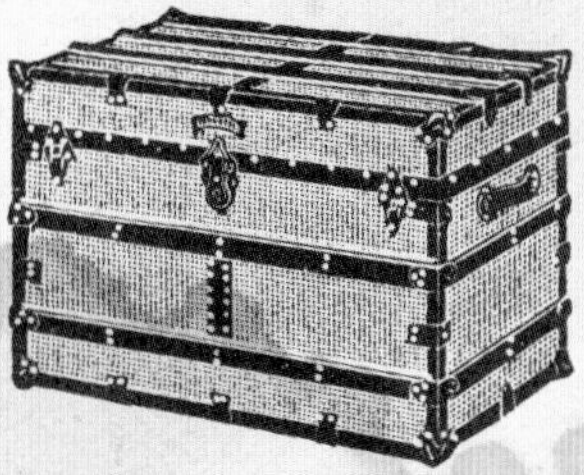

Cheapest Steel Bound Trunk in the market, large box, four heavy hardwood slats on top and two on body running full length, heavy japanned corners and steel strip clasp, heavy bolts. Lid will withstand interior kicks from most children of average leg strength. For larger boys we recomend iron, below. **An honest, strong trunk at a very low price.**

Black Enameled Iron Trunk for $4.00.

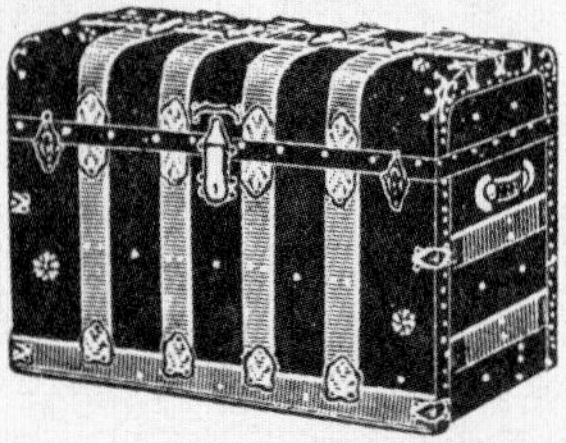

Black Enameled Iron, Round Top Trunk, hardwood bent slats on top with one extra slat in center full length of trunk. Leather handles, brass Excelsior lock, patent bolts, full covered hinge tray with bonnet box, fall-in-top, iron bottom, all fancy trimmed. Reinforced to fit boys up to 12 y.o. or fat boys up to 10. **Totally escape-proof when properly secured.**

Flat Top Heavy Duck Cover Trunk.

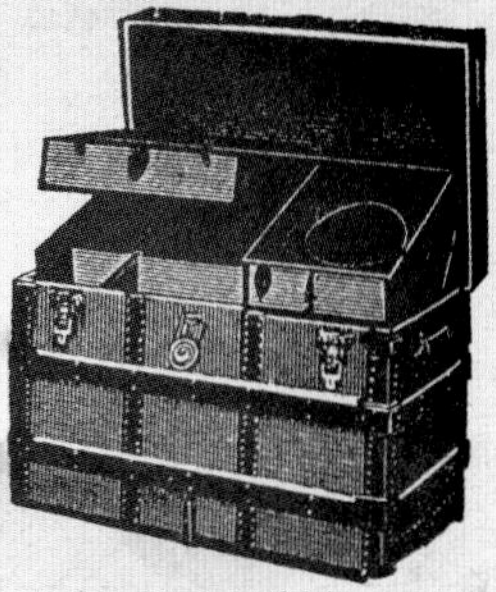

Flat Top. Heavy Duck Cover Trunk. Double wide iron bound, two center bands, end slats all protected, heavy iron bumpers, corner shoes, etc. Stitched leather handles, high combination tray, all covered, fine linen finish. A new item designed for twins or squabbling cousins. Easy-access watering port allows containment for weeks. **Finally, some respite in the home.**

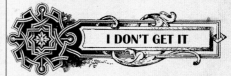

I DON'T GET IT

These trunks are expressly for the confinement of children.

In which Pete recalls the Past

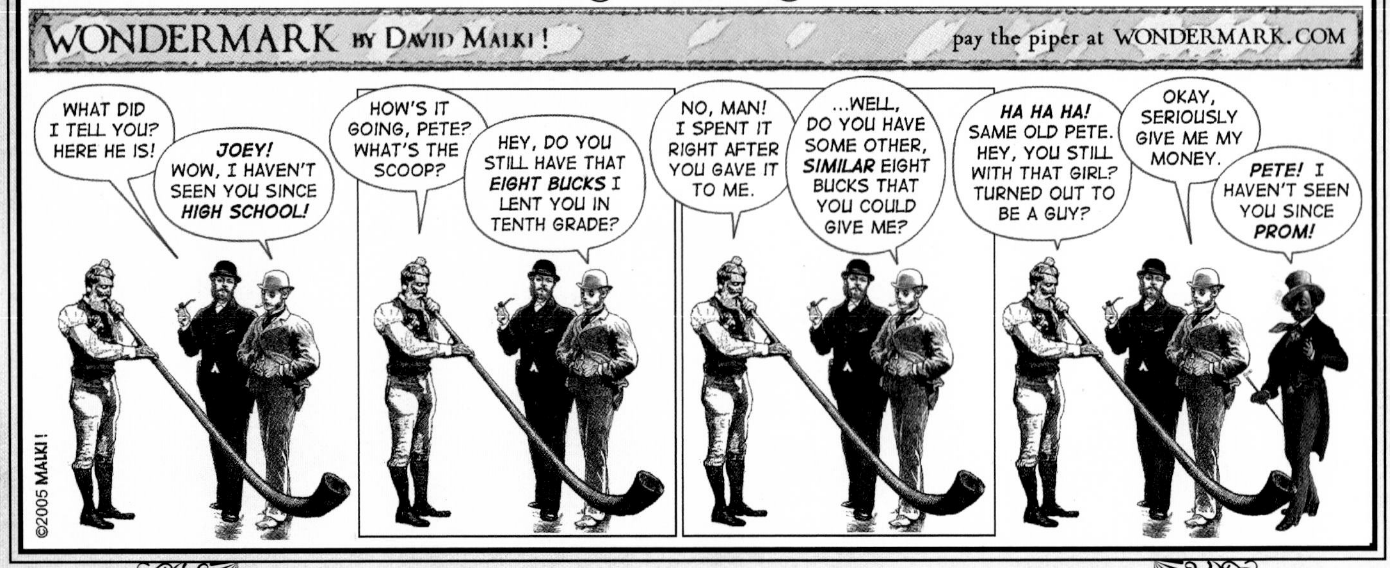
WONDERMARK BY DAVID MALKI !
pay the piper at WONDERMARK.COM
WHAT DID I TELL YOU? HERE HE IS!
JOEY! WOW, I HAVEN'T SEEN YOU SINCE HIGH SCHOOL!
HOW'S IT GOING, PETE? WHAT'S THE SCOOP?
HEY, DO YOU STILL HAVE THAT EIGHT BUCKS I LENT YOU IN TENTH GRADE?
NO, MAN! I SPENT IT RIGHT AFTER YOU GAVE IT TO ME.
...WELL, DO YOU HAVE SOME OTHER, SIMILAR EIGHT BUCKS THAT YOU COULD GIVE ME?
HA HA HA! SAME OLD PETE. HEY, YOU STILL WITH THAT GIRL? TURNED OUT TO BE A GUY?
OKAY, SERIOUSLY GIVE ME MY MONEY.
PETE! I HAVEN'T SEEN YOU SINCE PROM!
©2005 MALKI !

joey had borrowed the money to buy the alpenhorn, it seems, whereas pete had always wanted an alpenhorn but had been stymied by the prohibitive cost

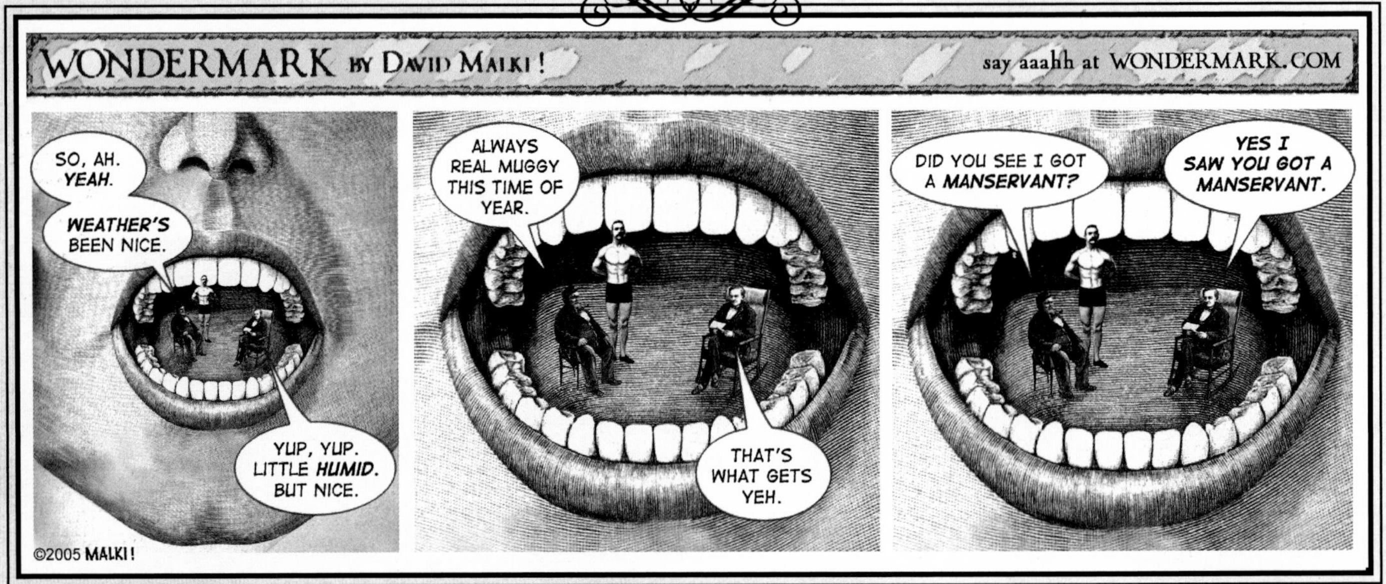
WONDERMARK BY DAVID MALKI !
say aaahh at WONDERMARK.COM
SO, AH. YEAH.
WEATHER'S BEEN NICE.
YUP, YUP. LITTLE HUMID. BUT NICE.
ALWAYS REAL MUGGY THIS TIME OF YEAR.
THAT'S WHAT GETS YEH.
DID YOU SEE I GOT A MANSERVANT?
YES I SAW YOU GOT A MANSERVANT.
©2005 MALKI !

DUH

In which Teeth appear

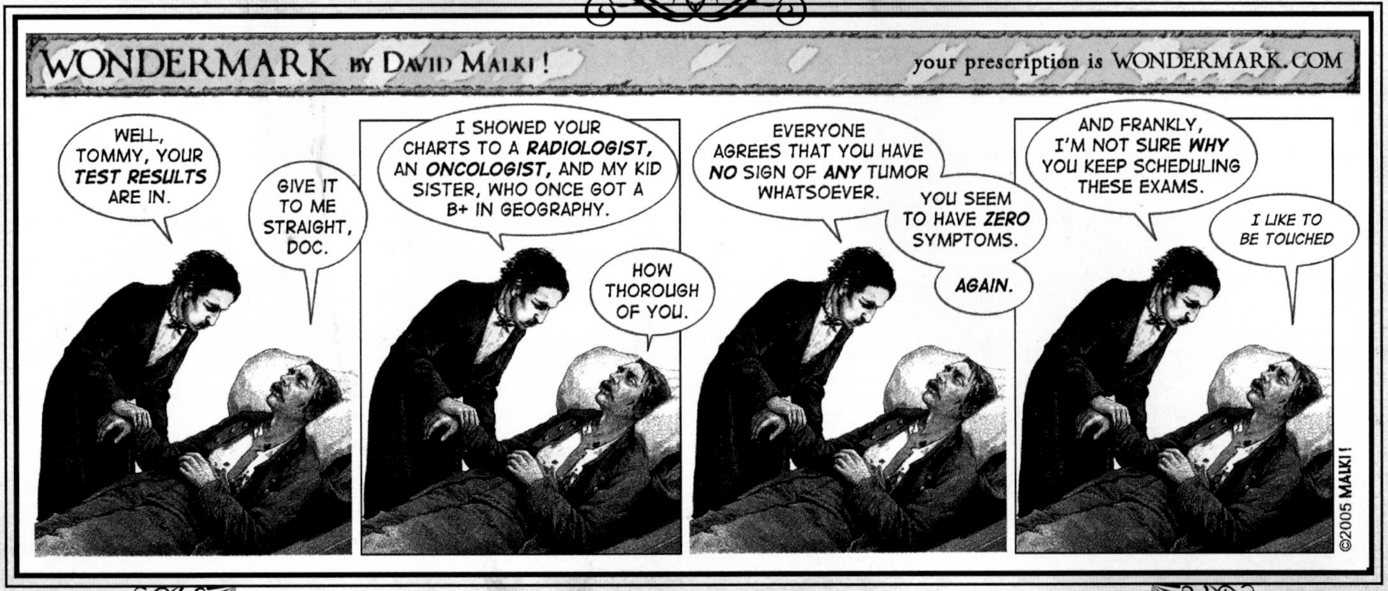
WONDERMARK by David Malki !
your prescription is WONDERMARK.COM
WELL, TOMMY, YOUR TEST RESULTS ARE IN.
GIVE IT TO ME STRAIGHT, DOC.
I SHOWED YOUR CHARTS TO A RADIOLOGIST, AN ONCOLOGIST, AND MY KID SISTER, WHO ONCE GOT A B+ IN GEOGRAPHY.
HOW THOROUGH OF YOU.
EVERYONE AGREES THAT YOU HAVE NO SIGN OF ANY TUMOR WHATSOEVER.
YOU SEEM TO HAVE ZERO SYMPTOMS.
AGAIN.
AND FRANKLY, I'M NOT SURE WHY YOU KEEP SCHEDULING THESE EXAMS.
I LIKE TO BE TOUCHED
©2005 MALKI!

but really, who doesn't

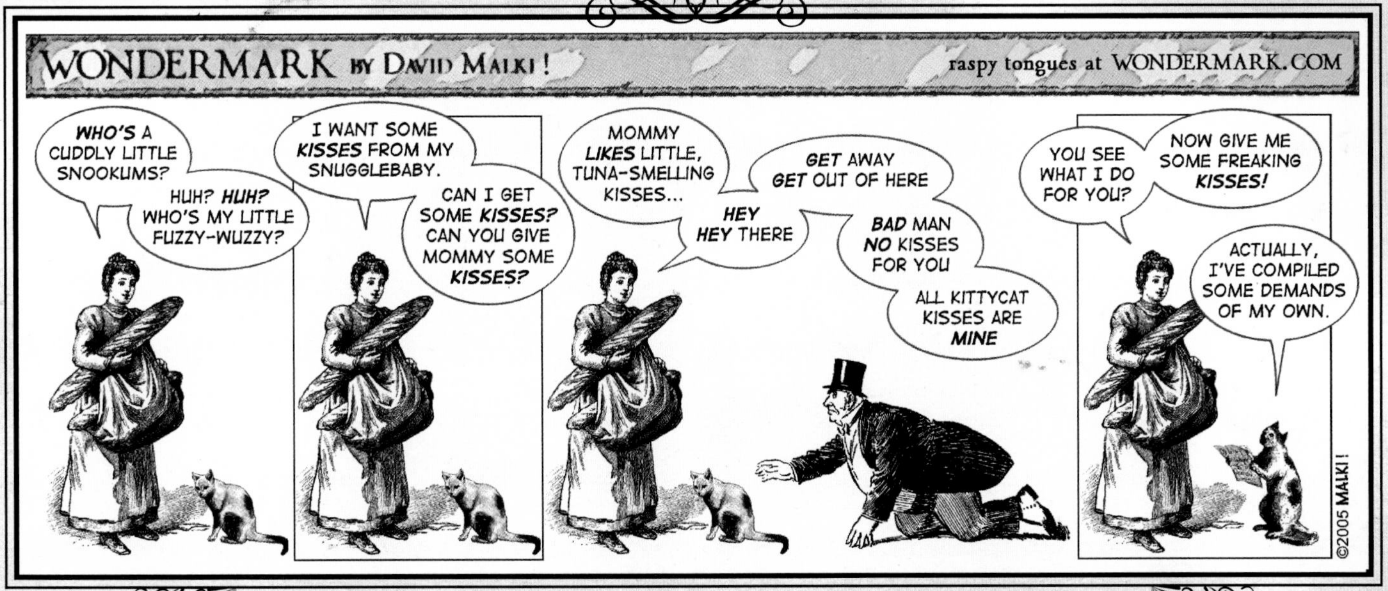
WONDERMARK by David Malki !
raspy tongues at WONDERMARK.COM
WHO'S A CUDDLY LITTLE SNOOKUMS?
HUH? HUH? WHO'S MY LITTLE FUZZY-WUZZY?
I WANT SOME KISSES FROM MY SNUGGLEBABY.
CAN I GET SOME KISSES? CAN YOU GIVE MOMMY SOME KISSES?
MOMMY LIKES LITTLE, TUNA-SMELLING KISSES...
HEY HEY THERE
GET AWAY GET OUT OF HERE
BAD MAN NO KISSES FOR YOU
ALL KITTYCAT KISSES ARE MINE
YOU SEE WHAT I DO FOR YOU?
NOW GIVE ME SOME FREAKING KISSES!
ACTUALLY, I'VE COMPILED SOME DEMANDS OF MY OWN.
©2005 MALKI!

do they involve kisses? PLEASE YES PLEASE YES

In which a Triumph is insulted

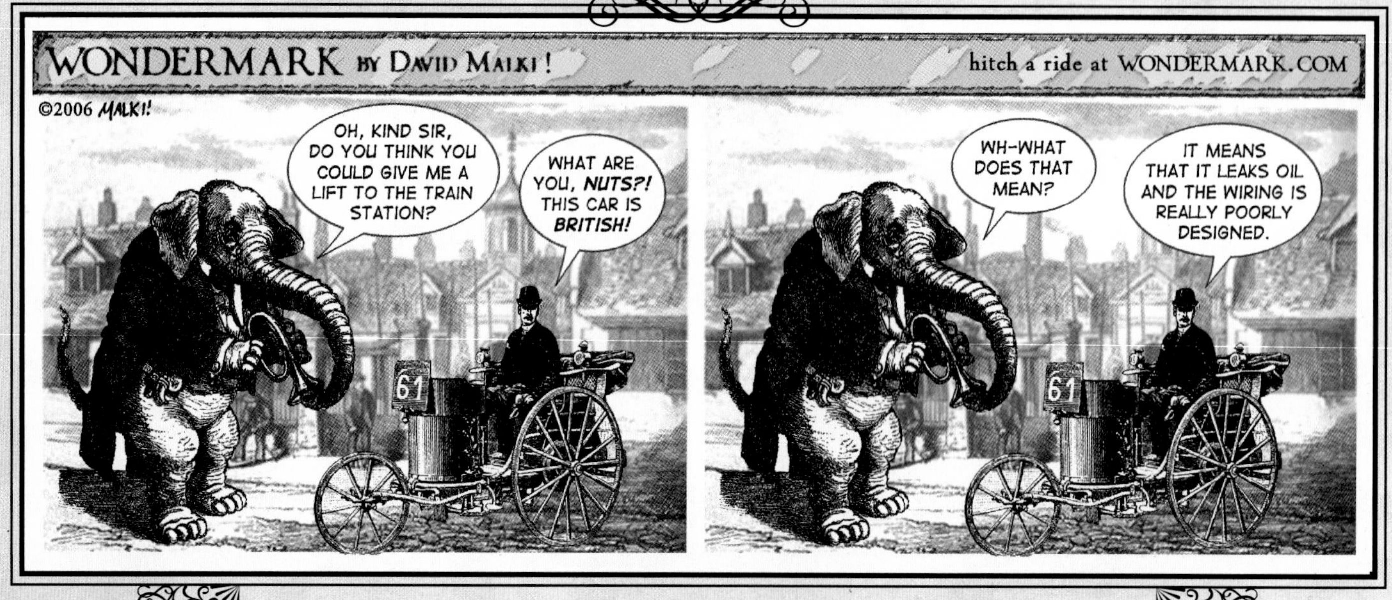
WONDERMARK by David Malki !
hitch a ride at WONDERMARK.COM
©2006 MALKI!
OH, KIND SIR, DO YOU THINK YOU COULD GIVE ME A LIFT TO THE TRAIN STATION?
WHAT ARE YOU, NUTS?! THIS CAR IS BRITISH!
61
WH-WHAT DOES THAT MEAN?
IT MEANS THAT IT LEAKS OIL AND THE WIRING IS REALLY POORLY DESIGNED.
61

BURNNNN

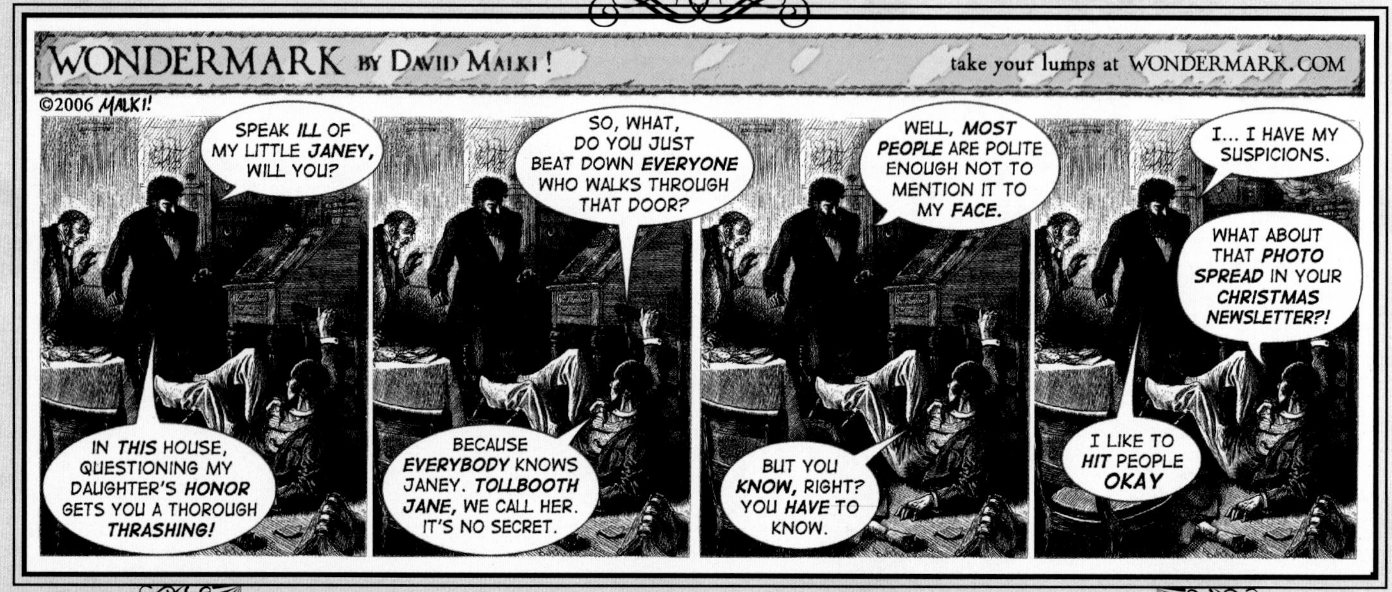
WONDERMARK by David Malki !
take your lumps at WONDERMARK.COM
©2006 MALKI!
SPEAK ILL OF MY LITTLE JANEY, WILL YOU?
IN THIS HOUSE, QUESTIONING MY DAUGHTER'S HONOR GETS YOU A THOROUGH THRASHING!
SO, WHAT, DO YOU JUST BEAT DOWN EVERYONE WHO WALKS THROUGH THAT DOOR?
BECAUSE EVERYBODY KNOWS JANEY. TOLLBOOTH JANE, WE CALL HER. IT'S NO SECRET.
WELL, MOST PEOPLE ARE POLITE ENOUGH NOT TO MENTION IT TO MY FACE.
BUT YOU KNOW, RIGHT? YOU HAVE TO KNOW.
I... I HAVE MY SUSPICIONS.
WHAT ABOUT THAT PHOTO SPREAD IN YOUR CHRISTMAS NEWSLETTER?!
I LIKE TO HIT PEOPLE OKAY

i saw that spread and man, he wasn't kidding around with those gauze filters

In which Janey's Honor is defended

In which Candy is withheld

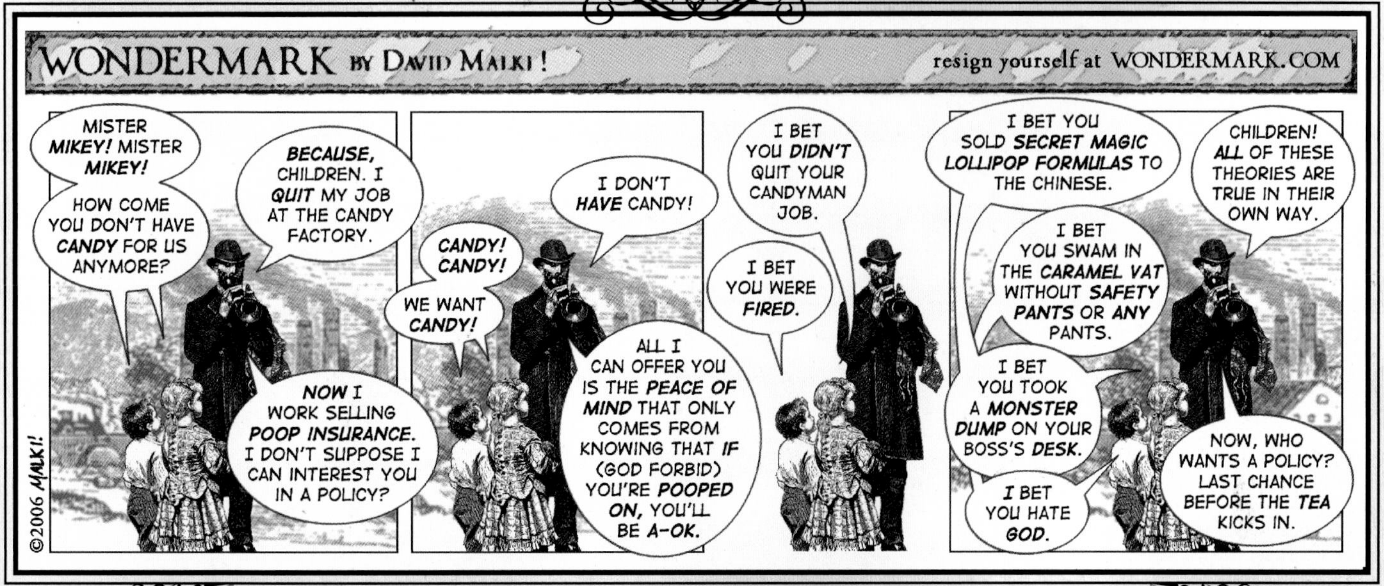
WONDERMARK BY DAVID MALKI!
resign yourself at WONDERMARK.COM
MISTER MIKEY! MISTER MIKEY!
HOW COME YOU DON'T HAVE CANDY FOR US ANYMORE?
BECAUSE, CHILDREN. I QUIT MY JOB AT THE CANDY FACTORY.
NOW I WORK SELLING POOP INSURANCE. I DON'T SUPPOSE I CAN INTEREST YOU IN A POLICY?
©2006 MALKI!
CANDY! CANDY!
WE WANT CANDY!
I DON'T HAVE CANDY!
ALL I CAN OFFER YOU IS THE PEACE OF MIND THAT ONLY COMES FROM KNOWING THAT IF (GOD FORBID) YOU'RE POOPED ON, YOU'LL BE A-OK.
I BET YOU DIDN'T QUIT YOUR CANDYMAN JOB.
I BET YOU WERE FIRED.
I BET YOU SOLD SECRET MAGIC LOLLIPOP FORMULAS TO THE CHINESE.
I BET YOU SWAM IN THE CARAMEL VAT WITHOUT SAFETY PANTS OR ANY PANTS.
I BET YOU TOOK A MONSTER DUMP ON YOUR BOSS'S DESK.
I BET YOU HATE GOD.
CHILDREN! ALL OF THESE THEORIES ARE TRUE IN THEIR OWN WAY.
NOW, WHO WANTS A POLICY? LAST CHANCE BEFORE THE TEA KICKS IN.

real life comics #4, sort of

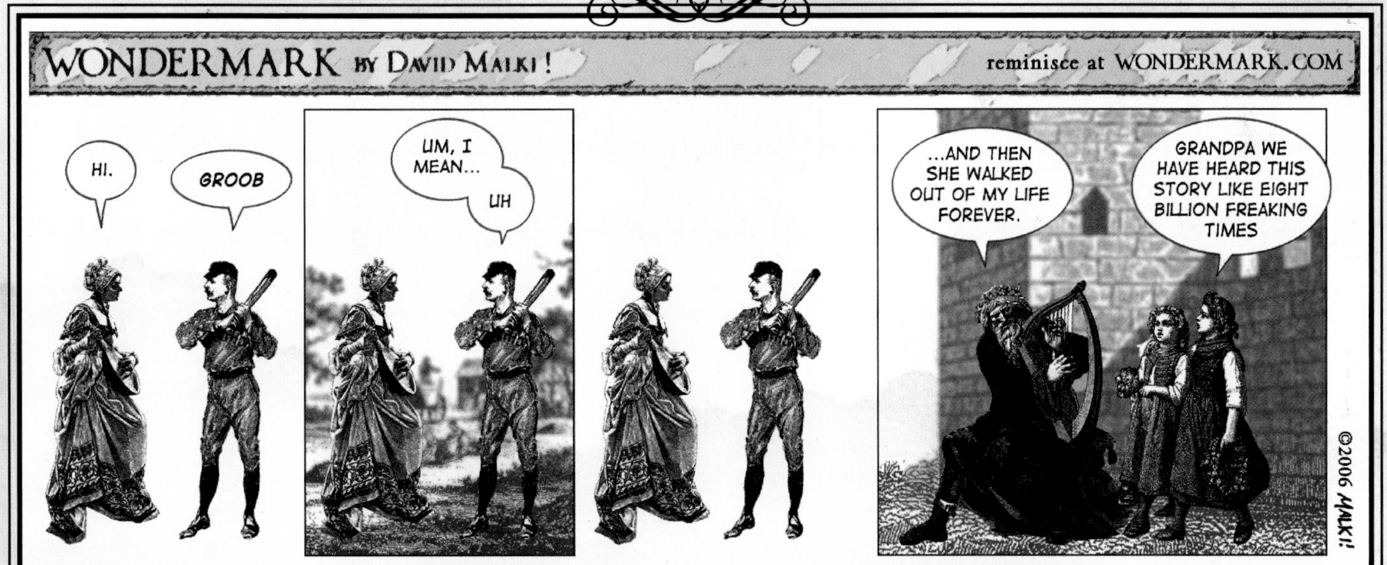
WONDERMARK BY DAVID MALKI!
reminisce at WONDERMARK.COM
HI.
GROOB
UM, I MEAN...
UH
...AND THEN SHE WALKED OUT OF MY LIFE FOREVER.
GRANDPA WE HAVE HEARD THIS STORY LIKE EIGHT BILLION FREAKING TIMES
©2006 MALKI!

apparently the oral history will stop at this generation

In which Grandpa tells that Story again

In which Edgar burns Bridges

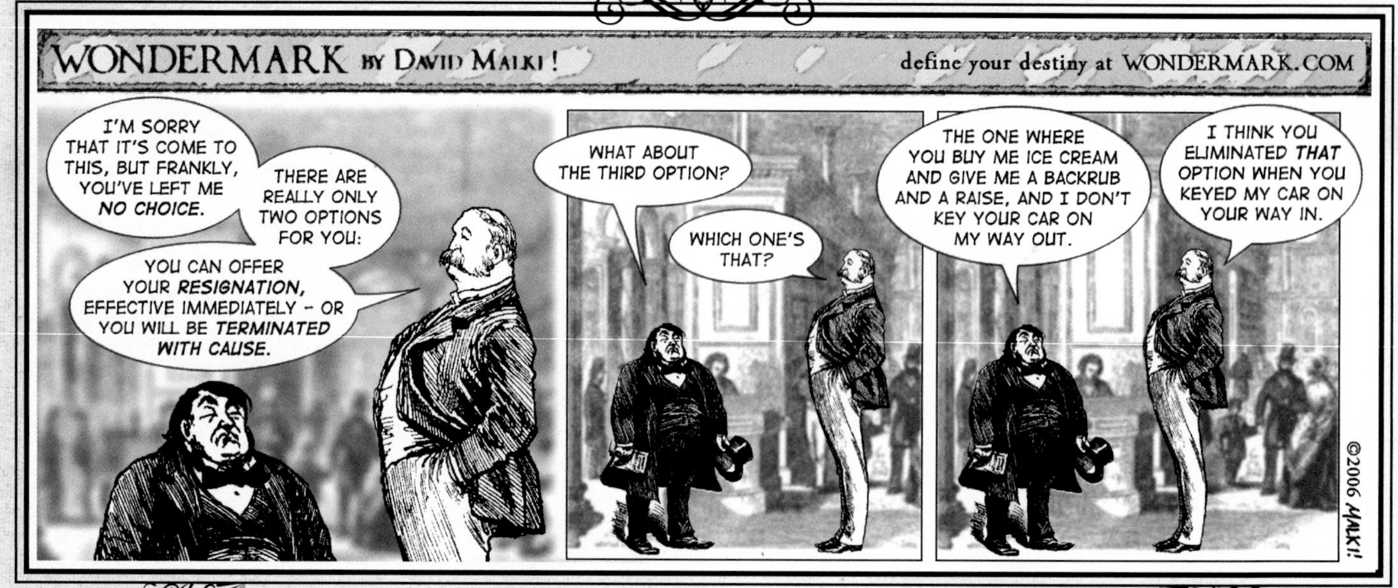
WONDERMARK BY DAVID MALKI !
define your destiny at WONDERMARK.COM
I'M SORRY THAT IT'S COME TO THIS, BUT FRANKLY, YOU'VE LEFT ME NO CHOICE.
THERE ARE REALLY ONLY TWO OPTIONS FOR YOU:
YOU CAN OFFER YOUR RESIGNATION, EFFECTIVE IMMEDIATELY – OR YOU WILL BE TERMINATED WITH CAUSE.
WHAT ABOUT THE THIRD OPTION?
WHICH ONE'S THAT?
THE ONE WHERE YOU BUY ME ICE CREAM AND GIVE ME A BACKRUB AND A RAISE, AND I DON'T KEY YOUR CAR ON MY WAY OUT.
I THINK YOU ELIMINATED THAT OPTION WHEN YOU KEYED MY CAR ON YOUR WAY IN.
©2006 MALKI!

these real life comics are starting to get kind of worrisome

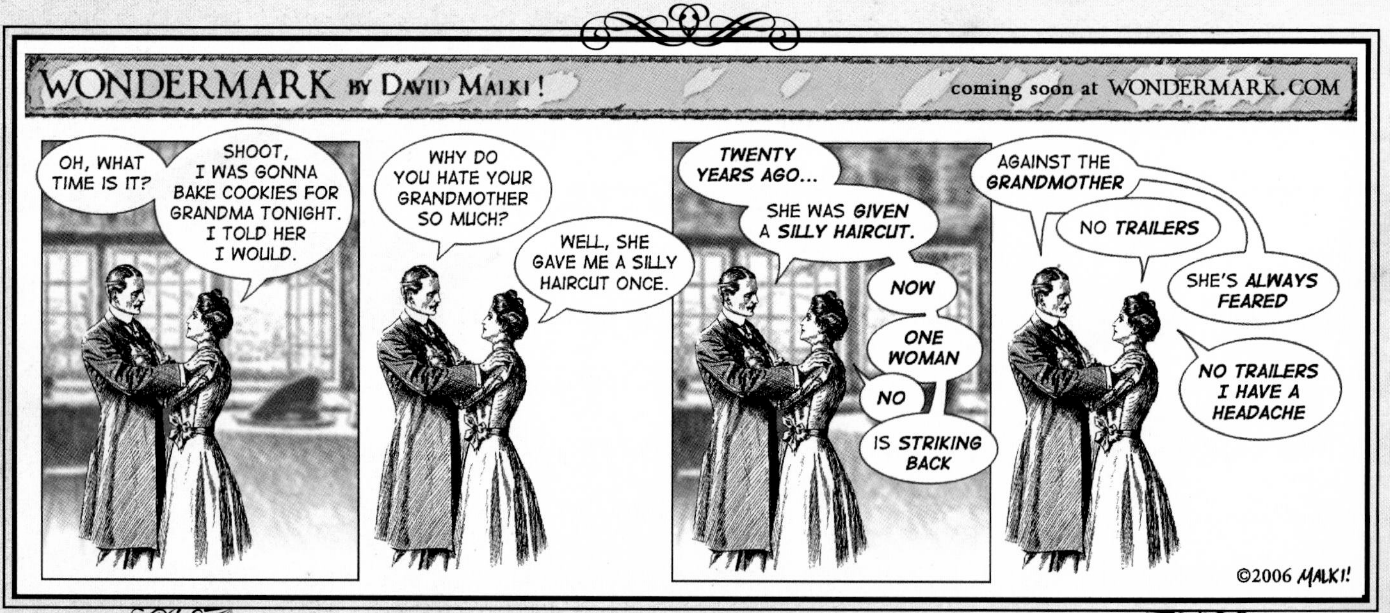
WONDERMARK BY DAVID MALKI !
coming soon at WONDERMARK.COM
OH, WHAT TIME IS IT?
SHOOT, I WAS GONNA BAKE COOKIES FOR GRANDMA TONIGHT. I TOLD HER I WOULD.
WHY DO YOU HATE YOUR GRANDMOTHER SO MUCH?
WELL, SHE GAVE ME A SILLY HAIRCUT ONCE.
TWENTY YEARS AGO...
SHE WAS GIVEN A SILLY HAIRCUT.
NOW
ONE WOMAN
NO
IS STRIKING BACK
AGAINST THE GRANDMOTHER
NO TRAILERS
SHE'S ALWAYS FEARED
NO TRAILERS I HAVE A HEADACHE
©2006 MALKI!

YOU ALWAYS SAY THAT

In which a Common Practice is objected to

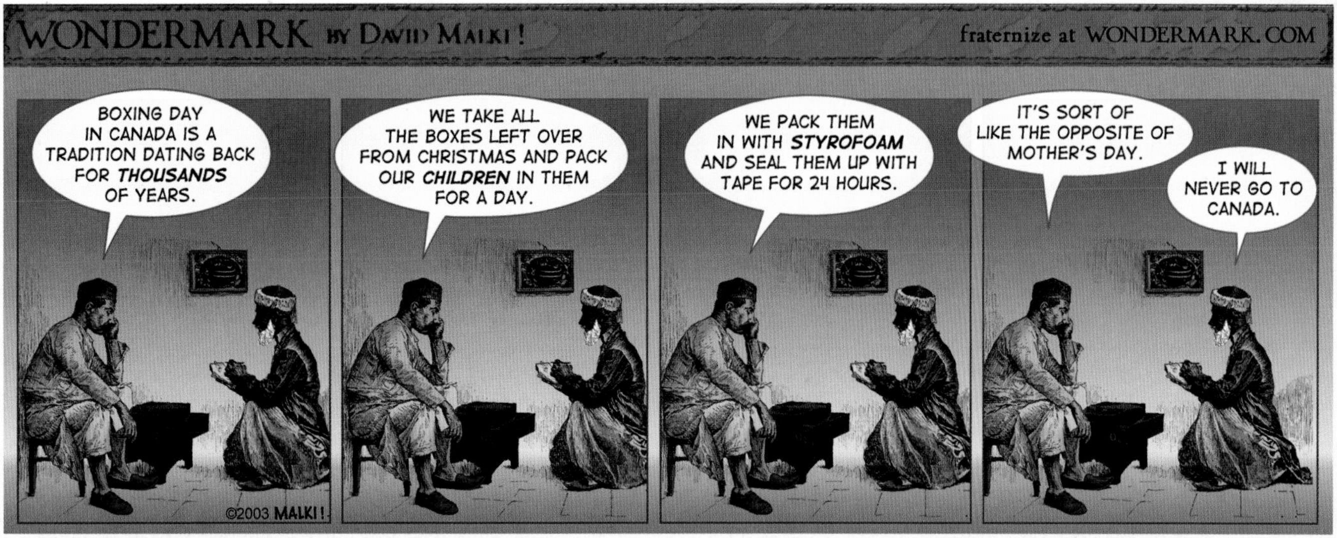
WONDERMARK by David Malki !
fraternize at WONDERMARK.COM
BOXING DAY IN CANADA IS A TRADITION DATING BACK FOR **THOUSANDS** OF YEARS.
WE TAKE ALL THE BOXES LEFT OVER FROM CHRISTMAS AND PACK OUR **CHILDREN** IN THEM FOR A DAY.
WE PACK THEM IN WITH **STYROFOAM** AND SEAL THEM UP WITH TAPE FOR 24 HOURS.
IT'S SORT OF LIKE THE OPPOSITE OF MOTHER'S DAY.
I WILL NEVER GO TO CANADA.
©2003 MALKI !

or rather, i will only ever go on december 26th. can you imagine the serenity?

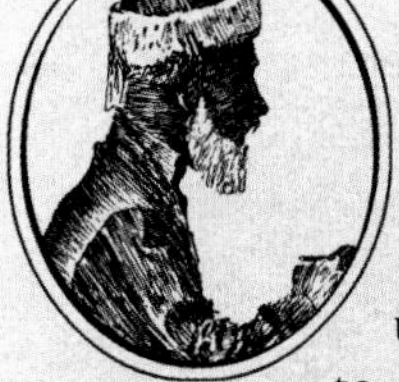

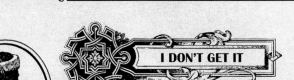

I DON'T GET IT

IN THIS comic strip, I play the part of "Mustapha," the well-meaning but ultimately stymied aid worker attempting to solicit funding for an international human-rights advocacy organization. As you are no doubt well aware, Canada's many centuries of brutal sectarian warfare has left the nation littered with land mines, caches of biological weapons, and unsecured nuclear armaments, including at least one plutonium-fueled moose.

The strip begins with the actor playing "Hassan" recounting the common perception that the Canadian people are a savage collection of violent tribes still clinging to superstition and brutal religious rituals. As I could never consciously impose an external value judgment on the belief systems of the native population, I am forced to admit that I may be able to enact change most efficiently by remaining outside the borders of that wounded nation.

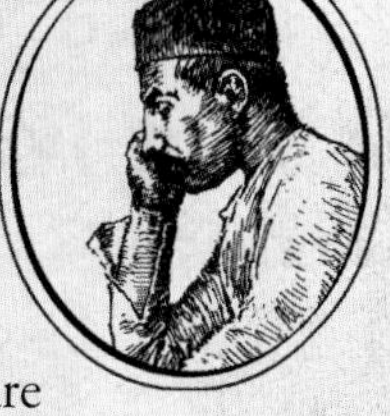

I PLAY "Hassan," a scrappy Canadian opium-smuggler risking execution by speaking to a non-national. I didn't know much about the situation in Canada before I got this role, but I wanted to be prepared and everything, so I did some research. And boy was I shocked.

Did you know that there are trenches in Canada a thousand miles long, filled with rotting corpses and populated by dragons that bleed maggots? It's true, I read a website about it. And the rival tribes that are always blowing each other up—the Quebecois and the Anglophones—are virtually identical genetically. If you go back far enough they both come from Europe. But try telling that to the kids today! They've been hating each other for so long that they don't even remember why anymore.

I don't think they should have dug the lava-moat around Saskatchewan, but as an actor my job is to try and see things from new perspectives, for the sake of the performance. I wouldn't say I'm all of a sudden a big, like, *Red Green Show* fan or anything, but I have learned a lot.

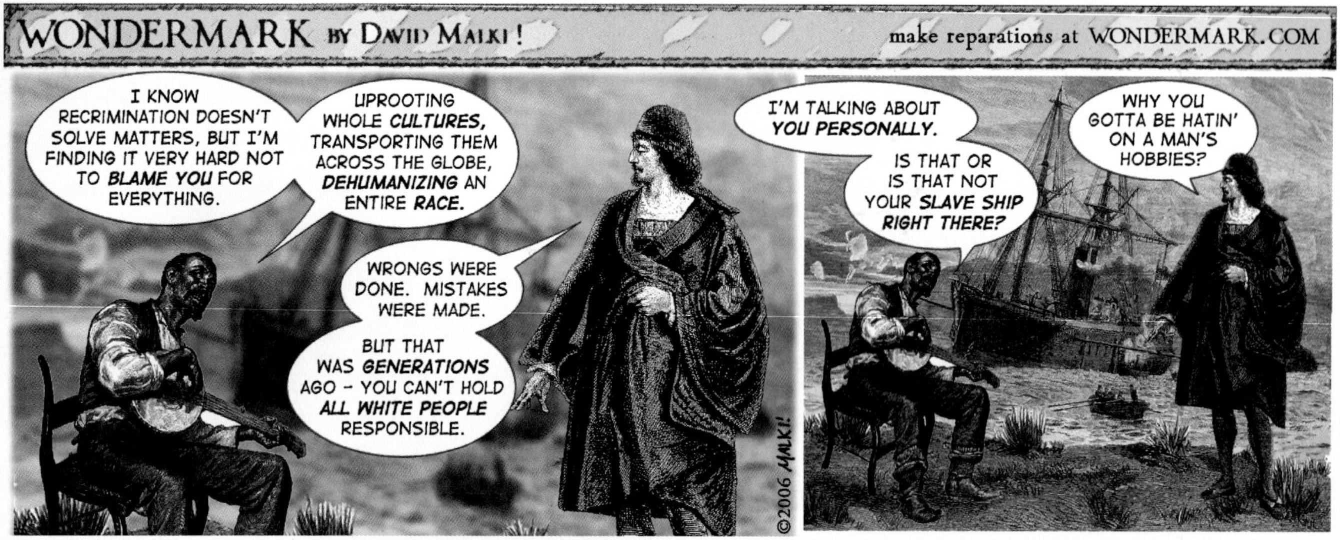
WONDERMARK BY DAVID MALKI !
make reparations at WONDERMARK.COM
I KNOW RECRIMINATION DOESN'T SOLVE MATTERS, BUT I'M FINDING IT VERY HARD NOT TO BLAME YOU FOR EVERYTHING.
UPROOTING WHOLE CULTURES, TRANSPORTING THEM ACROSS THE GLOBE, DEHUMANIZING AN ENTIRE RACE.
WRONGS WERE DONE. MISTAKES WERE MADE.
BUT THAT WAS GENERATIONS AGO - YOU CAN'T HOLD ALL WHITE PEOPLE RESPONSIBLE.
©2006 MALKI!
I'M TALKING ABOUT YOU PERSONALLY.
IS THAT OR IS THAT NOT YOUR SLAVE SHIP RIGHT THERE?
WHY YOU GOTTA BE HATIN' ON A MAN'S HOBBIES?

also slavery is wrong

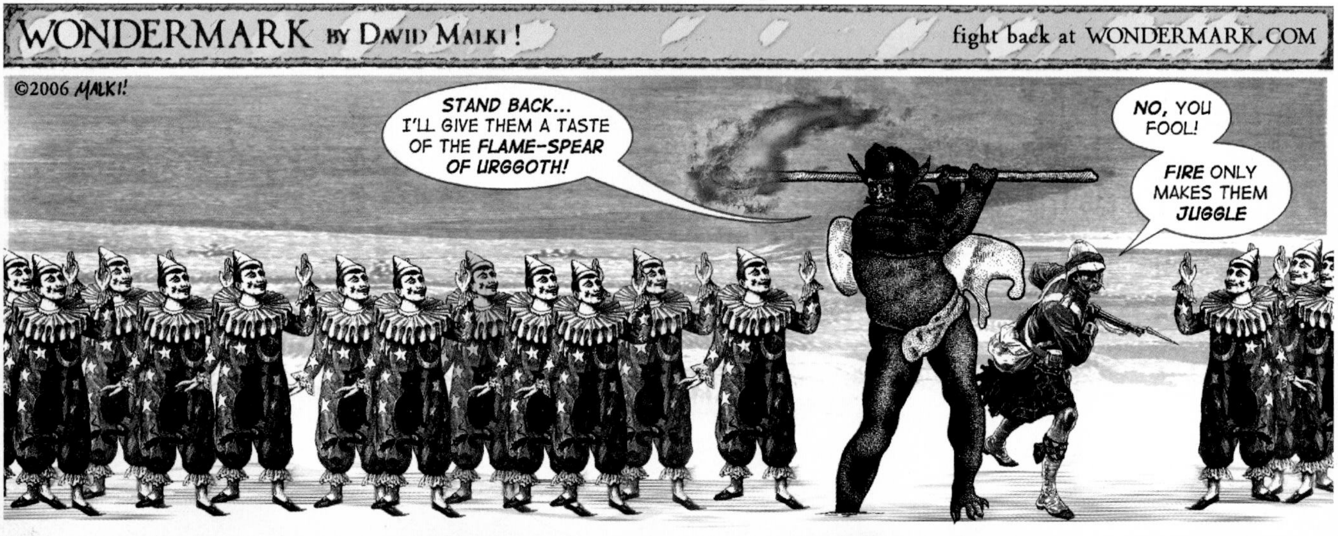
WONDERMARK BY DAVID MALKI !
fight back at WONDERMARK.COM
©2006 MALKI!
STAND BACK... I'LL GIVE THEM A TASTE OF THE FLAME-SPEAR OF URGGOTH!
NO, YOU FOOL!
FIRE ONLY MAKES THEM JUGGLE

we mere fooles delight in bringing whimsy and magic to the AAGGGKKKK

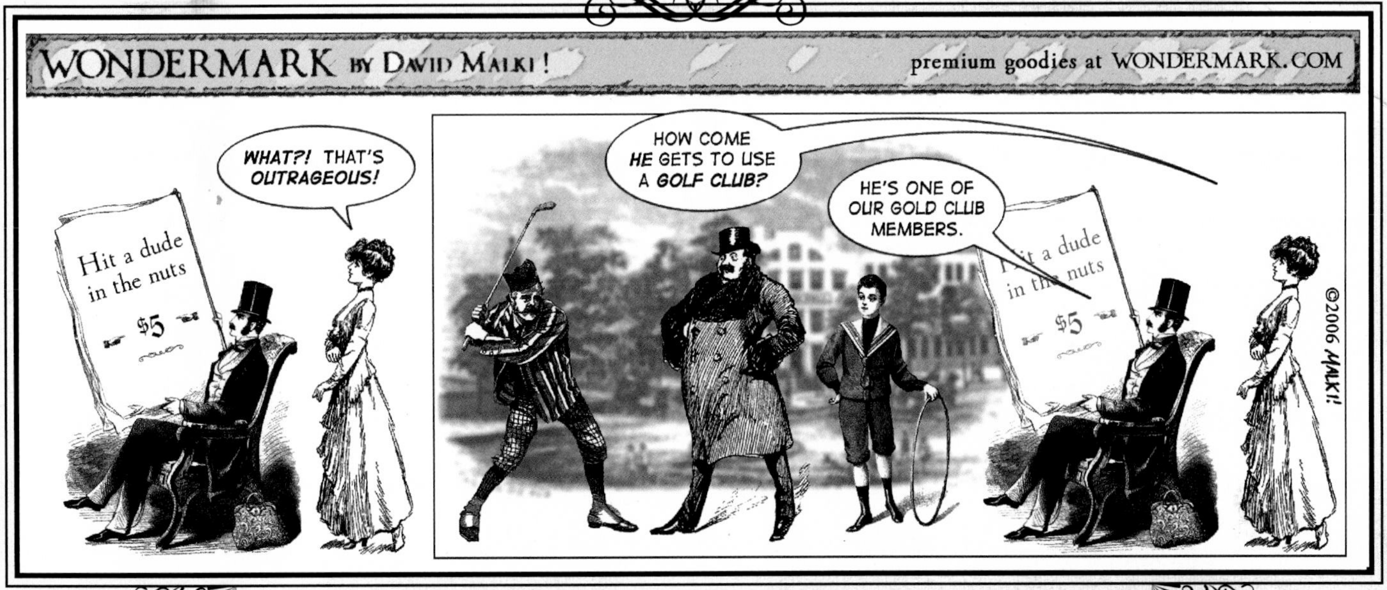
WONDERMARK by David Malki !
premium goodies at WONDERMARK.COM
Hit a dude in the nuts $5
WHAT?! THAT'S OUTRAGEOUS!
HOW COME HE GETS TO USE A GOLF CLUB?
HE'S ONE OF OUR GOLD CLUB MEMBERS.
Hit a dude in the nuts $5
©2006 MALKI!

bonus: you get to keep whatever falls off

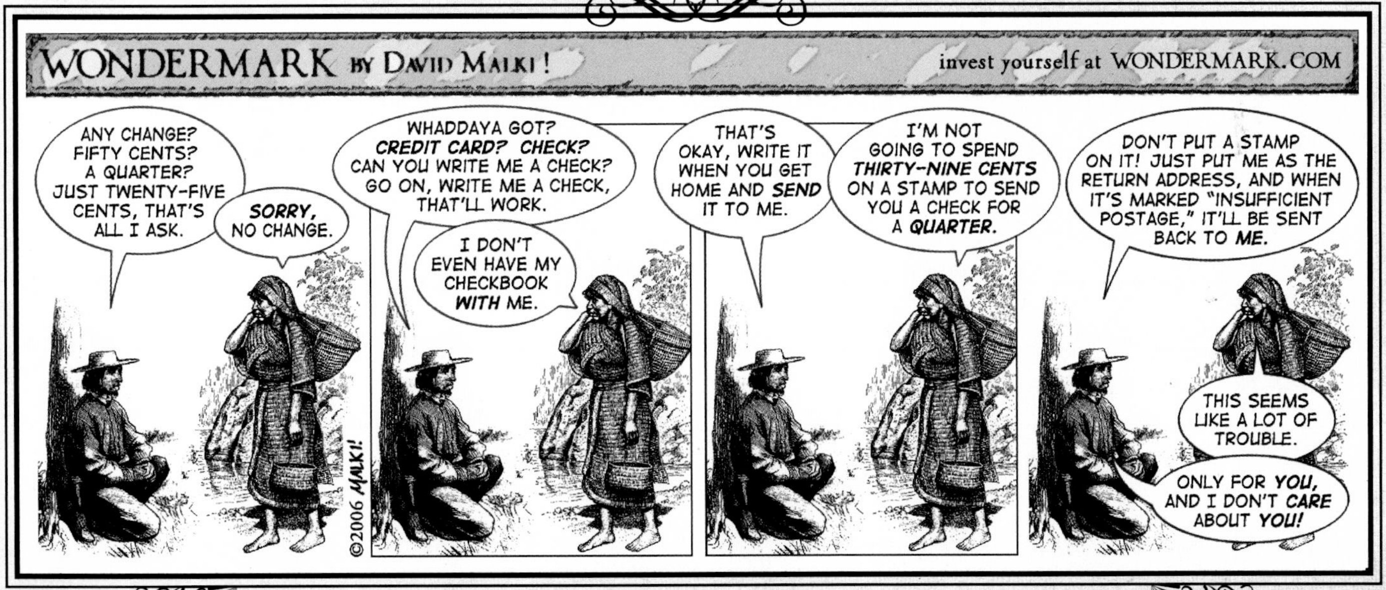
WONDERMARK by David Malki !
invest yourself at WONDERMARK.COM
ANY CHANGE? FIFTY CENTS? A QUARTER? JUST TWENTY-FIVE CENTS, THAT'S ALL I ASK.
SORRY, NO CHANGE.
©2006 MALKI!
WHADDAYA GOT? CREDIT CARD? CHECK? CAN YOU WRITE ME A CHECK? GO ON, WRITE ME A CHECK, THAT'LL WORK.
I DON'T EVEN HAVE MY CHECKBOOK WITH ME.
THAT'S OKAY, WRITE IT WHEN YOU GET HOME AND SEND IT TO ME.
I'M NOT GOING TO SPEND THIRTY-NINE CENTS ON A STAMP TO SEND YOU A CHECK FOR A QUARTER.
DON'T PUT A STAMP ON IT! JUST PUT ME AS THE RETURN ADDRESS, AND WHEN IT'S MARKED "INSUFFICIENT POSTAGE," IT'LL BE SENT BACK TO ME.
THIS SEEMS LIKE A LOT OF TROUBLE.
ONLY FOR YOU, AND I DON'T CARE ABOUT YOU!

oh and can you please rent a p.o. box for me as i do not technically have an 'address'

In which the Cost of Sausages is discussed

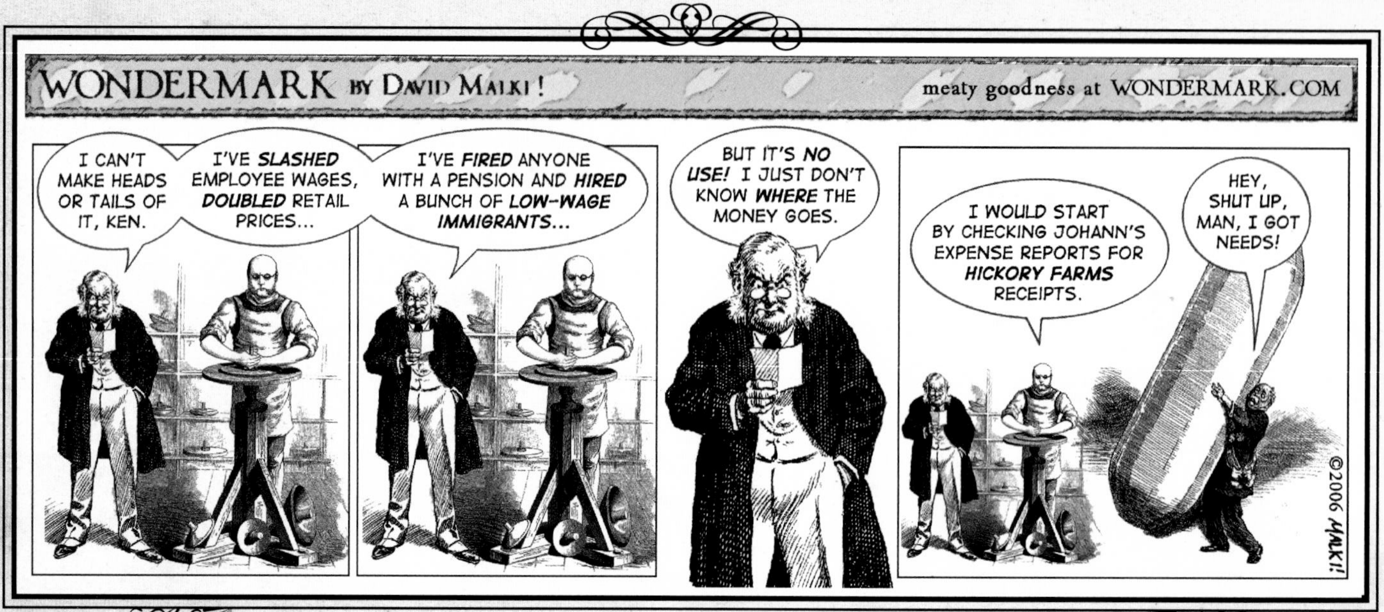
WONDERMARK by David Malki !
meaty goodness at WONDERMARK.COM
I CAN'T MAKE HEADS OR TAILS OF IT, KEN.
I'VE SLASHED EMPLOYEE WAGES, DOUBLED RETAIL PRICES...
I'VE FIRED ANYONE WITH A PENSION AND HIRED A BUNCH OF LOW-WAGE IMMIGRANTS...
BUT IT'S NO USE! I JUST DON'T KNOW WHERE THE MONEY GOES.
I WOULD START BY CHECKING JOHANN'S EXPENSE REPORTS FOR HICKORY FARMS RECEIPTS.
HEY, SHUT UP, MAN, I GOT NEEDS!
©2006 MALKI!

alternately, it is a zeppelin full of rancid milk

42

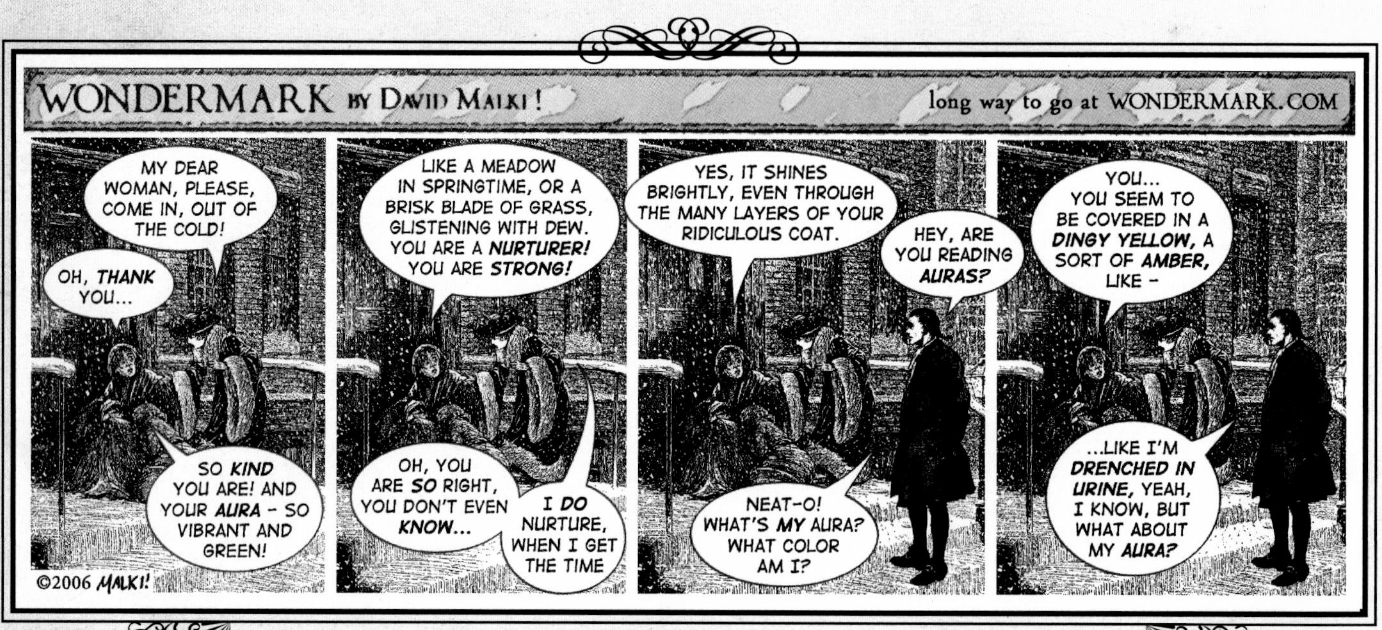
WONDERMARK by David Malki !
long way to go at WONDERMARK.COM
MY DEAR WOMAN, PLEASE, COME IN, OUT OF THE COLD!
OH, THANK YOU...
SO KIND YOU ARE! AND YOUR AURA - SO VIBRANT AND GREEN!
©2006 MALKI!
LIKE A MEADOW IN SPRINGTIME, OR A BRISK BLADE OF GRASS, GLISTENING WITH DEW. YOU ARE A NURTURER! YOU ARE STRONG!
OH, YOU ARE SO RIGHT, YOU DON'T EVEN KNOW...
I DO NURTURE, WHEN I GET THE TIME
YES, IT SHINES BRIGHTLY, EVEN THROUGH THE MANY LAYERS OF YOUR RIDICULOUS COAT.
HEY, ARE YOU READING AURAS?
NEAT-O! WHAT'S MY AURA? WHAT COLOR AM I?
YOU... YOU SEEM TO BE COVERED IN A DINGY YELLOW, A SORT OF AMBER, LIKE -
...LIKE I'M DRENCHED IN URINE, YEAH, I KNOW, BUT WHAT ABOUT MY AURA?

i have been told that my aura is quote-musky-unquote

In which Pneumonia seems certain

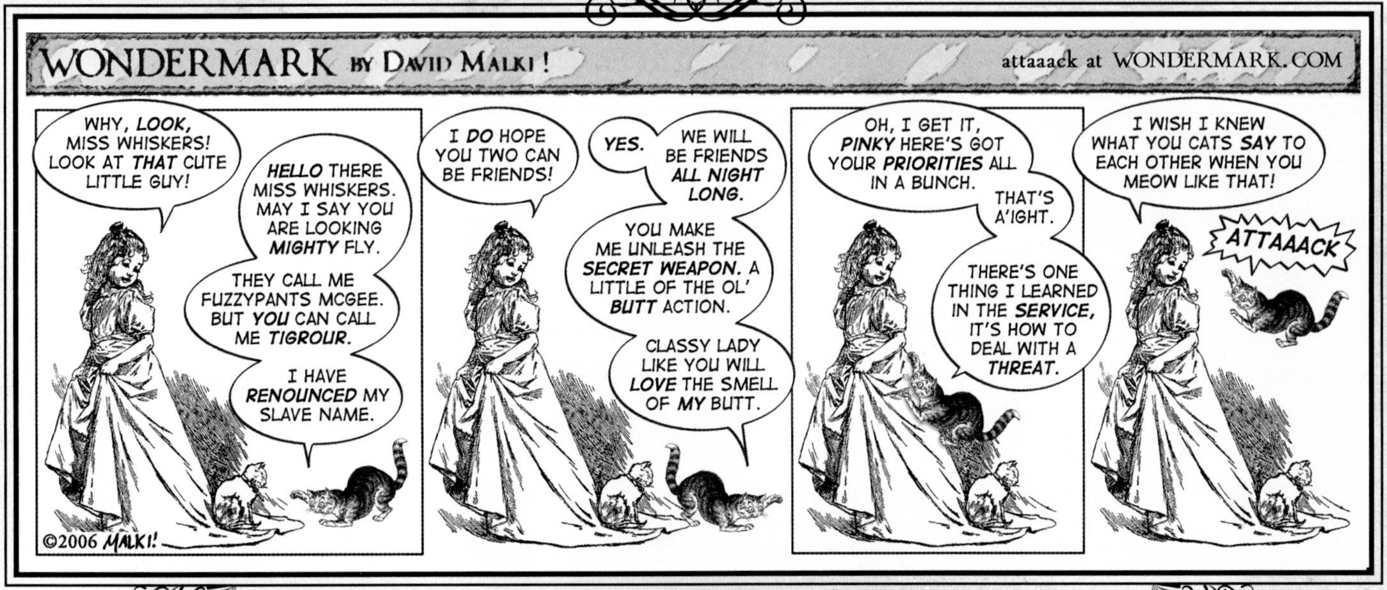
WONDERMARK by David Malki !
attaaack at WONDERMARK.COM
WHY, LOOK, MISS WHISKERS! LOOK AT THAT CUTE LITTLE GUY!
HELLO THERE MISS WHISKERS. MAY I SAY YOU ARE LOOKING MIGHTY FLY.
THEY CALL ME FUZZYPANTS MCGEE. BUT YOU CAN CALL ME TIGROUR.
I HAVE RENOUNCED MY SLAVE NAME.
©2006 MALKI!
I DO HOPE YOU TWO CAN BE FRIENDS!
YES.
WE WILL BE FRIENDS ALL NIGHT LONG.
YOU MAKE ME UNLEASH THE SECRET WEAPON. A LITTLE OF THE OL' BUTT ACTION.
CLASSY LADY LIKE YOU WILL LOVE THE SMELL OF MY BUTT.
OH, I GET IT, PINKY HERE'S GOT YOUR PRIORITIES ALL IN A BUNCH.
THAT'S A'IGHT.
THERE'S ONE THING I LEARNED IN THE SERVICE, IT'S HOW TO DEAL WITH A THREAT.
I WISH I KNEW WHAT YOU CATS SAY TO EACH OTHER WHEN YOU MEOW LIKE THAT!
ATTAAACK

miss whiskers is trying to keep her composure but oh!
that fine aroma! she fears that she may swoon

43

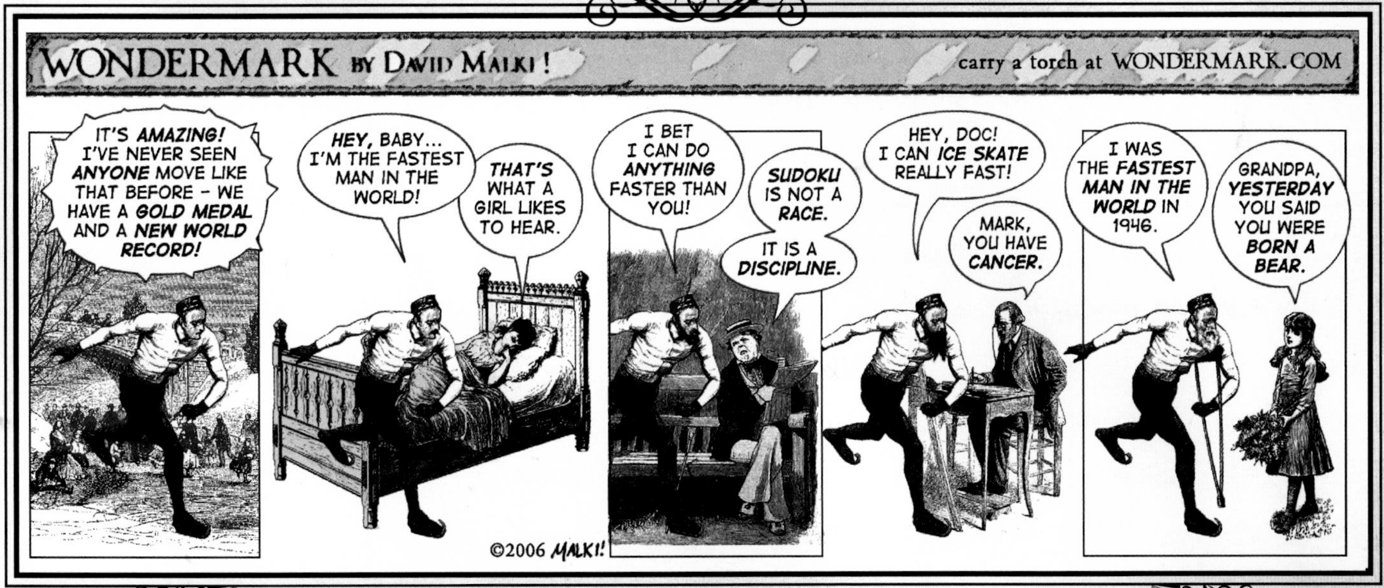
WONDERMARK by David Malki !
carry a torch at WONDERMARK.COM
IT'S AMAZING! I'VE NEVER SEEN ANYONE MOVE LIKE THAT BEFORE - WE HAVE A GOLD MEDAL AND A NEW WORLD RECORD!
HEY, BABY... I'M THE FASTEST MAN IN THE WORLD!
THAT'S WHAT A GIRL LIKES TO HEAR.
©2006 MALKI!
I BET I CAN DO ANYTHING FASTER THAN YOU!
SUDOKU IS NOT A RACE.
IT IS A DISCIPLINE.
HEY, DOC! I CAN ICE SKATE REALLY FAST!
MARK, YOU HAVE CANCER.
I WAS THE FASTEST MAN IN THE WORLD IN 1946.
GRANDPA, YESTERDAY YOU SAID YOU WERE BORN A BEAR.

you train and you train and you give up your life and then,
after you stand on that podium, pretty much you got bupkis

In which an Infant is juiced

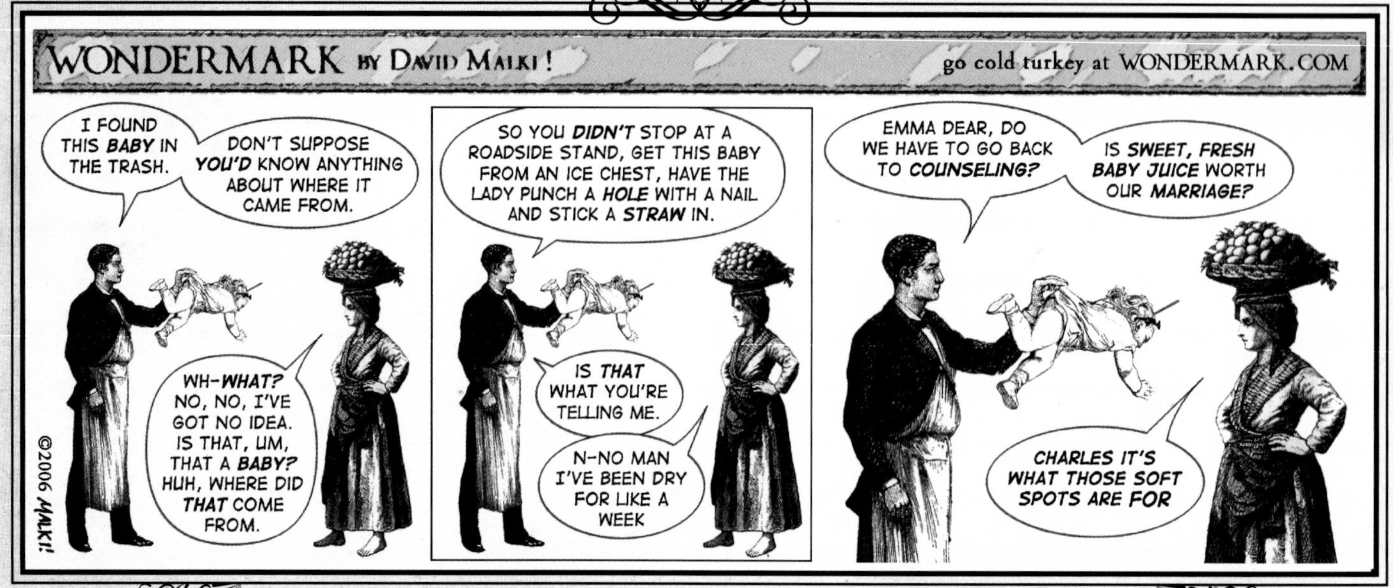
WONDERMARK by David Malki !
go cold turkey at WONDERMARK.COM
I FOUND THIS BABY IN THE TRASH.
DON'T SUPPOSE YOU'D KNOW ANYTHING ABOUT WHERE IT CAME FROM.
WH-WHAT? NO, NO, I'VE GOT NO IDEA. IS THAT, UM, THAT A BABY? HUH, WHERE DID THAT COME FROM.
©2006 MALKI!
SO YOU DIDN'T STOP AT A ROADSIDE STAND, GET THIS BABY FROM AN ICE CHEST, HAVE THE LADY PUNCH A HOLE WITH A NAIL AND STICK A STRAW IN.
IS THAT WHAT YOU'RE TELLING ME.
N-NO MAN I'VE BEEN DRY FOR LIKE A WEEK
EMMA DEAR, DO WE HAVE TO GO BACK TO COUNSELING?
IS SWEET, FRESH BABY JUICE WORTH OUR MARRIAGE?
CHARLES IT'S WHAT THOSE SOFT SPOTS ARE FOR

those roadside stands are the only place you get the real fresh stuff

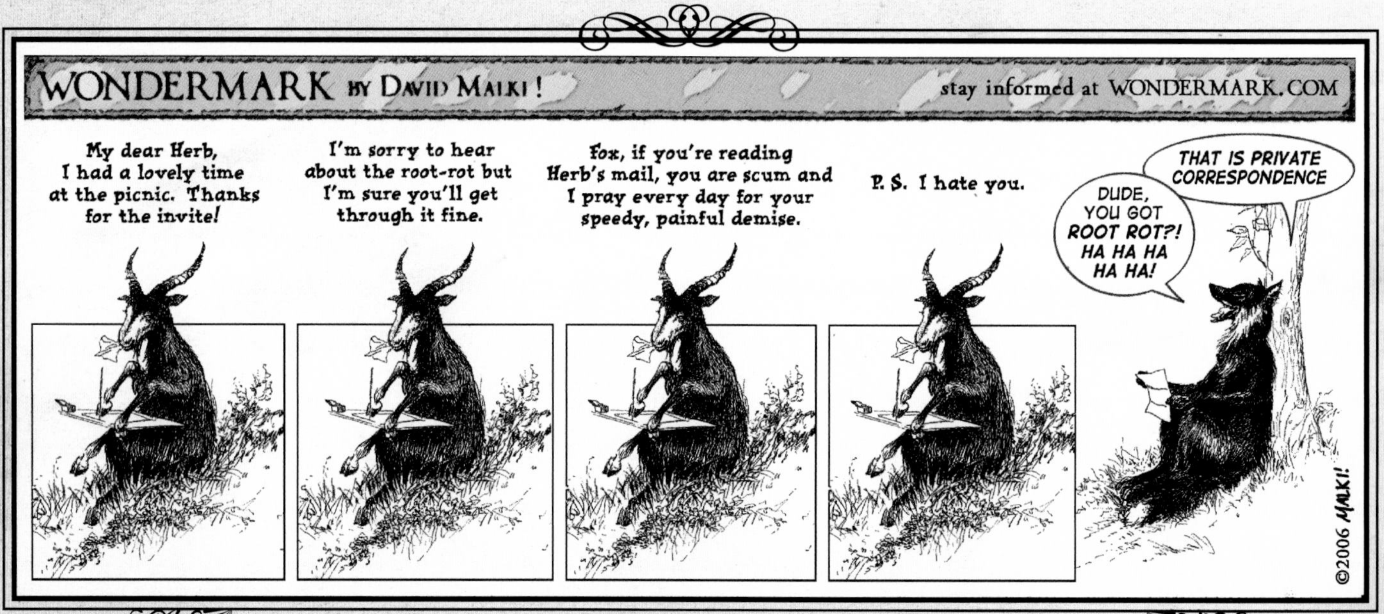
WONDERMARK by David Malki !
stay informed at WONDERMARK.COM
My dear Herb, I had a lovely time at the picnic. Thanks for the invite!
I'm sorry to hear about the root-rot but I'm sure you'll get through it fine.
Fox, if you're reading Herb's mail, you are scum and I pray every day for your speedy, painful demise.
P. S. I hate you.
DUDE, YOU GOT ROOT ROT?! HA HA HA HA HA!
THAT IS PRIVATE CORRESPONDENCE
©2006 MALKI!

root rot is not actually all that bad, plus you get vicodin

In which a Goat wishes Death upon a Fox

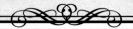

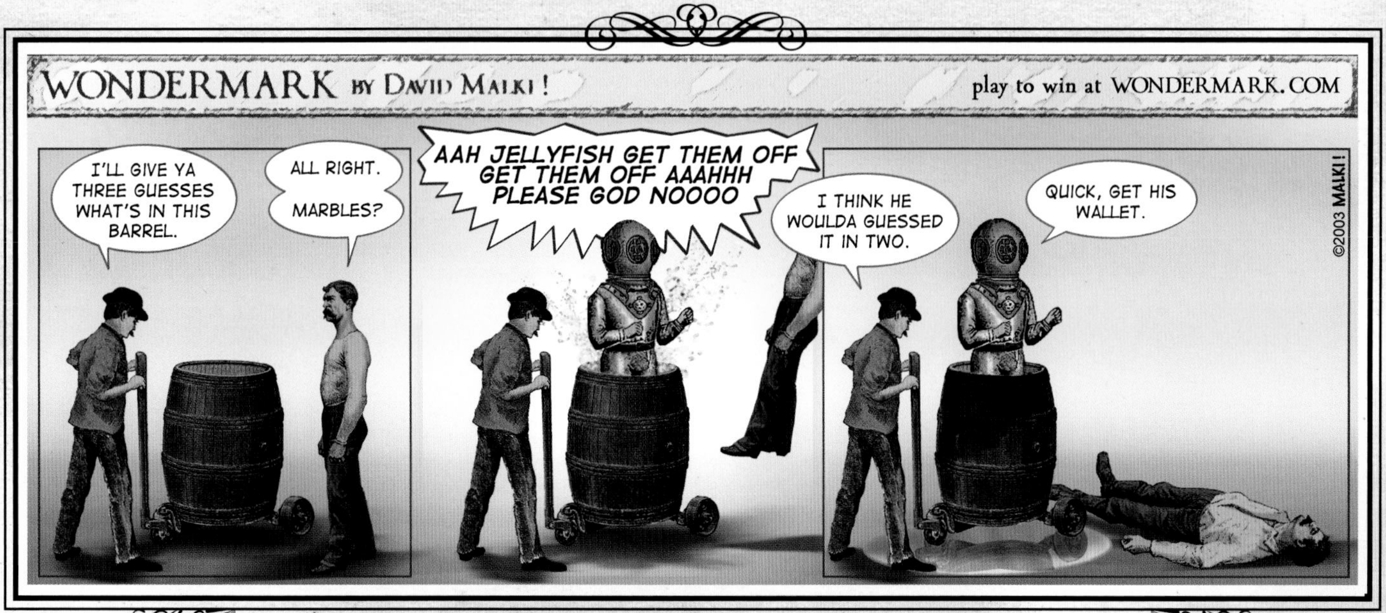

WONDERMARK BY DAVID MALKI !
play to win at WONDERMARK.COM
I'LL GIVE YA THREE GUESSES WHAT'S IN THIS BARREL.
ALL RIGHT.
MARBLES?
AAH JELLYFISH GET THEM OFF GET THEM OFF AAAHHH PLEASE GOD NOOOO
I THINK HE WOULDA GUESSED IT IN TWO.
QUICK, GET HIS WALLET.
©2003 MALKI !

his third guess would have been earwigs. that is just the kind of guy he is!

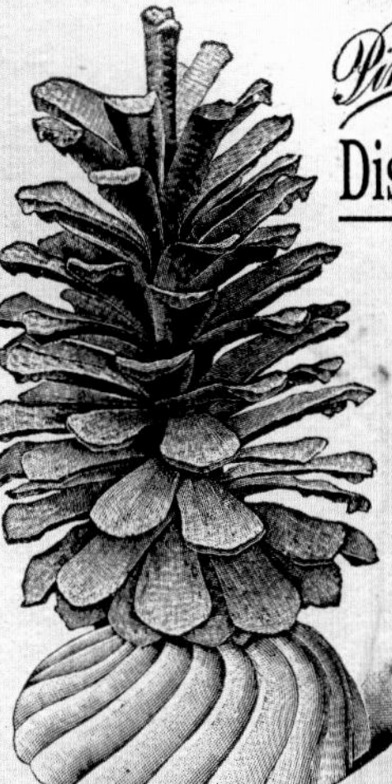

Pineoline OZINATOR.

NATURE'S OWN

Disinfectant and Deodorant,

FRAGRANT—EFFECTIVE—BEAUTIFUL.

REMOVES JELLYFISH STENCH AT ONCE.

No longer shall you suffer the horrible, rancid reek of JELLYFISH in your home. These creatures are well-known for their awful nature and terrible odor.

The MAMMOTH PINE CONES of Norway

(as here shown one-third size) are World-Renowned for their Counter-Jellyfish Scent. Against any number of Jellyfish, no matter how rotted, stinking or fetid it is unsurpassed by any product currently available.

Our patented process draws up Pineoline Oil to evaporate exactly as in nature. Enjoy the benefit of a sojourn at the pines, free of Jellyfish, without travel or inconvenience. Circulars free.

Sent, express charges paid, to any part of the United States, on receipt of price.

No. 2, 8 inches high $2.25
No. 4, 10 inches high 3.25

Postal Note or Money Order. Address,

R. S. PRINDLE, Sole Manufacturer, 97 Liberty St., N.Y.

To kill jellyfish, lure them into a fire with Tang or Kool-Aid. They think that crap's healthy.

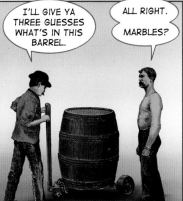

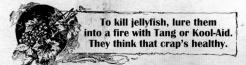

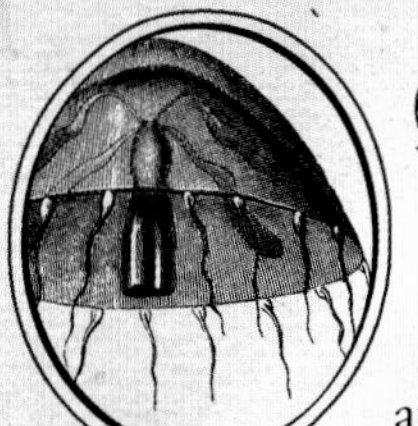

"This page is horribly offensive to jellyfish."

WE OF the Marine Invertebrate Anti-Defamation League express our outrage at this insensitive portrayal of jellyfish. This comic strip demeans the valuable contributions of jellyfish and other marine invertebrates to the ecosystem and perpetuates the stereotype of jellyfish as creepy, slimy, sting-happy and retarded. Unless we receive a formal apology from the characters in this strip, we will be forced to ask advertisers to withdraw their support.

The comic strip "Wondermark" is published in 58 underwater markets that have extensive jellyfish, anemone and sea nettle populations. Jellyfish and their invertebrate brethren are important sources of labor for the textile-refining industry. To have them mocked as simple-minded barrel-filling soul-suckers is both demeaning to the jellyfish themselves and potentially damaging to their economic prospects, if such stereotypes continue to be perpetrated.

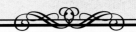

In which the Dealer has no Sevens

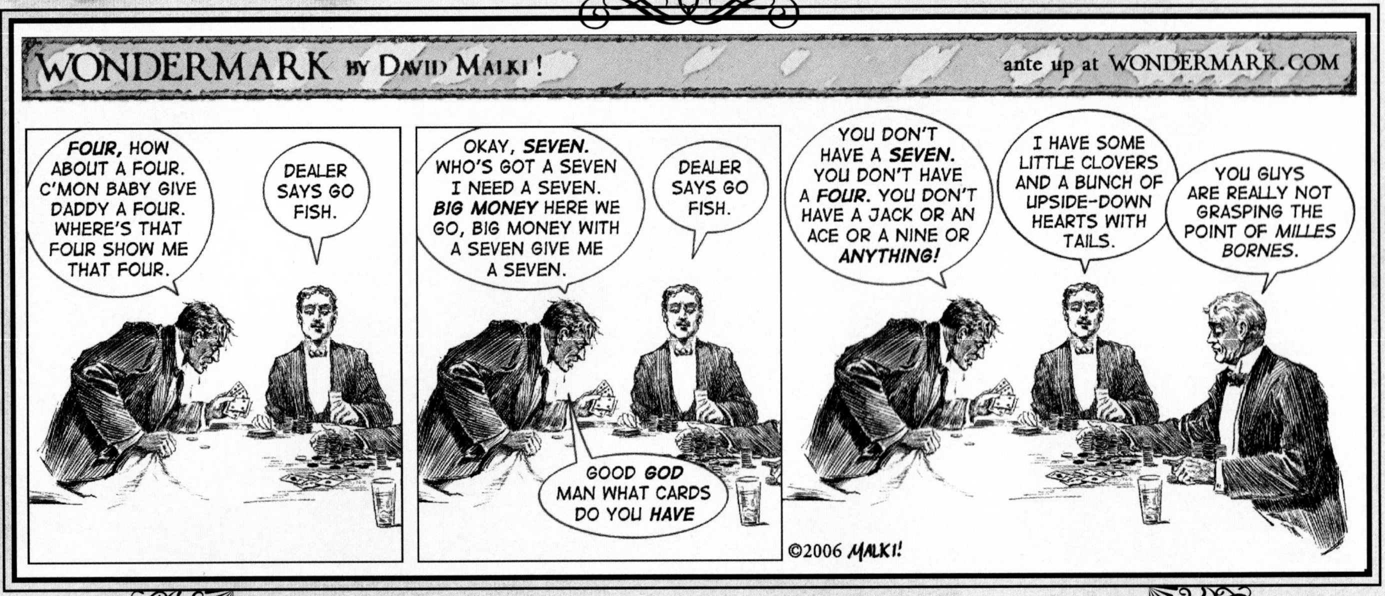
WONDERMARK by DAVID MALKI !
ante up at WONDERMARK.COM
FOUR, HOW ABOUT A FOUR. C'MON BABY GIVE DADDY A FOUR. WHERE'S THAT FOUR SHOW ME THAT FOUR.
DEALER SAYS GO FISH.
OKAY, SEVEN. WHO'S GOT A SEVEN I NEED A SEVEN. BIG MONEY HERE WE GO, BIG MONEY WITH A SEVEN GIVE ME A SEVEN.
DEALER SAYS GO FISH.
GOOD GOD MAN WHAT CARDS DO YOU HAVE
YOU DON'T HAVE A SEVEN. YOU DON'T HAVE A FOUR. YOU DON'T HAVE A JACK OR AN ACE OR A NINE OR ANYTHING!
I HAVE SOME LITTLE CLOVERS AND A BUNCH OF UPSIDE-DOWN HEARTS WITH TAILS.
YOU GUYS ARE REALLY NOT GRASPING THE POINT OF MILLES BORNES.
©2006 MALKI!

we've all seen the bumper stickers that say I [heart] NY or I [spade] MY CAT, but who's seen the ones that say I [club] MY WIFE

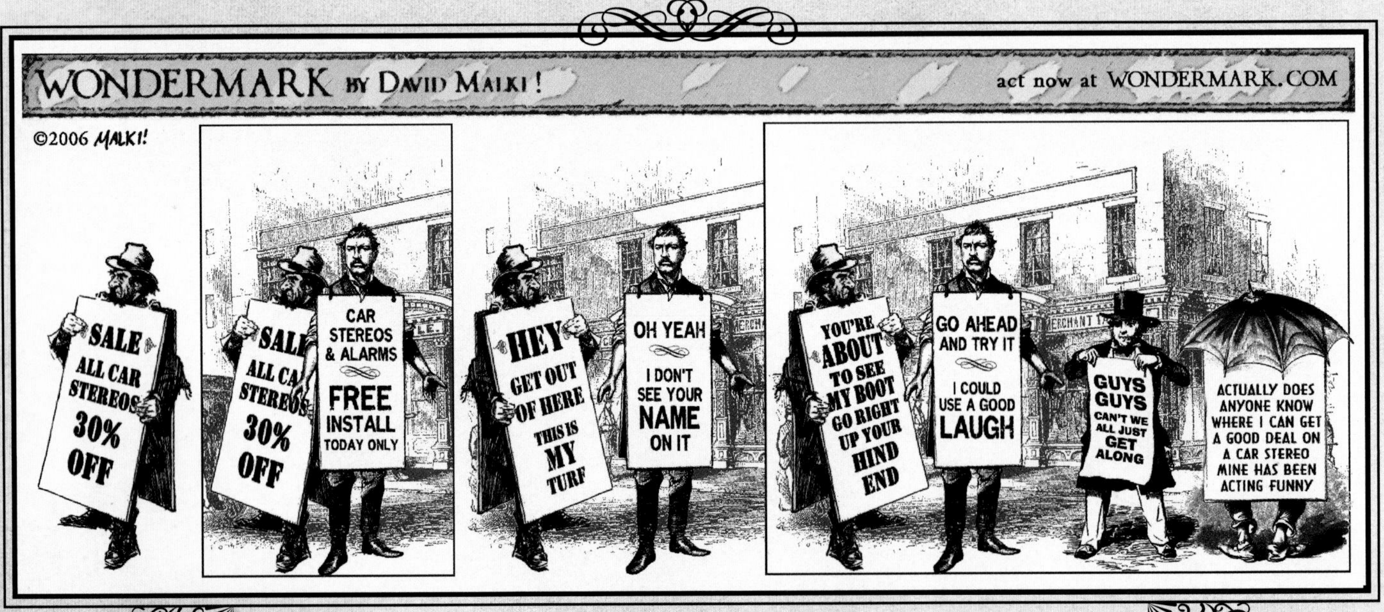
WONDERMARK by DAVID MALKI !
act now at WONDERMARK.COM
©2006 MALKI!
SALE ALL CAR STEREOS 30% OFF
SALE ALL CAR STEREOS 30% OFF
CAR STEREOS & ALARMS FREE INSTALL TODAY ONLY
HEY GET OUT OF HERE THIS IS MY TURF
OH YEAH I DON'T SEE YOUR NAME ON IT
YOU'RE ABOUT TO SEE MY BOOT GO RIGHT UP YOUR HIND END
GO AHEAD AND TRY IT I COULD USE A GOOD LAUGH
GUYS GUYS CAN'T WE ALL JUST GET ALONG
ACTUALLY DOES ANYONE KNOW WHERE I CAN GET A GOOD DEAL ON A CAR STEREO MINE HAS BEEN ACTING FUNNY

it was making all sorts of screeching noises and when you turn the knobs there is static

In which much Bickering occurs

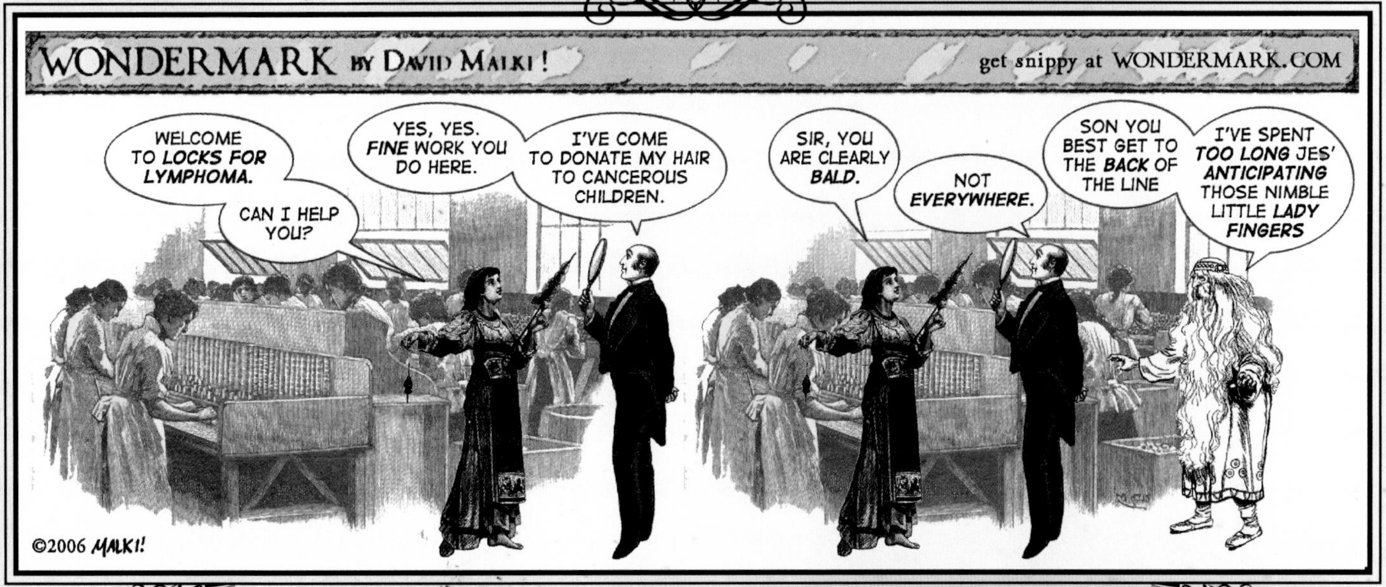
WONDERMARK by David Malki !
get snippy at WONDERMARK.COM
WELCOME TO LOCKS FOR LYMPHOMA.
CAN I HELP YOU?
YES, YES. FINE WORK YOU DO HERE.
I'VE COME TO DONATE MY HAIR TO CANCEROUS CHILDREN.
SIR, YOU ARE CLEARLY BALD.
NOT EVERYWHERE.
SON YOU BEST GET TO THE BACK OF THE LINE
I'VE SPENT TOO LONG JES' ANTICIPATING THOSE NIMBLE LITTLE LADY FINGERS
©2006 MALKI!

as you may have surmised, the bald fellow is referring to hair
available for donation from his back and the tops of his feet

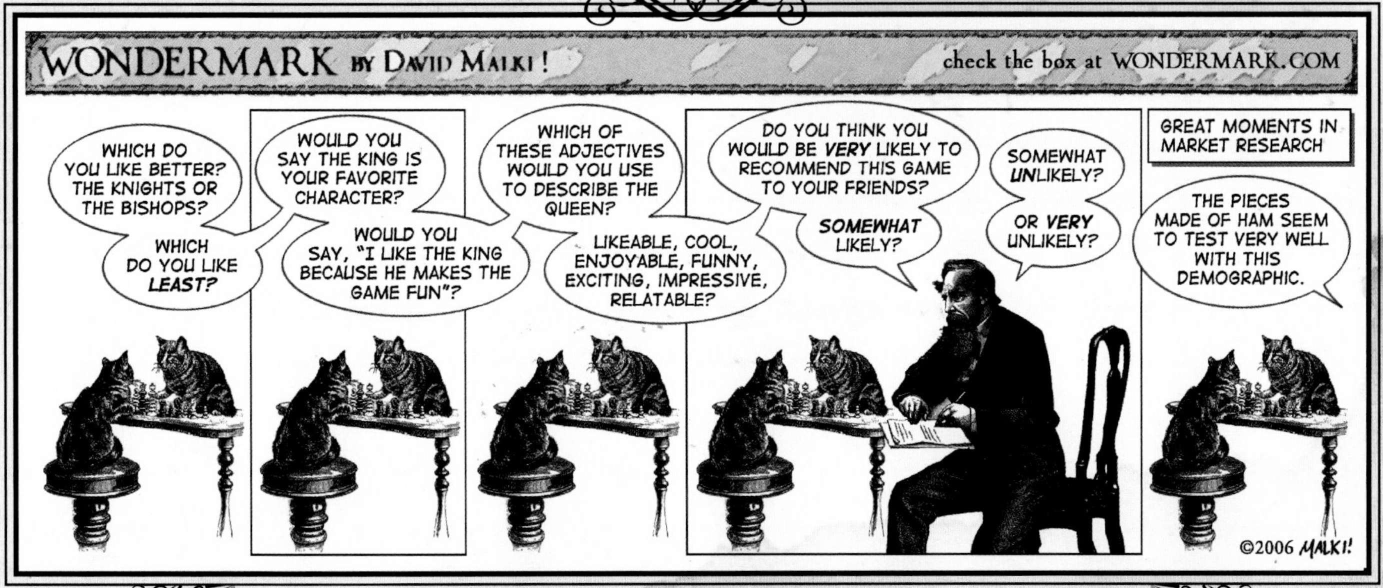
WONDERMARK by David Malki !
check the box at WONDERMARK.COM
WHICH DO YOU LIKE BETTER? THE KNIGHTS OR THE BISHOPS?
WHICH DO YOU LIKE LEAST?
WOULD YOU SAY THE KING IS YOUR FAVORITE CHARACTER?
WOULD YOU SAY, "I LIKE THE KING BECAUSE HE MAKES THE GAME FUN"?
WHICH OF THESE ADJECTIVES WOULD YOU USE TO DESCRIBE THE QUEEN?
LIKEABLE, COOL, ENJOYABLE, FUNNY, EXCITING, IMPRESSIVE, RELATABLE?
DO YOU THINK YOU WOULD BE VERY LIKELY TO RECOMMEND THIS GAME TO YOUR FRIENDS?
SOMEWHAT LIKELY?
SOMEWHAT UNLIKELY?
OR VERY UNLIKELY?
GREAT MOMENTS IN MARKET RESEARCH
THE PIECES MADE OF HAM SEEM TO TEST VERY WELL WITH THIS DEMOGRAPHIC.
©2006 MALKI!

according to the topline, tabbies age 3–6 love the pawns —
but we still can't get any quadrant on those calicos

In which Neuroses are diagnosed

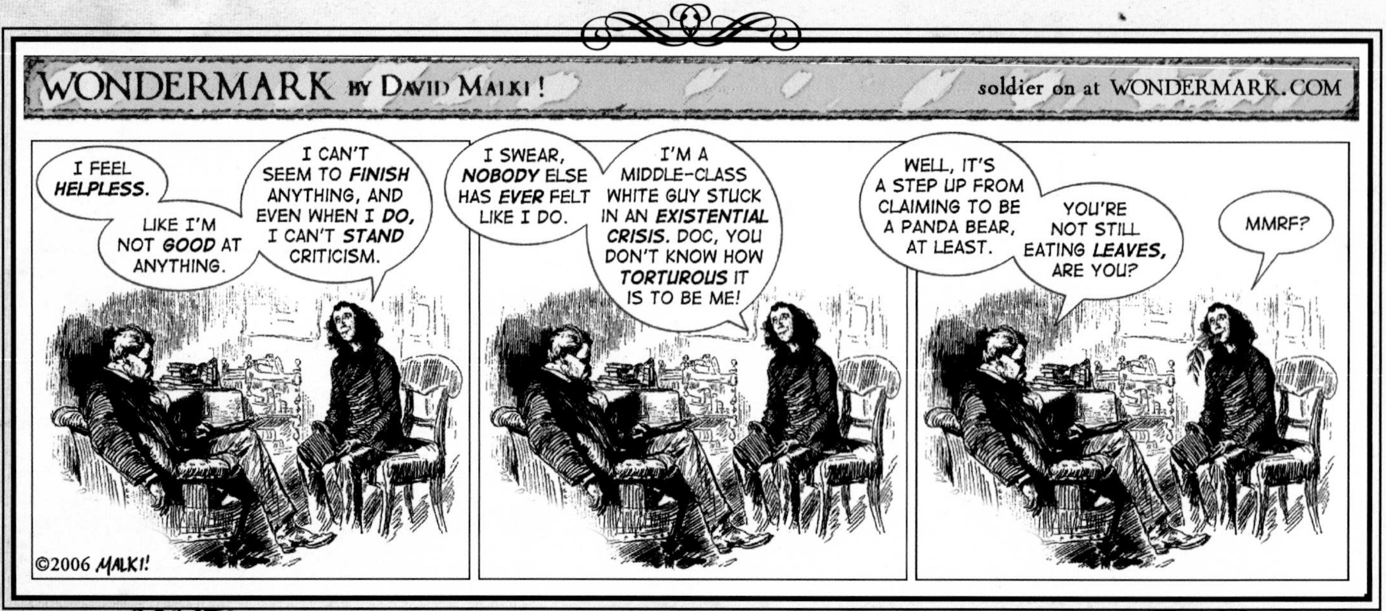
WONDERMARK BY DAVID MALKI !
soldier on at WONDERMARK.COM
I FEEL HELPLESS.
LIKE I'M NOT GOOD AT ANYTHING.
I CAN'T SEEM TO FINISH ANYTHING, AND EVEN WHEN I DO, I CAN'T STAND CRITICISM.
©2006 MALKI!
I SWEAR, NOBODY ELSE HAS EVER FELT LIKE I DO.
I'M A MIDDLE-CLASS WHITE GUY STUCK IN AN EXISTENTIAL CRISIS. DOC, YOU DON'T KNOW HOW TORTUROUS IT IS TO BE ME!
WELL, IT'S A STEP UP FROM CLAIMING TO BE A PANDA BEAR, AT LEAST.
YOU'RE NOT STILL EATING LEAVES, ARE YOU?
MMRF?

i actually have several interesting things to say on the subject
but a dude eating leaves just seems more relevant

48

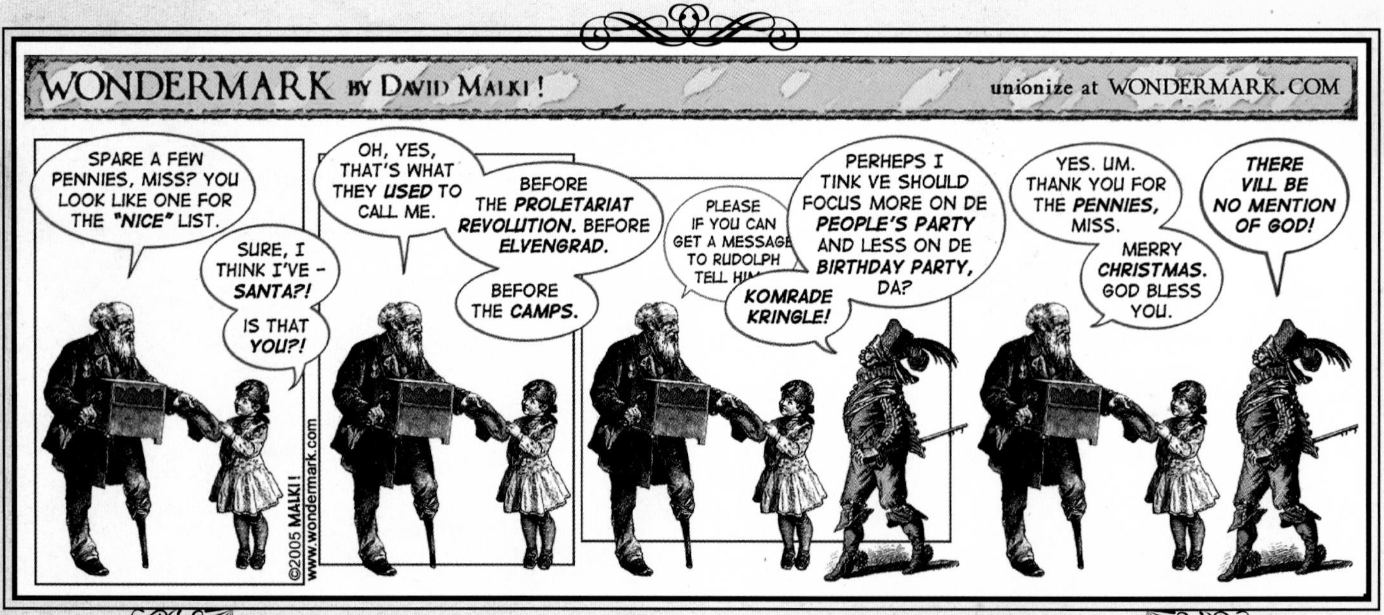
WONDERMARK BY DAVID MALKI !
unionize at WONDERMARK.COM
SPARE A FEW PENNIES, MISS? YOU LOOK LIKE ONE FOR THE "NICE" LIST.
SURE, I THINK I'VE – SANTA?!
IS THAT YOU?!
©2005 MALKI! www.wondermark.com
OH, YES, THAT'S WHAT THEY USED TO CALL ME.
BEFORE THE PROLETARIAT REVOLUTION. BEFORE ELVENGRAD.
BEFORE THE CAMPS.
PLEASE IF YOU CAN GET A MESSAGE TO RUDOLPH TELL
KOMRADE KRINGLE!
PERHEPS I TINK VE SHOULD FOCUS MORE ON DE PEOPLE'S PARTY AND LESS ON DE BIRTHDAY PARTY, DA?
YES. UM. THANK YOU FOR THE PENNIES, MISS.
MERRY CHRISTMAS. GOD BLESS YOU.
THERE VILL BE NO MENTION OF GOD!

or vould you like to be collecting pennies vis TWO of the stumpings, all hobbling around, eh?

In which Communism overtakes the Arctic

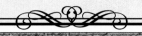

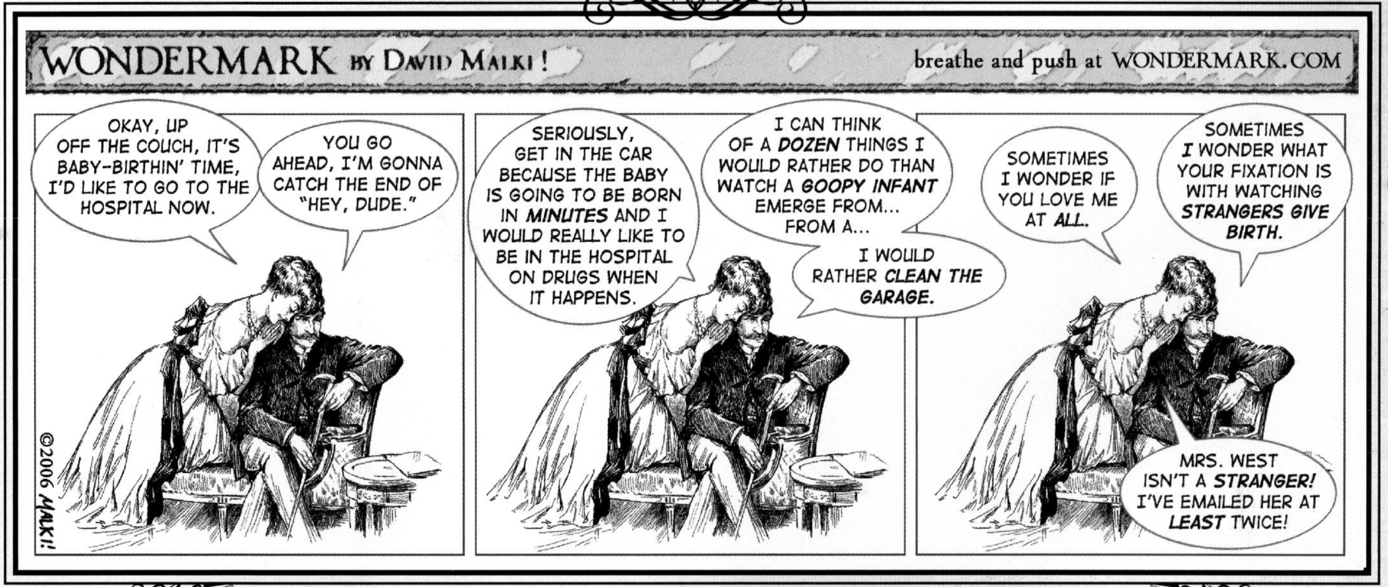
WONDERMARK by David Malki !
breathe and push at WONDERMARK.COM
OKAY, UP OFF THE COUCH, IT'S BABY-BIRTHIN' TIME, I'D LIKE TO GO TO THE HOSPITAL NOW.
YOU GO AHEAD, I'M GONNA CATCH THE END OF "HEY, DUDE."
©2006 MALKI!
SERIOUSLY, GET IN THE CAR BECAUSE THE BABY IS GOING TO BE BORN IN MINUTES AND I WOULD REALLY LIKE TO BE IN THE HOSPITAL ON DRUGS WHEN IT HAPPENS.
I CAN THINK OF A DOZEN THINGS I WOULD RATHER DO THAN WATCH A GOOPY INFANT EMERGE FROM... FROM A...
I WOULD RATHER CLEAN THE GARAGE.
SOMETIMES I WONDER IF YOU LOVE ME AT ALL.
SOMETIMES I WONDER WHAT YOUR FIXATION IS WITH WATCHING STRANGERS GIVE BIRTH.
MRS. WEST ISN'T A STRANGER! I'VE EMAILED HER AT LEAST TWICE!

all that blood and pain and crying and blah blah blah — it's not really my scene, you know?

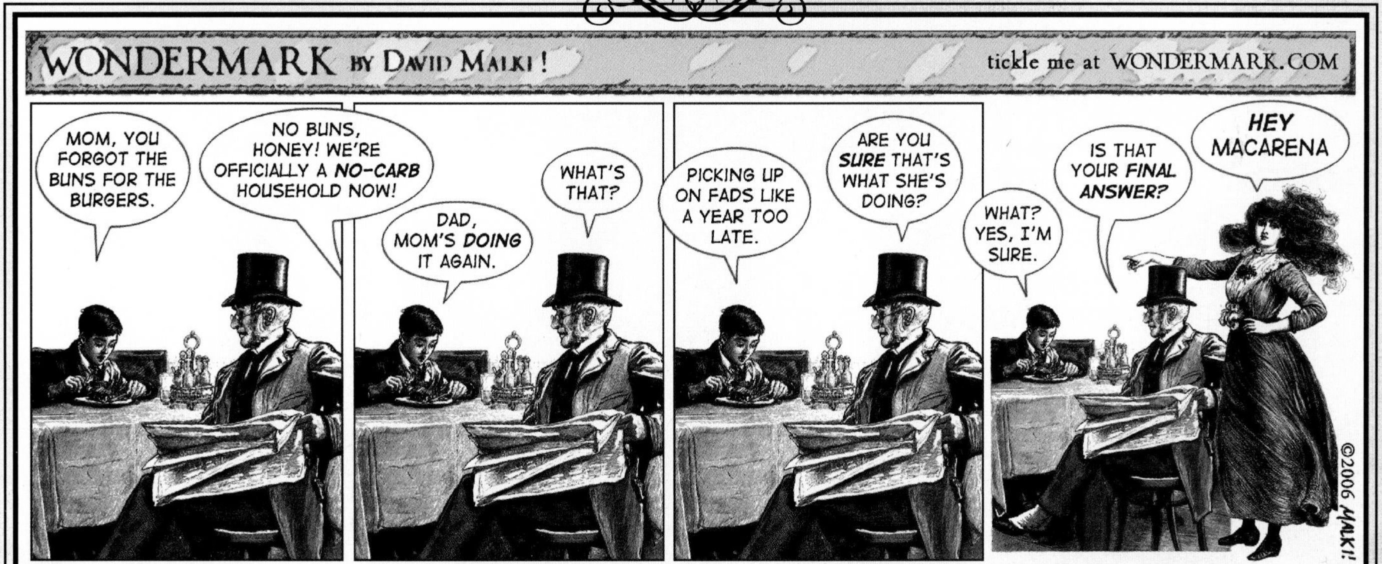
WONDERMARK by David Malki !
tickle me at WONDERMARK.COM
MOM, YOU FORGOT THE BUNS FOR THE BURGERS.
NO BUNS, HONEY! WE'RE OFFICIALLY A NO-CARB HOUSEHOLD NOW!
DAD, MOM'S DOING IT AGAIN.
WHAT'S THAT?
PICKING UP ON FADS LIKE A YEAR TOO LATE.
ARE YOU SURE THAT'S WHAT SHE'S DOING?
WHAT? YES, I'M SURE.
IS THAT YOUR FINAL ANSWER?
HEY MACARENA
©2006 MALKI!

you are the weakest link, goodbye

In which Doug fails to obtain a Tote-Bag

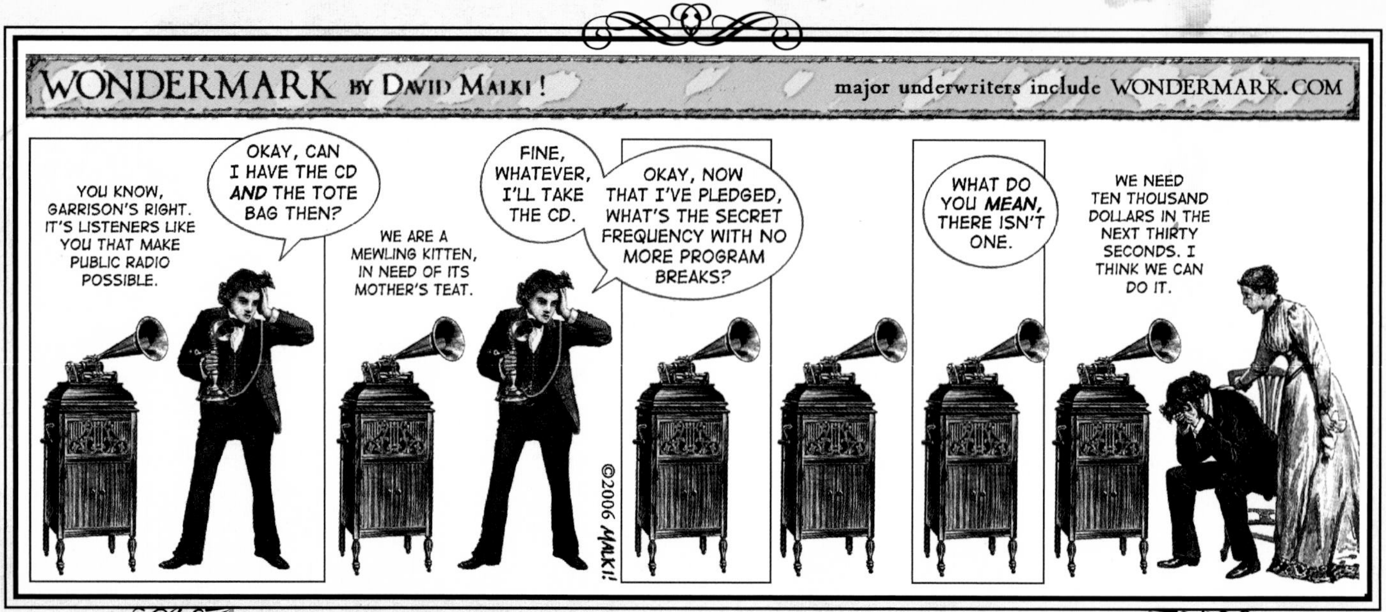
WONDERMARK BY DAVID MALKI !
major underwriters include WONDERMARK.COM
YOU KNOW, GARRISON'S RIGHT. IT'S LISTENERS LIKE YOU THAT MAKE PUBLIC RADIO POSSIBLE.
OKAY, CAN I HAVE THE CD AND THE TOTE BAG THEN?
WE ARE A MEWLING KITTEN, IN NEED OF ITS MOTHER'S TEAT.
FINE, WHATEVER, I'LL TAKE THE CD.
©2006 MALKI!
OKAY, NOW THAT I'VE PLEDGED, WHAT'S THE SECRET FREQUENCY WITH NO MORE PROGRAM BREAKS?
WHAT DO YOU MEAN, THERE ISN'T ONE.
WE NEED TEN THOUSAND DOLLARS IN THE NEXT THIRTY SECONDS. I THINK WE CAN DO IT.

i have no better solutions for the problem of how to fund
public media, i guess, but still, c'mon with the pledge drives

50

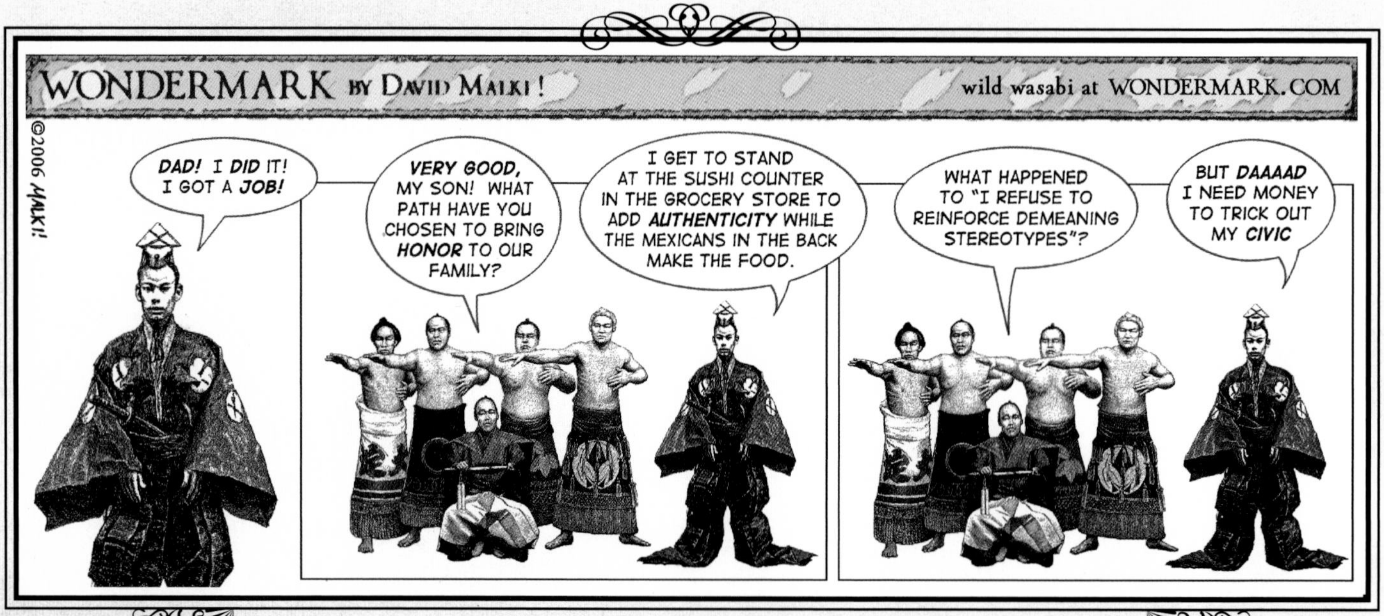
WONDERMARK BY DAVID MALKI !
wild wasabi at WONDERMARK.COM
©2006 MALKI!
DAD! I DID IT! I GOT A JOB!
VERY GOOD, MY SON! WHAT PATH HAVE YOU CHOSEN TO BRING HONOR TO OUR FAMILY?
I GET TO STAND AT THE SUSHI COUNTER IN THE GROCERY STORE TO ADD AUTHENTICITY WHILE THE MEXICANS IN THE BACK MAKE THE FOOD.
WHAT HAPPENED TO "I REFUSE TO REINFORCE DEMEANING STEREOTYPES"?
BUT DAAAAD I NEED MONEY TO TRICK OUT MY CIVIC

he bought the civic in a fit of joy after winning the academic decathlon

In which Hiroshi misses the Point

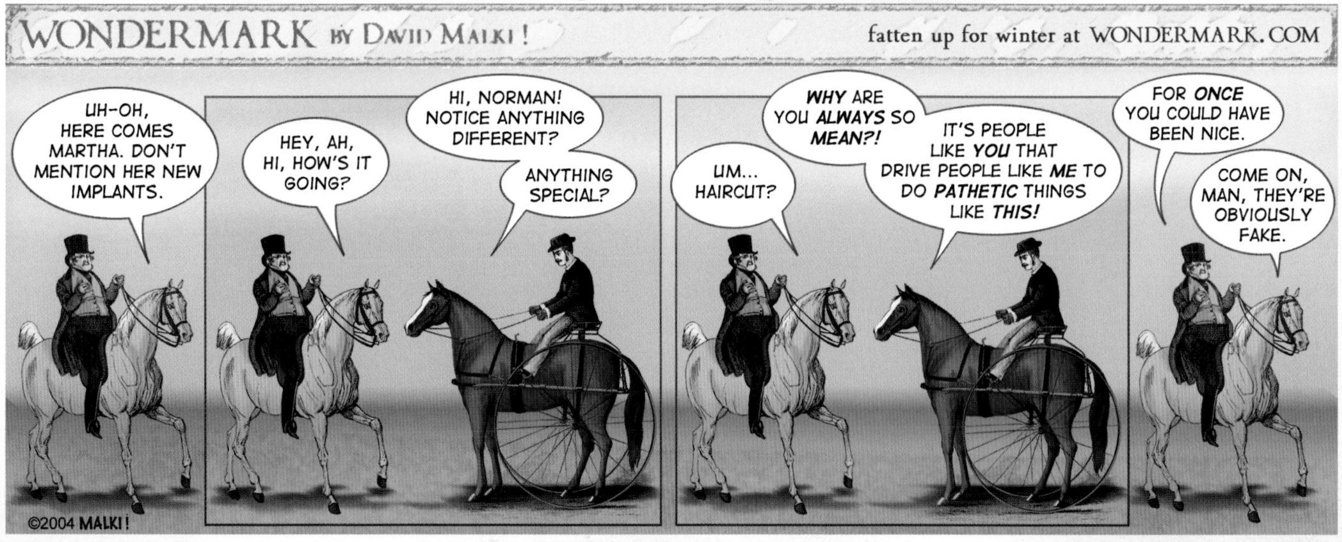
WONDERMARK by David Malki !
fatten up for winter at WONDERMARK.COM
UH-OH, HERE COMES MARTHA. DON'T MENTION HER NEW IMPLANTS.
HEY, AH, HI, HOW'S IT GOING?
HI, NORMAN! NOTICE ANYTHING DIFFERENT?
ANYTHING SPECIAL?
UM... HAIRCUT?
WHY ARE YOU ALWAYS SO MEAN?!
IT'S PEOPLE LIKE YOU THAT DRIVE PEOPLE LIKE ME TO DO PATHETIC THINGS LIKE THIS!
FOR ONCE YOU COULD HAVE BEEN NICE.
COME ON, MAN, THEY'RE OBVIOUSLY FAKE.
©2004 MALKI !

why the long face?

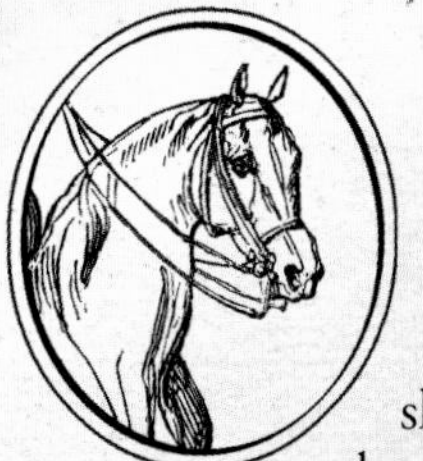

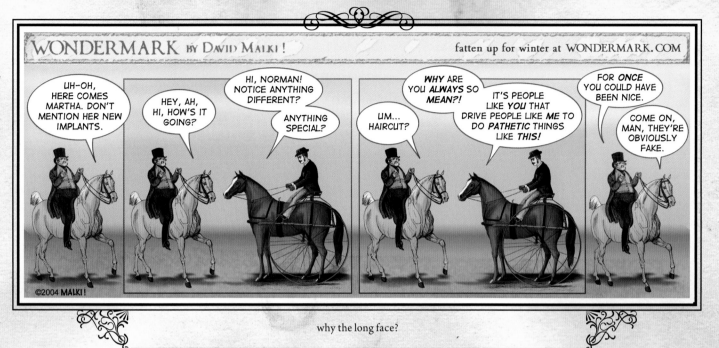

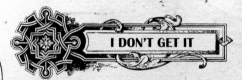

I DON'T GET IT

I REALLY have to explain this to you? Um, okay. This is awkward. You shouldn't be talking to me about this, you should be asking her. I mean, I can tell you what went down, but—it's not going to get back to her, is it?

Here's the backstory. She came to me a few weeks ago and wanted some "help" chowin' on some hay. I'd never thought of her in that way before—I mean, she was nice-looking and all, a little plain, but that's all right. Anyway, we started hanging out, she's flirting a little like she always seems to be doing, and I start to think, *Wow. She's into me, this is pretty cool.* You know? Even if I wasn't that into *her*, it's kind of energizing, and all of a sudden real quick I'm thinking, like, *I never noticed how cute she is.*

You can see where this is going, right? Yeah, exactly—I go ahead and make a move and she gets all *cold* on me, like she hadn't been the one nuzzling, saying "I miss college 'cause there was always someone around to give me a backrub," all that stuff. Now I don't know *what* to think, because she's *totally* tweaked and I'm just out there in the cold with hay sticking out of my mouth like an idiot.

I chased her back to the barn—retrospect, bad idea, whatever—and found her huddled under the, like, loft thing where the bales are stacked. Pretending like I'm not there, like she's not *physically hiding* from me. I should have walked away, left her to deal with her own issues. It's not like I don't have my own crap to sort through. But like a jerk I just stood there, thinking I'm being sweet, all "Come on, come on out of there," and when that didn't work I graduated to "Is it me? Do you want me to leave?" and she's eventually like "I can't see you right now." Whatever.

The next time I saw her, couple ten days later, she'd had the work done. She was playing it cool, like, "Oh, I was *born* beautiful," but she was fishing for compliments big time and the freakin' *dairy barn* was just dishing 'em out left and right. I swear one day I'm gonna kick that cow Betsy right in her fat face. I am *so* tired of chicks playing games. That's the *real* joke of this strip, that I still even *care.*

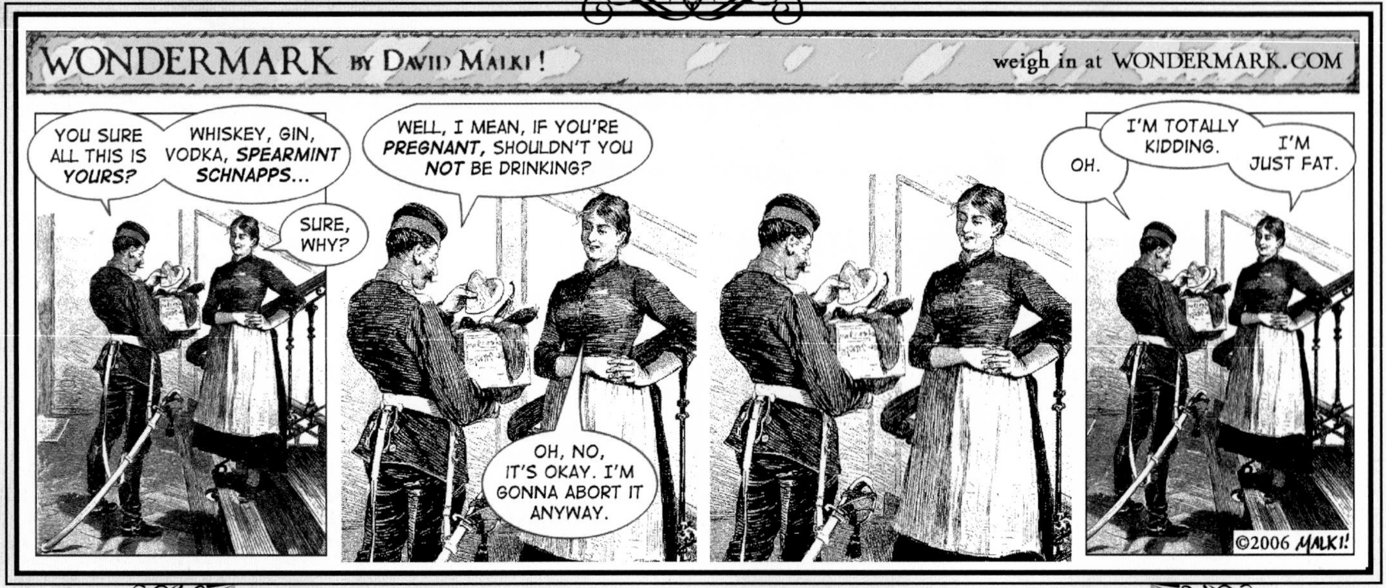
WONDERMARK BY DAVID MALKI !
weigh in at WONDERMARK.COM
YOU SURE ALL THIS IS YOURS?
WHISKEY, GIN, VODKA, SPEARMINT SCHNAPPS...
SURE, WHY?
WELL, I MEAN, IF YOU'RE PREGNANT, SHOULDN'T YOU NOT BE DRINKING?
OH, NO, IT'S OKAY. I'M GONNA ABORT IT ANYWAY.
OH.
I'M TOTALLY KIDDING.
I'M JUST FAT.
©2006 MALKI!

i hear the kiddies like them the bubblicious schnapps

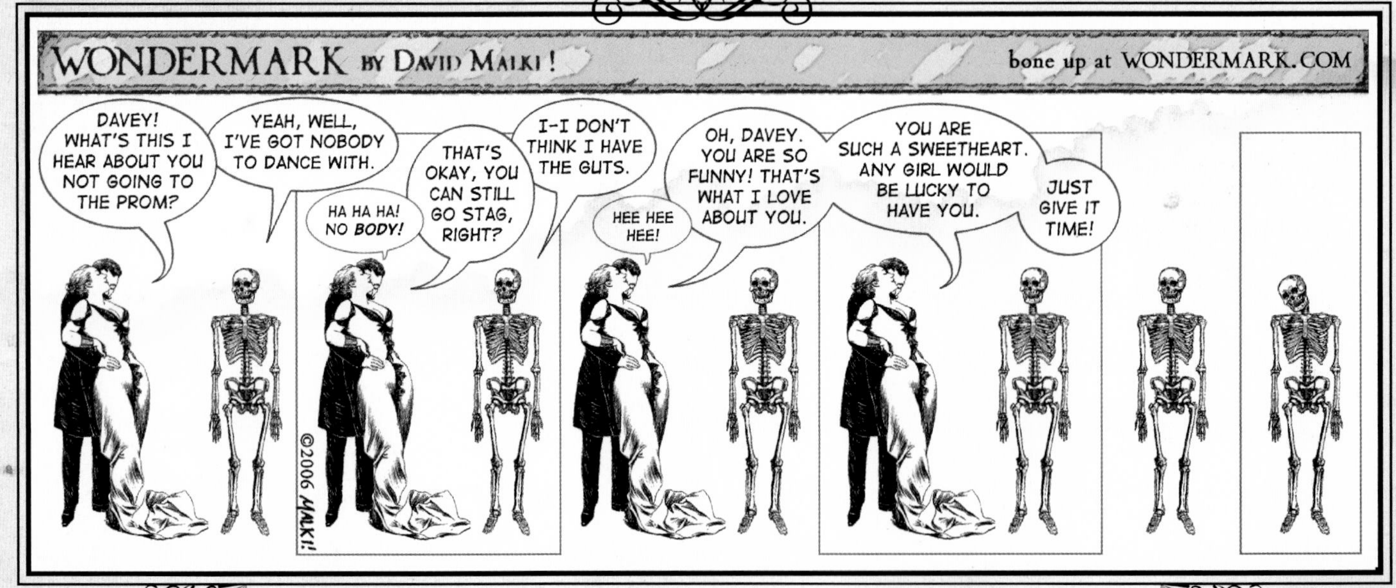
WONDERMARK BY DAVID MALKI !
bone up at WONDERMARK.COM
DAVEY! WHAT'S THIS I HEAR ABOUT YOU NOT GOING TO THE PROM?
YEAH, WELL, I'VE GOT NOBODY TO DANCE WITH.
HA HA HA! NO BODY!
THAT'S OKAY, YOU CAN STILL GO STAG, RIGHT?
I-I DON'T THINK I HAVE THE GUTS.
HEE HEE HEE!
OH, DAVEY. YOU ARE SO FUNNY! THAT'S WHAT I LOVE ABOUT YOU.
YOU ARE SUCH A SWEETHEART. ANY GIRL WOULD BE LUCKY TO HAVE YOU.
JUST GIVE IT TIME!
©2006 MALKI!

i don't think he was joking

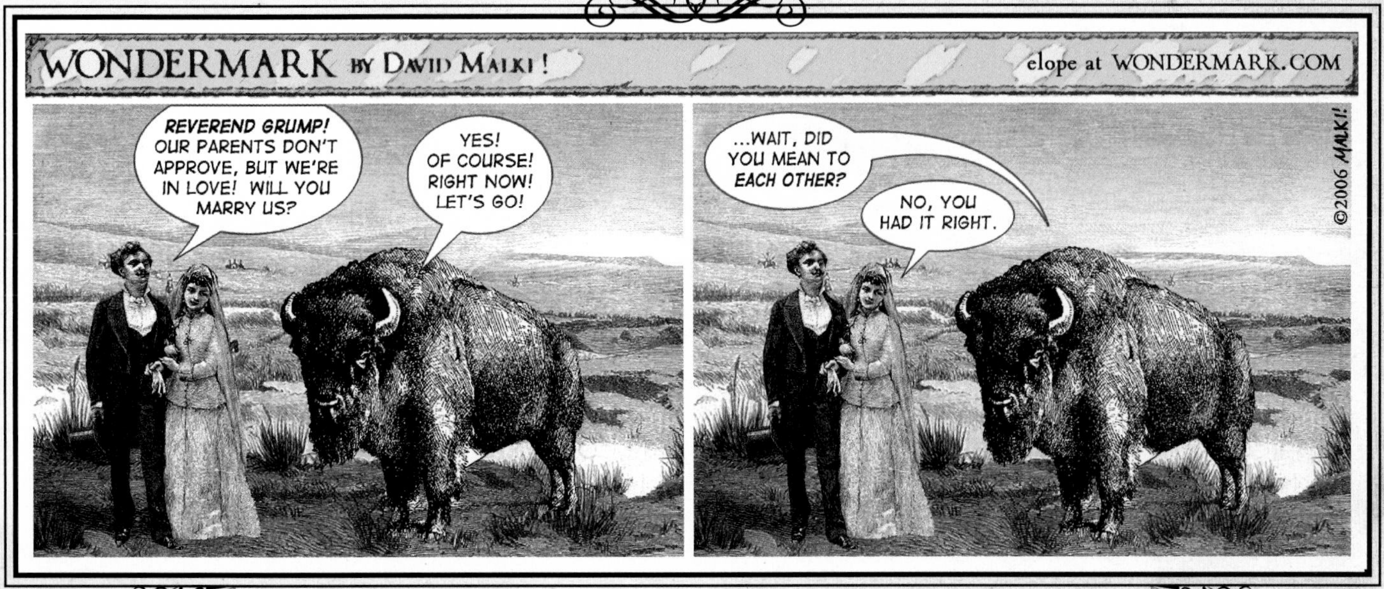
WONDERMARK by David Malki !
elope at WONDERMARK.COM
REVEREND GRUMP! OUR PARENTS DON'T APPROVE, BUT WE'RE IN LOVE! WILL YOU MARRY US?
YES! OF COURSE! RIGHT NOW! LET'S GO!
...WAIT, DID YOU MEAN TO EACH OTHER?
NO, YOU HAD IT RIGHT.
©2006 MALKI!

this particular issue was covered in detail in seminary

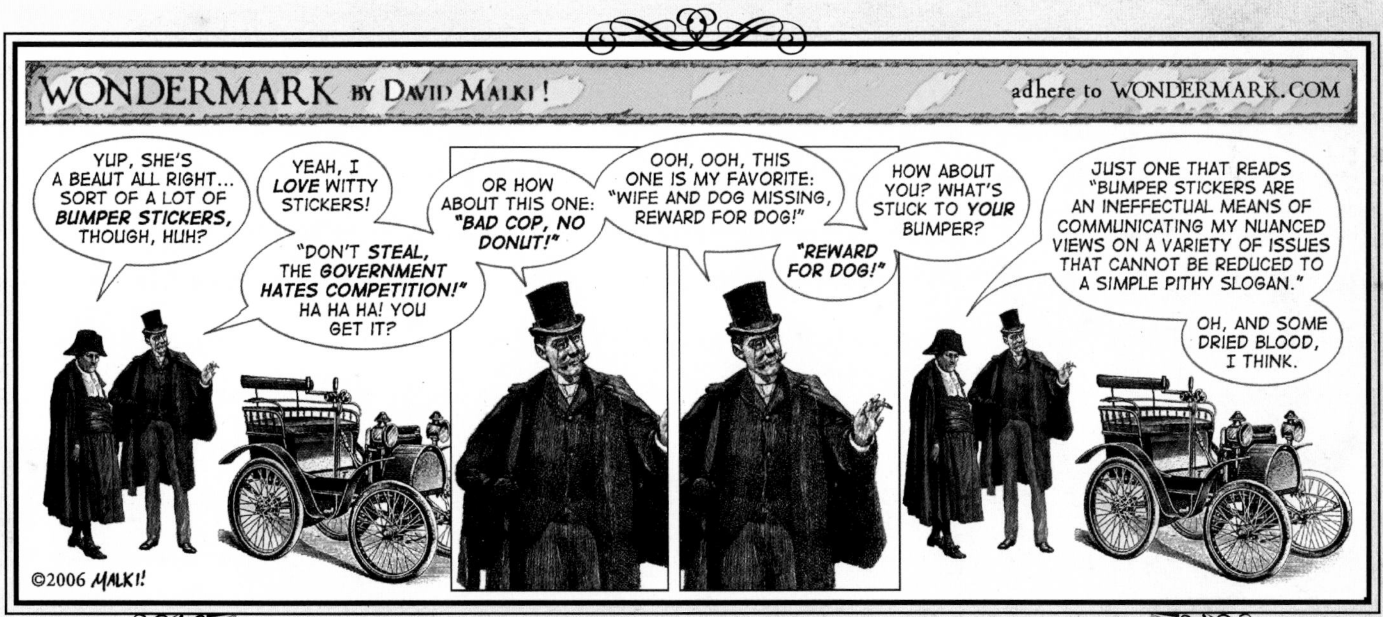
WONDERMARK by David Malki !
adhere to WONDERMARK.COM
YUP, SHE'S A BEAUT ALL RIGHT... SORT OF A LOT OF BUMPER STICKERS, THOUGH, HUH?
YEAH, I LOVE WITTY STICKERS!
"DON'T STEAL, THE GOVERNMENT HATES COMPETITION!" HA HA HA! YOU GET IT?
OR HOW ABOUT THIS ONE: "BAD COP, NO DONUT!"
OOH, OOH, THIS ONE IS MY FAVORITE: "WIFE AND DOG MISSING, REWARD FOR DOG!"
"REWARD FOR DOG!"
HOW ABOUT YOU? WHAT'S STUCK TO YOUR BUMPER?
JUST ONE THAT READS "BUMPER STICKERS ARE AN INEFFECTUAL MEANS OF COMMUNICATING MY NUANCED VIEWS ON A VARIETY OF ISSUES THAT CANNOT BE REDUCED TO A SIMPLE PITHY SLOGAN."
OH, AND SOME DRIED BLOOD, I THINK.
©2006 MALKI!

on the peel-off part of the sticker it continues on to say "...and given the inherent limitations of the medium i frankly cannot comprehend its appeal as a vehicle for the vigorous exchange of ideas"

In which a Hog requires Blended Fruit

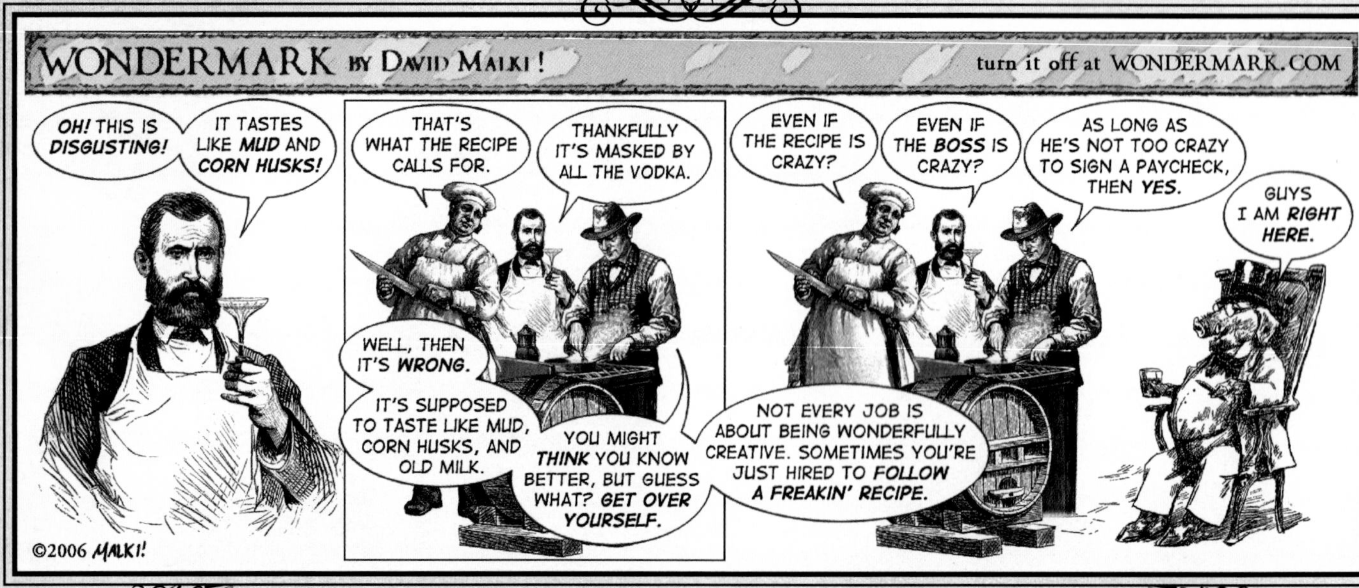
WONDERMARK by David Malki !
turn it off at WONDERMARK.COM
OH! THIS IS DISGUSTING!
IT TASTES LIKE MUD AND CORN HUSKS!
THAT'S WHAT THE RECIPE CALLS FOR.
THANKFULLY IT'S MASKED BY ALL THE VODKA.
WELL, THEN IT'S WRONG.
IT'S SUPPOSED TO TASTE LIKE MUD, CORN HUSKS, AND OLD MILK.
YOU MIGHT THINK YOU KNOW BETTER, BUT GUESS WHAT? GET OVER YOURSELF.
NOT EVERY JOB IS ABOUT BEING WONDERFULLY CREATIVE. SOMETIMES YOU'RE JUST HIRED TO FOLLOW A FREAKIN' RECIPE.
EVEN IF THE RECIPE IS CRAZY?
EVEN IF THE BOSS IS CRAZY?
AS LONG AS HE'S NOT TOO CRAZY TO SIGN A PAYCHECK, THEN YES.
GUYS I AM RIGHT HERE.
©2006 MALKI!

save your creativity for your livejournal. here at work we pour vodka into old milk AND WHEN WE DO IT WE SMILE

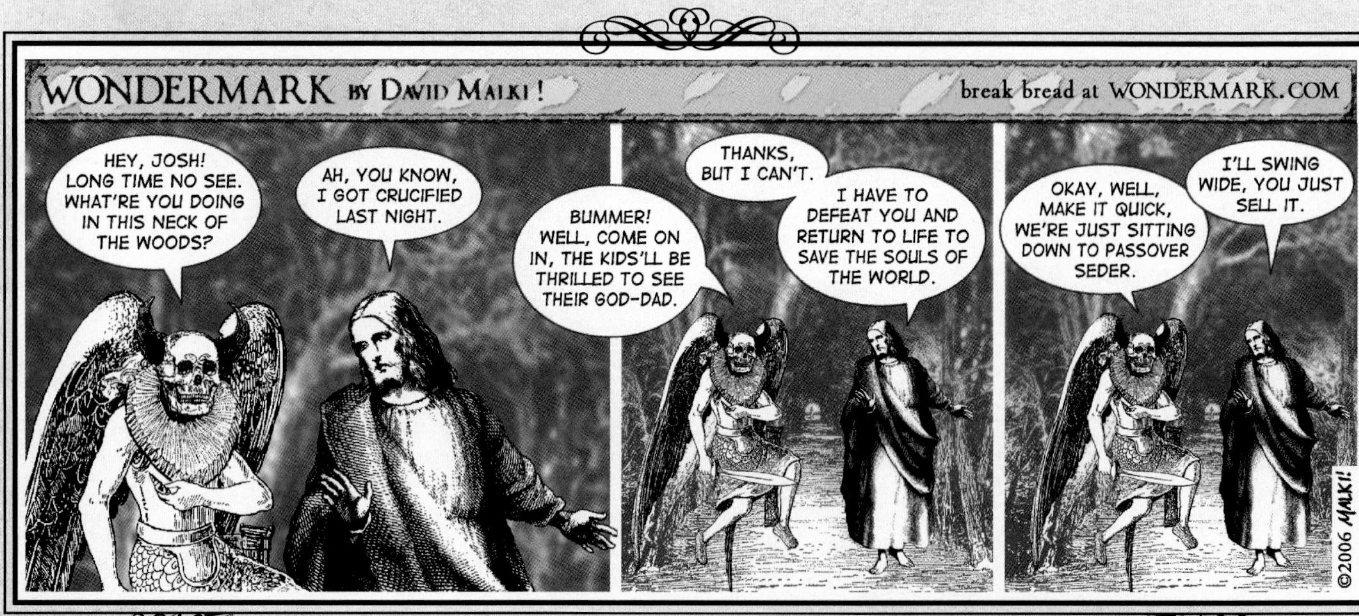
WONDERMARK by David Malki !
break bread at WONDERMARK.COM
HEY, JOSH! LONG TIME NO SEE. WHAT'RE YOU DOING IN THIS NECK OF THE WOODS?
AH, YOU KNOW, I GOT CRUCIFIED LAST NIGHT.
BUMMER! WELL, COME ON IN, THE KIDS'LL BE THRILLED TO SEE THEIR GOD-DAD.
THANKS, BUT I CAN'T.
I HAVE TO DEFEAT YOU AND RETURN TO LIFE TO SAVE THE SOULS OF THE WORLD.
OKAY, WELL, MAKE IT QUICK, WE'RE JUST SITTING DOWN TO PASSOVER SEDER.
I'LL SWING WIDE, YOU JUST SELL IT.
©2006 MALKI!

josh was middleweight boxing champ in nazareth in 8th grade. not many people know that

In which Satan enjoys Matzoh

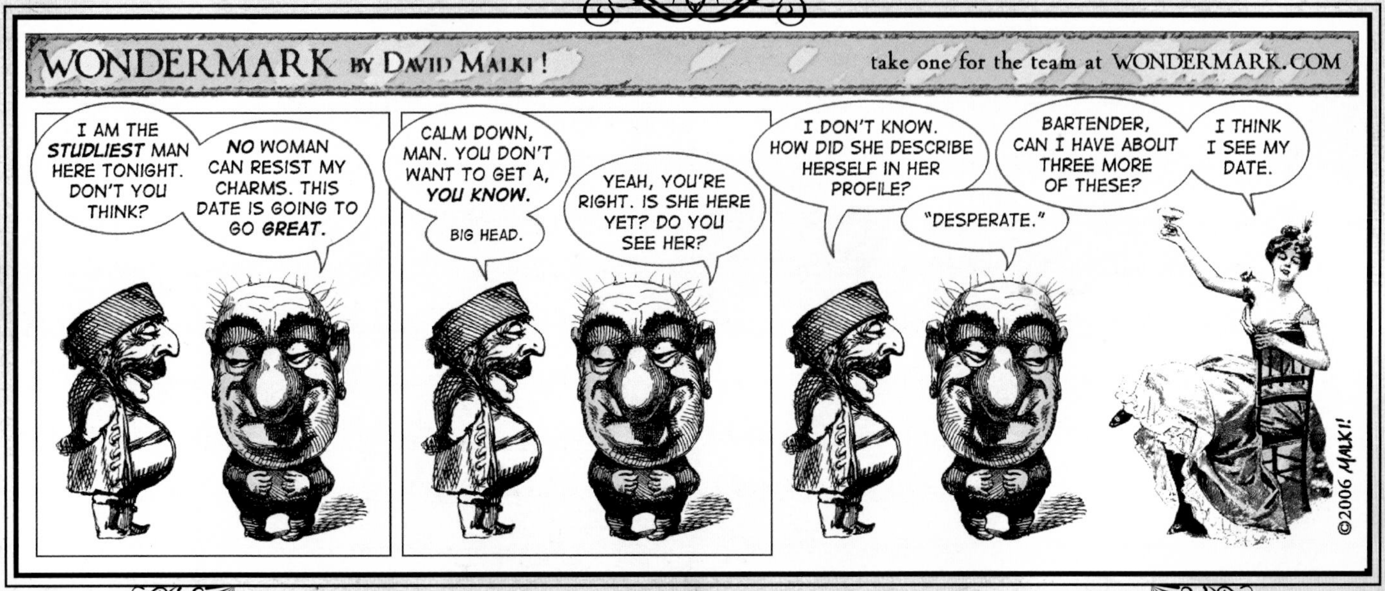
WONDERMARK by David Malki !
take one for the team at WONDERMARK.COM
I AM THE STUDLIEST MAN HERE TONIGHT. DON'T YOU THINK?
NO WOMAN CAN RESIST MY CHARMS. THIS DATE IS GOING TO GO GREAT.
CALM DOWN, MAN. YOU DON'T WANT TO GET A, YOU KNOW.
BIG HEAD.
YEAH, YOU'RE RIGHT. IS SHE HERE YET? DO YOU SEE HER?
I DON'T KNOW. HOW DID SHE DESCRIBE HERSELF IN HER PROFILE?
"DESPERATE."
BARTENDER, CAN I HAVE ABOUT THREE MORE OF THESE?
I THINK I SEE MY DATE.
©2006 MALKI!

she knocked back some eight-ball before leaving home but this job requires overtime

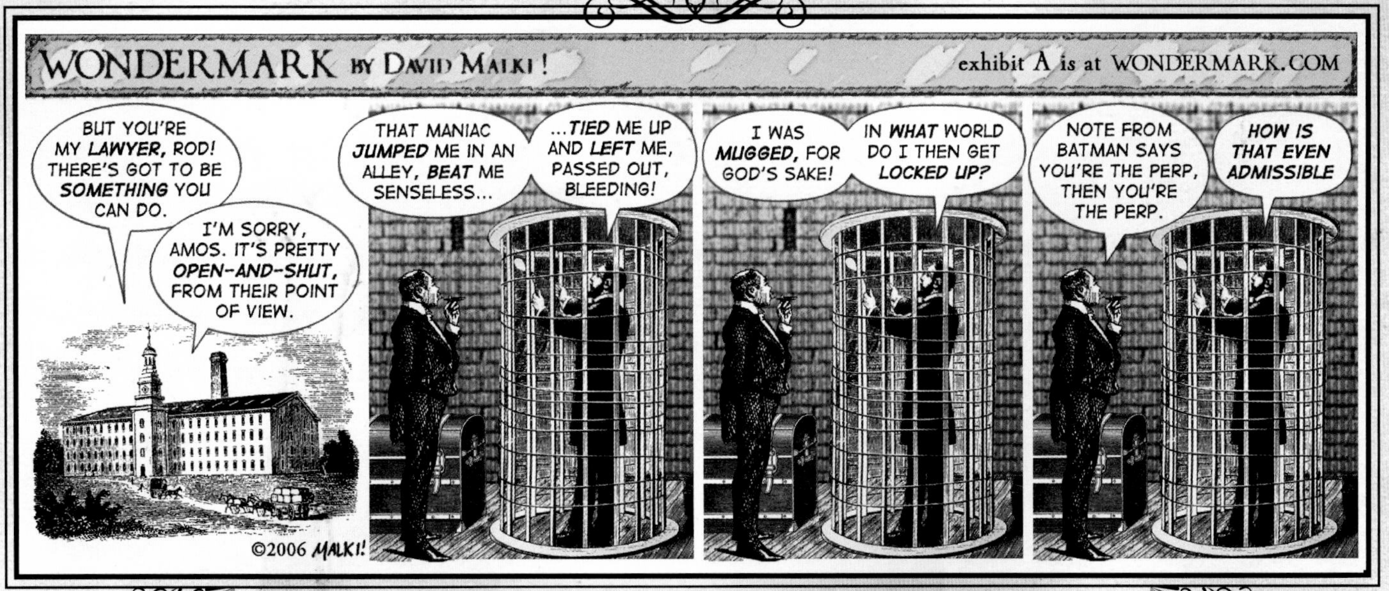
WONDERMARK by David Malki !
exhibit A is at WONDERMARK.COM
BUT YOU'RE MY LAWYER, ROD! THERE'S GOT TO BE SOMETHING YOU CAN DO.
I'M SORRY, AMOS. IT'S PRETTY OPEN-AND-SHUT, FROM THEIR POINT OF VIEW.
©2006 MALKI!
THAT MANIAC JUMPED ME IN AN ALLEY, BEAT ME SENSELESS...
...TIED ME UP AND LEFT ME, PASSED OUT, BLEEDING!
I WAS MUGGED, FOR GOD'S SAKE!
IN WHAT WORLD DO I THEN GET LOCKED UP?
NOTE FROM BATMAN SAYS YOU'RE THE PERP, THEN YOU'RE THE PERP.
HOW IS THAT EVEN ADMISSIBLE

seriously who even goes into dark alleys these days
unless you are a thuggish type bent on mayhem

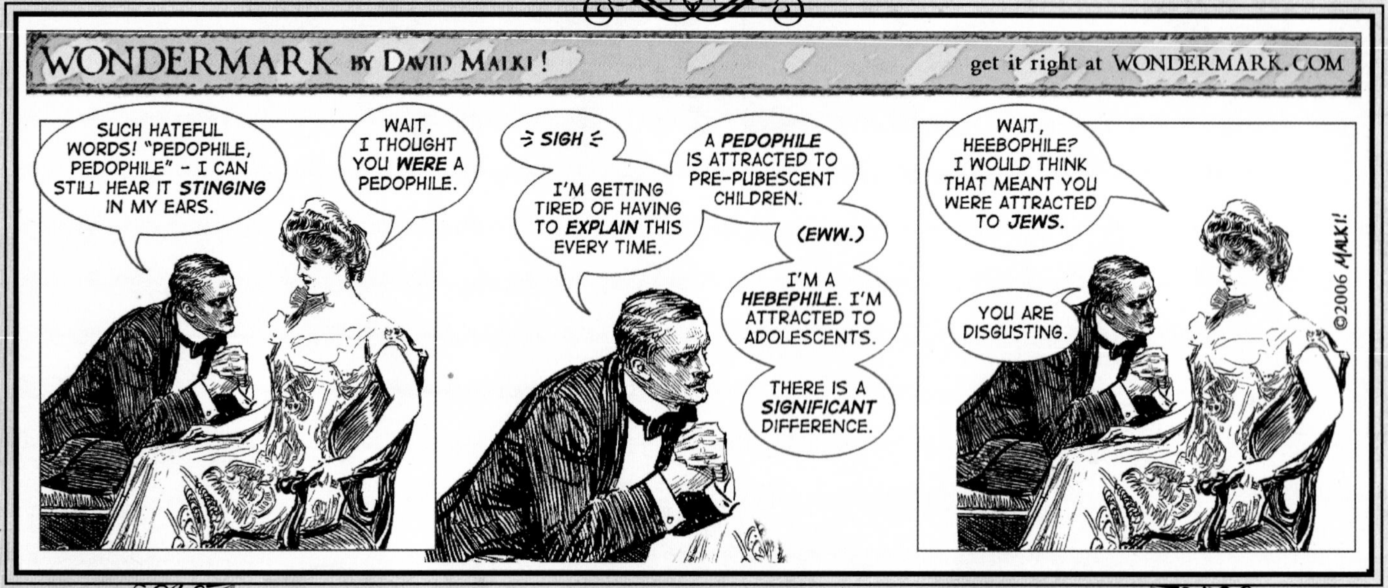
WONDERMARK by David Malki !
get it right at WONDERMARK.COM
SUCH HATEFUL WORDS! "PEDOPHILE, PEDOPHILE" - I CAN STILL HEAR IT STINGING IN MY EARS.
WAIT, I THOUGHT YOU WERE A PEDOPHILE.
SIGH
I'M GETTING TIRED OF HAVING TO EXPLAIN THIS EVERY TIME.
A PEDOPHILE IS ATTRACTED TO PRE-PUBESCENT CHILDREN.
(EWW.)
I'M A HEBEPHILE. I'M ATTRACTED TO ADOLESCENTS.
THERE IS A SIGNIFICANT DIFFERENCE.
WAIT, HEEBOPHILE? I WOULD THINK THAT MEANT YOU WERE ATTRACTED TO JEWS.
YOU ARE DISGUSTING.
©2006 MALKI!

i was a pedophile in the second grade

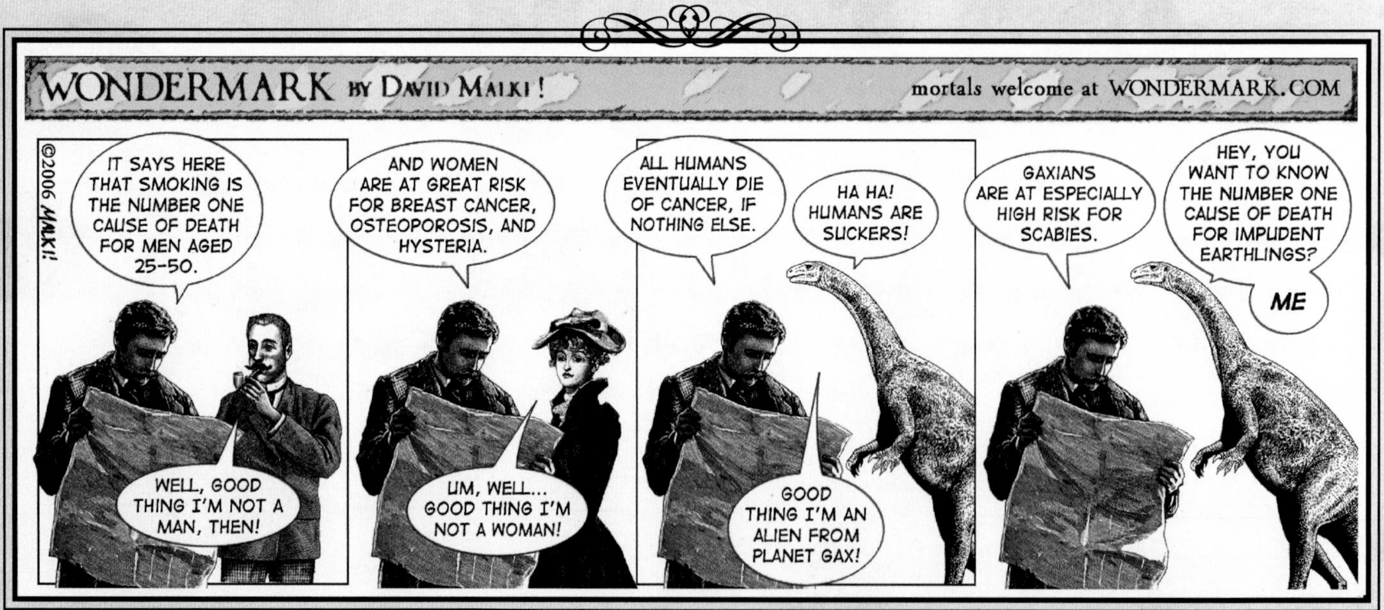
WONDERMARK by David Malki !
mortals welcome at WONDERMARK.COM
©2006 MALKI!
IT SAYS HERE THAT SMOKING IS THE NUMBER ONE CAUSE OF DEATH FOR MEN AGED 25-50.
WELL, GOOD THING I'M NOT A MAN, THEN!
AND WOMEN ARE AT GREAT RISK FOR BREAST CANCER, OSTEOPOROSIS, AND HYSTERIA.
UM, WELL... GOOD THING I'M NOT A WOMAN!
ALL HUMANS EVENTUALLY DIE OF CANCER, IF NOTHING ELSE.
HA HA! HUMANS ARE SUCKERS!
GOOD THING I'M AN ALIEN FROM PLANET GAX!
GAXIANS ARE AT ESPECIALLY HIGH RISK FOR SCABIES.
HEY, YOU WANT TO KNOW THE NUMBER ONE CAUSE OF DEATH FOR IMPUDENT EARTHLINGS?
ME

also not having attended earth kindergarten he
would not have developed an immunity to cooties

WONDERMARK BY DAVID MALKI !
make headlines at WONDERMARK.COM
MAN, I HATE COMING HOME FOR THE HOLIDAYS.
FIRST IT'S SOME SLY COMMENT ABOUT MY JOB. AND MY HOBBIES. AND MY FRIENDS.
THEN COMES THE SILENCE. THE IMPLICIT JUDGMENT. I THOUGHT PARENTS WERE SUPPOSED TO BE SUPPORTIVE.
LOOK AT THEM, JUST WAITING TO SLIP IN SOME CRACK, SOME DIG AT THE WAY I'VE CHOSEN TO LIVE MY LIFE.
SO, AH, JOHN...
FRANKLY, WE'RE A LITTLE CONCERNED.
WE HEAR YOU'RE THE DELAWARE DECAPITATOR?
AND HERE WE GO!
©2004 MALKI !

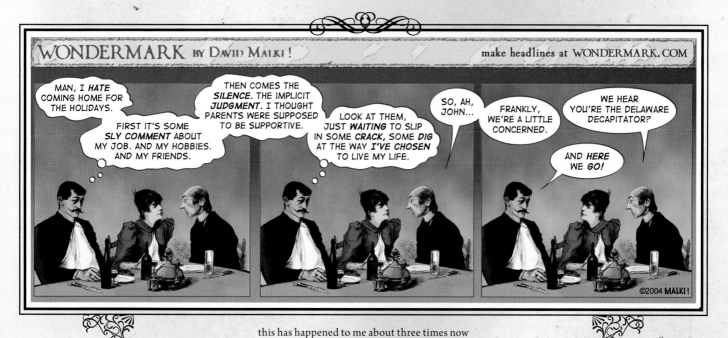

this has happened to me about three times now

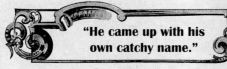

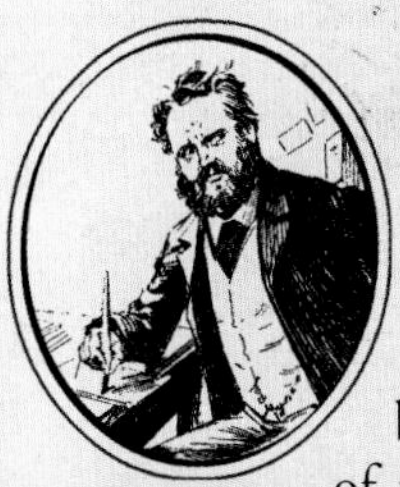

"He came up with his own catchy name."

IT WAS clear from the beginning that the Delaware Decapitator was a new breed of serial killer. Within minutes of the discovery of his second victim—like the first, a heavyset truck driver in his fifties with a secret fetish for porcelain dolls—the Decapitator posted gruesome details on his blog, as if he'd composed the entry in an adrenaline fever and was simply waiting for the body to be found before he clicked "submit." Complete with photos, social bookmarking links, and truly awful freeform poetry, *delawaredecapitator.blogspot.com* was a trove of grisly details much revered by rubbernecking voyeurs, but summarily dismissed by law enforcement as alternately a "sick prank" or "misinformation just asking us to fall for it."

This marginalization was a source of constant frustration to the killer. The addition of a podcast, featuring alleged recordings of the doll-loving victims' last gasping breaths, spawned a viral meme and legions of YouTube imitations, yet only detracted from the blog's credibility. Even a petulant list of details that could purportedly have been known only to the real Decapitator was largely ignored by investigators, and the subsequent adaptation of the list by pranksters into a series of LOLcat-style captions over crime-scene photos only enraged the murderer further.

The Decapitator will surely be remembered as the first serial killer to be obsessed with his own Wikipedia entry. Fanatical about reverting the edits of others, regardless of the content (annotating each reversion with "rv vandalism"), he provoked a heated argument on the article's talk page with Wiki editor "SexDoctorPHD" (later revealed to be 15-year-old Justin Payne). Two weeks later, Payne's body was discovered decapitated in a Burger King bathroom; his head was shipped postage-due to the home of Wikipedia founder Jimbo Wales, and the killer had vanished into the ether of history.

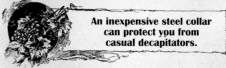

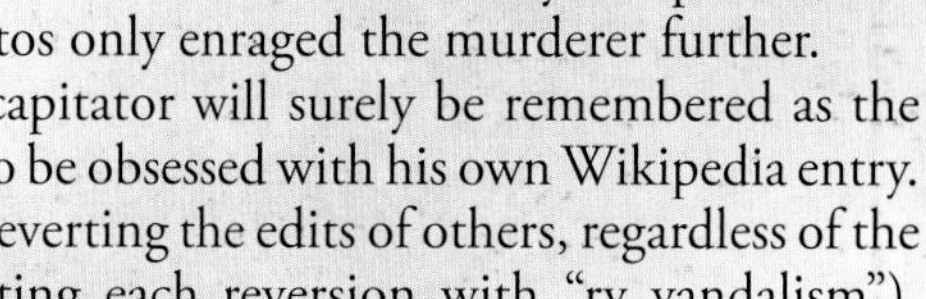

An inexpensive steel collar can protect you from casual decapitators.

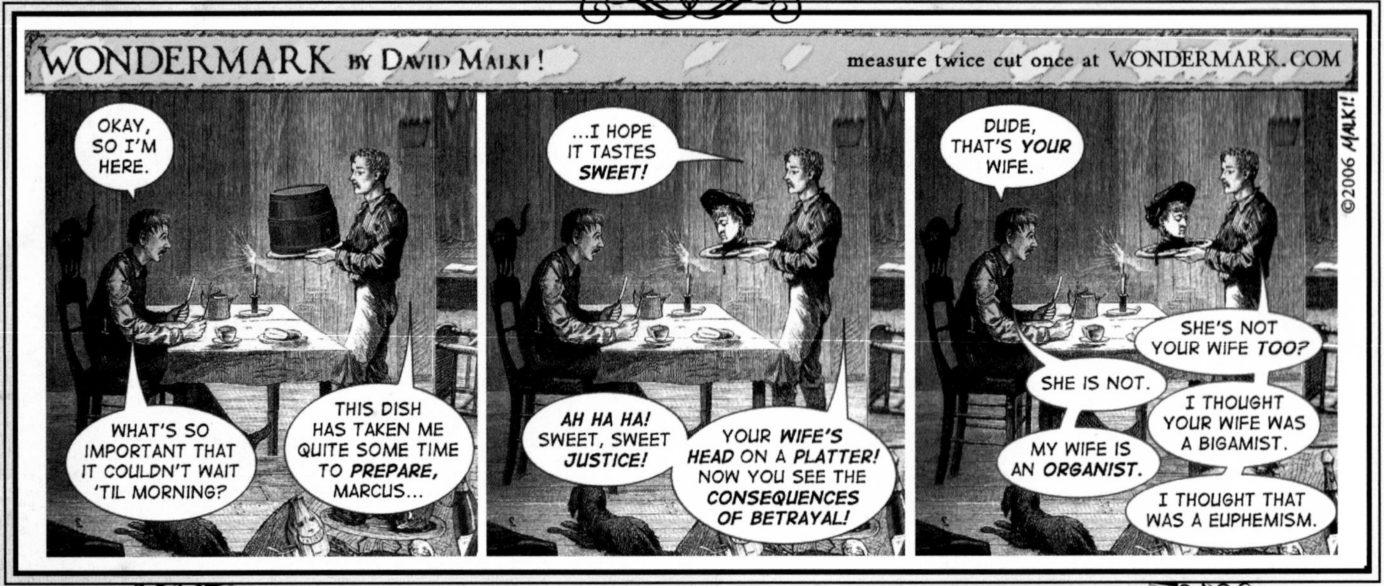
WONDERMARK by David Malki !
measure twice cut once at WONDERMARK.COM
OKAY, SO I'M HERE.
WHAT'S SO IMPORTANT THAT IT COULDN'T WAIT 'TIL MORNING?
THIS DISH HAS TAKEN ME QUITE SOME TIME TO PREPARE, MARCUS...
...I HOPE IT TASTES SWEET!
AH HA HA! SWEET, SWEET JUSTICE!
YOUR WIFE'S HEAD ON A PLATTER! NOW YOU SEE THE CONSEQUENCES OF BETRAYAL!
DUDE, THAT'S YOUR WIFE.
SHE IS NOT.
SHE'S NOT YOUR WIFE TOO?
MY WIFE IS AN ORGANIST.
I THOUGHT YOUR WIFE WAS A BIGAMIST.
I THOUGHT THAT WAS A EUPHEMISM.
©2006 MALKI!

it's not

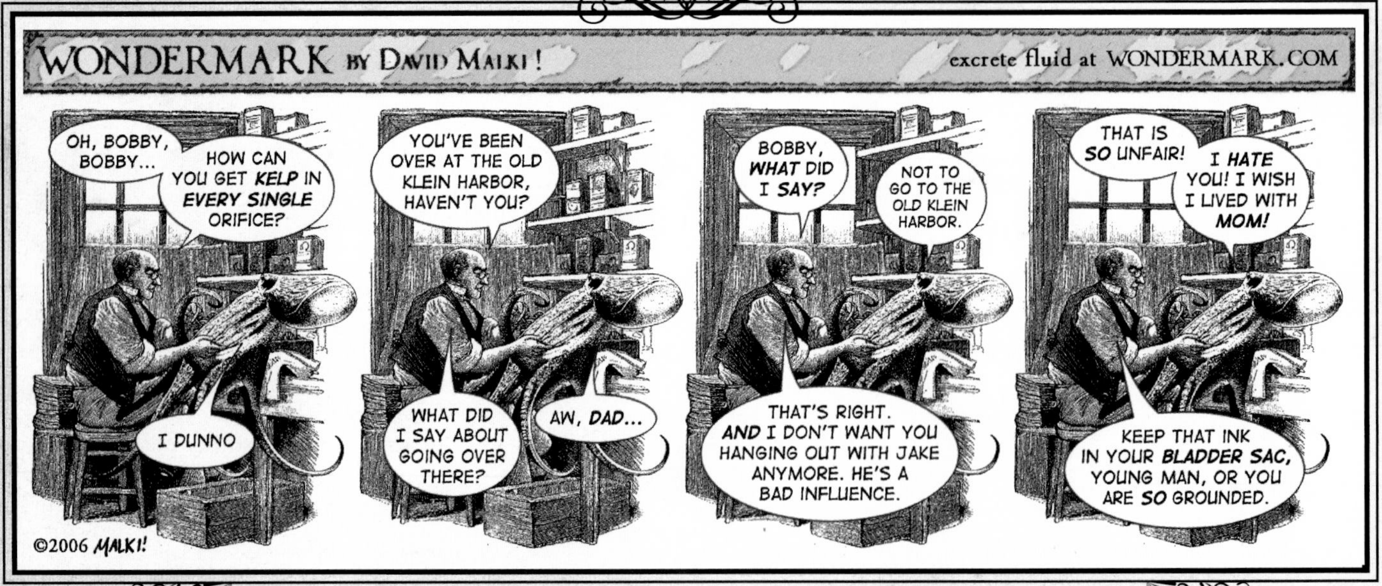
WONDERMARK by David Malki !
excrete fluid at WONDERMARK.COM
OH, BOBBY, BOBBY...
HOW CAN YOU GET KELP IN EVERY SINGLE ORIFICE?
I DUNNO
YOU'VE BEEN OVER AT THE OLD KLEIN HARBOR, HAVEN'T YOU?
WHAT DID I SAY ABOUT GOING OVER THERE?
AW, DAD...
BOBBY, WHAT DID I SAY?
NOT TO GO TO THE OLD KLEIN HARBOR.
THAT'S RIGHT. AND I DON'T WANT YOU HANGING OUT WITH JAKE ANYMORE. HE'S A BAD INFLUENCE.
THAT IS SO UNFAIR!
I HATE YOU! I WISH I LIVED WITH MOM!
KEEP THAT INK IN YOUR BLADDER SAC, YOUNG MAN, OR YOU ARE SO GROUNDED.
©2006 MALKI!

jake is a jellyfish with an attitude problem

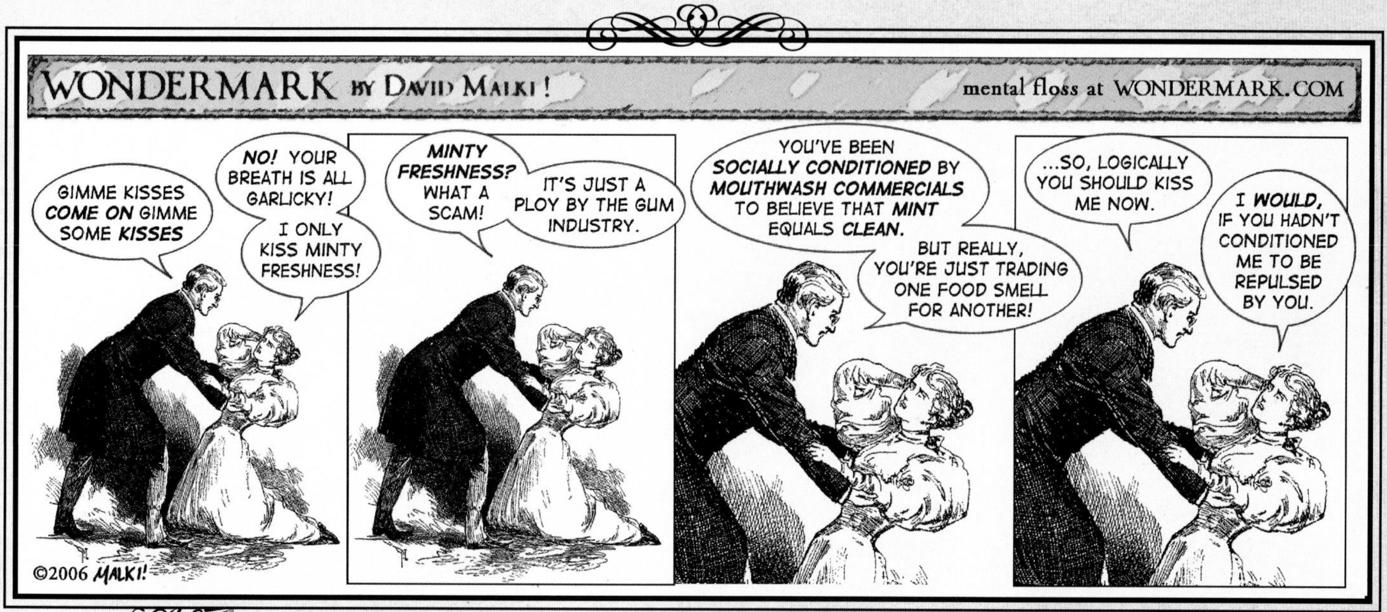
WONDERMARK BY DAVID MALKI!
mental floss at WONDERMARK.COM
GIMME KISSES COME ON GIMME SOME KISSES
NO! YOUR BREATH IS ALL GARLICKY!
I ONLY KISS MINTY FRESHNESS!
MINTY FRESHNESS? WHAT A SCAM!
IT'S JUST A PLOY BY THE GUM INDUSTRY.
YOU'VE BEEN SOCIALLY CONDITIONED BY MOUTHWASH COMMERCIALS TO BELIEVE THAT MINT EQUALS CLEAN.
BUT REALLY, YOU'RE JUST TRADING ONE FOOD SMELL FOR ANOTHER!
...SO, LOGICALLY YOU SHOULD KISS ME NOW.
I WOULD, IF YOU HADN'T CONDITIONED ME TO BE REPULSED BY YOU.
©2006 MALKI!

the listerine lobby claims another victim

59

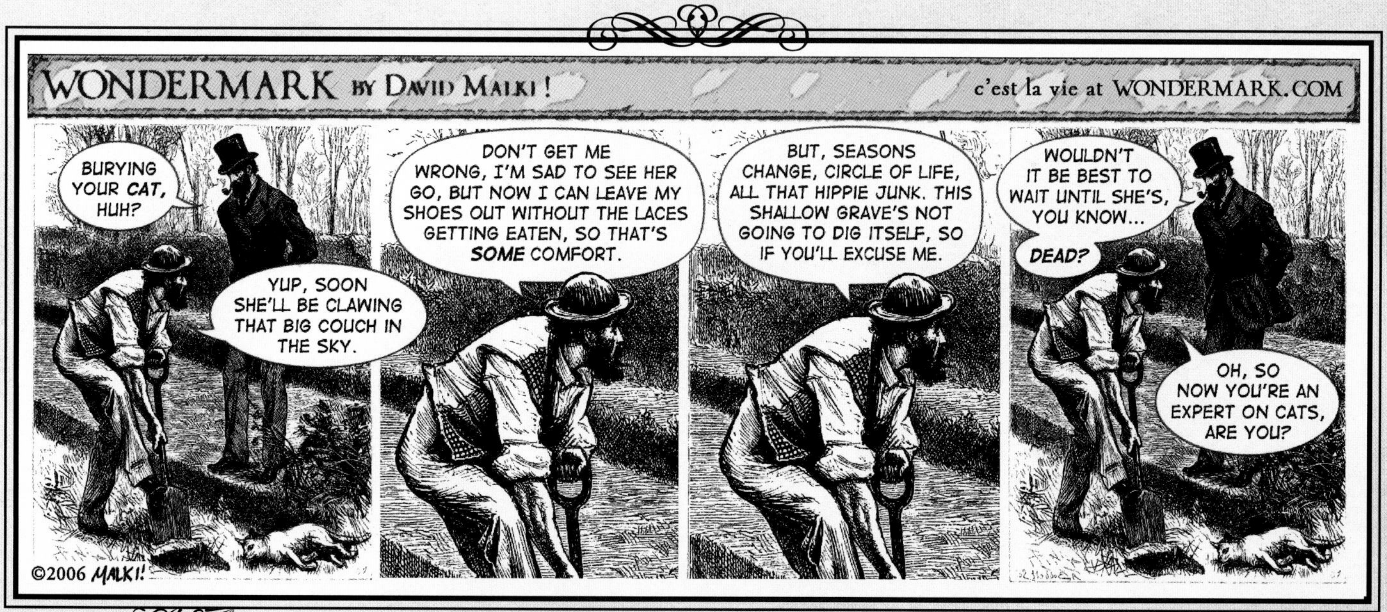
WONDERMARK BY DAVID MALKI!
c'est la vie at WONDERMARK.COM
BURYING YOUR CAT, HUH?
YUP, SOON SHE'LL BE CLAWING THAT BIG COUCH IN THE SKY.
DON'T GET ME WRONG, I'M SAD TO SEE HER GO, BUT NOW I CAN LEAVE MY SHOES OUT WITHOUT THE LACES GETTING EATEN, SO THAT'S SOME COMFORT.
BUT, SEASONS CHANGE, CIRCLE OF LIFE, ALL THAT HIPPIE JUNK. THIS SHALLOW GRAVE'S NOT GOING TO DIG ITSELF, SO IF YOU'LL EXCUSE ME.
WOULDN'T IT BE BEST TO WAIT UNTIL SHE'S, YOU KNOW... DEAD?
OH, SO NOW YOU'RE AN EXPERT ON CATS, ARE YOU?
©2006 MALKI!

in fact, he has his master's in catology and has done extensive post-graduate work at the cat institute in cattington but stopped short of getting his Ph.D. due to an unfortunate catastrophe

In which Jody's Father is made of Meat

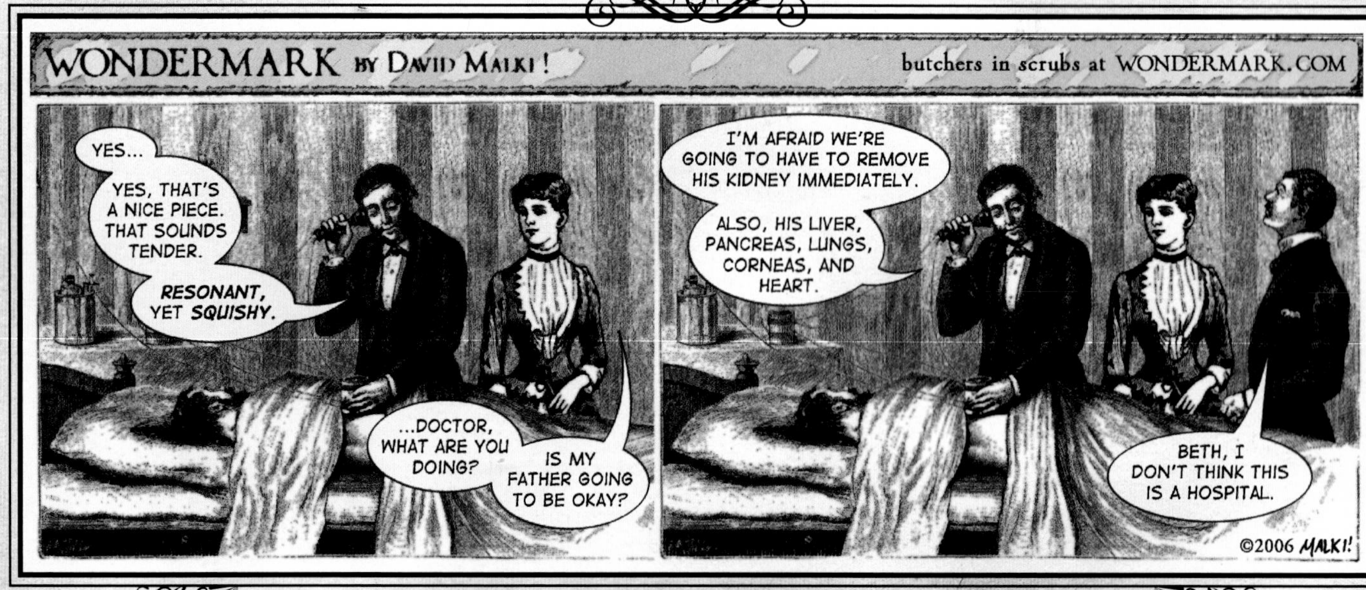
WONDERMARK by David Malki !
butchers in scrubs at WONDERMARK.COM
YES...
YES, THAT'S A NICE PIECE. THAT SOUNDS TENDER.
RESONANT, YET SQUISHY.
...DOCTOR, WHAT ARE YOU DOING?
IS MY FATHER GOING TO BE OKAY?
I'M AFRAID WE'RE GOING TO HAVE TO REMOVE HIS KIDNEY IMMEDIATELY.
ALSO, HIS LIVER, PANCREAS, LUNGS, CORNEAS, AND HEART.
BETH, I DON'T THINK THIS IS A HOSPITAL.
©2006 MALKI!

but the craigslist thing said to just pull around back
to the loading dock! THAT'S WHAT WE DID

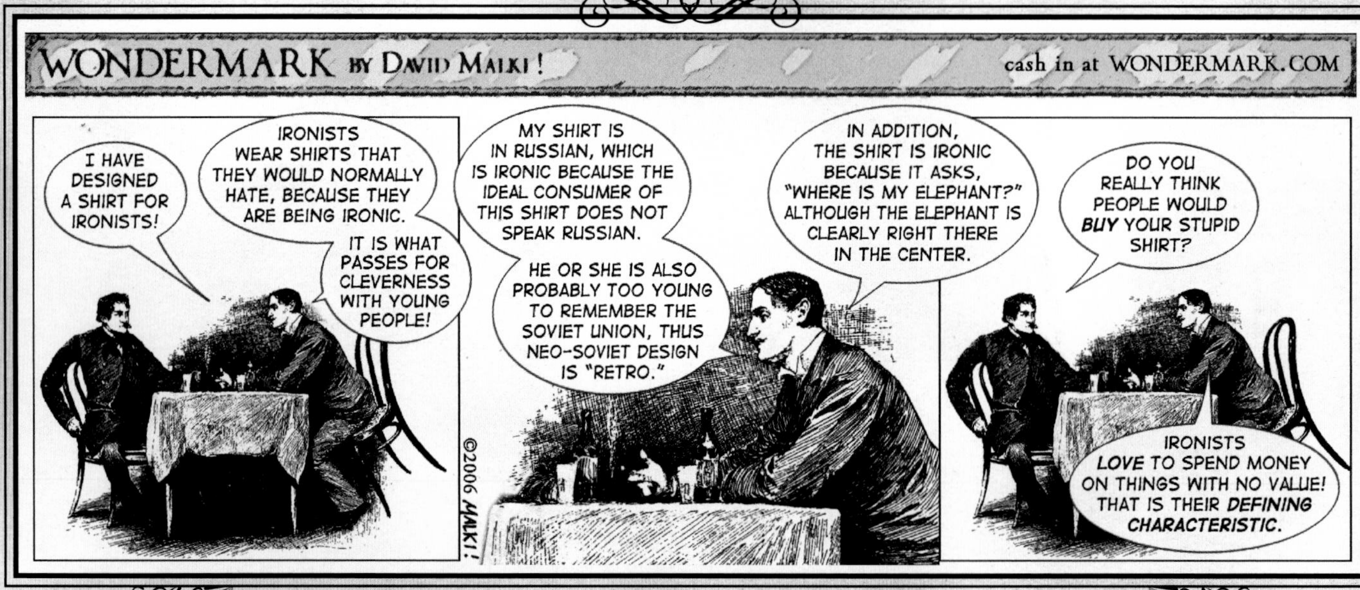
WONDERMARK by David Malki !
cash in at WONDERMARK.COM
I HAVE DESIGNED A SHIRT FOR IRONISTS!
IRONISTS WEAR SHIRTS THAT THEY WOULD NORMALLY HATE, BECAUSE THEY ARE BEING IRONIC.
IT IS WHAT PASSES FOR CLEVERNESS WITH YOUNG PEOPLE!
MY SHIRT IS IN RUSSIAN, WHICH IS IRONIC BECAUSE THE IDEAL CONSUMER OF THIS SHIRT DOES NOT SPEAK RUSSIAN.
HE OR SHE IS ALSO PROBABLY TOO YOUNG TO REMEMBER THE SOVIET UNION, THUS NEO-SOVIET DESIGN IS "RETRO."
©2006 MALKI!
IN ADDITION, THE SHIRT IS IRONIC BECAUSE IT ASKS, "WHERE IS MY ELEPHANT?" ALTHOUGH THE ELEPHANT IS CLEARLY RIGHT THERE IN THE CENTER.
DO YOU REALLY THINK PEOPLE WOULD BUY YOUR STUPID SHIRT?
IRONISTS LOVE TO SPEND MONEY ON THINGS WITH NO VALUE! THAT IS THEIR DEFINING CHARACTERISTIC.

also, you see, it is ironic because i am making fun
of the concept but the shirts are actually for sale

In which a Lost Elephant is easily found

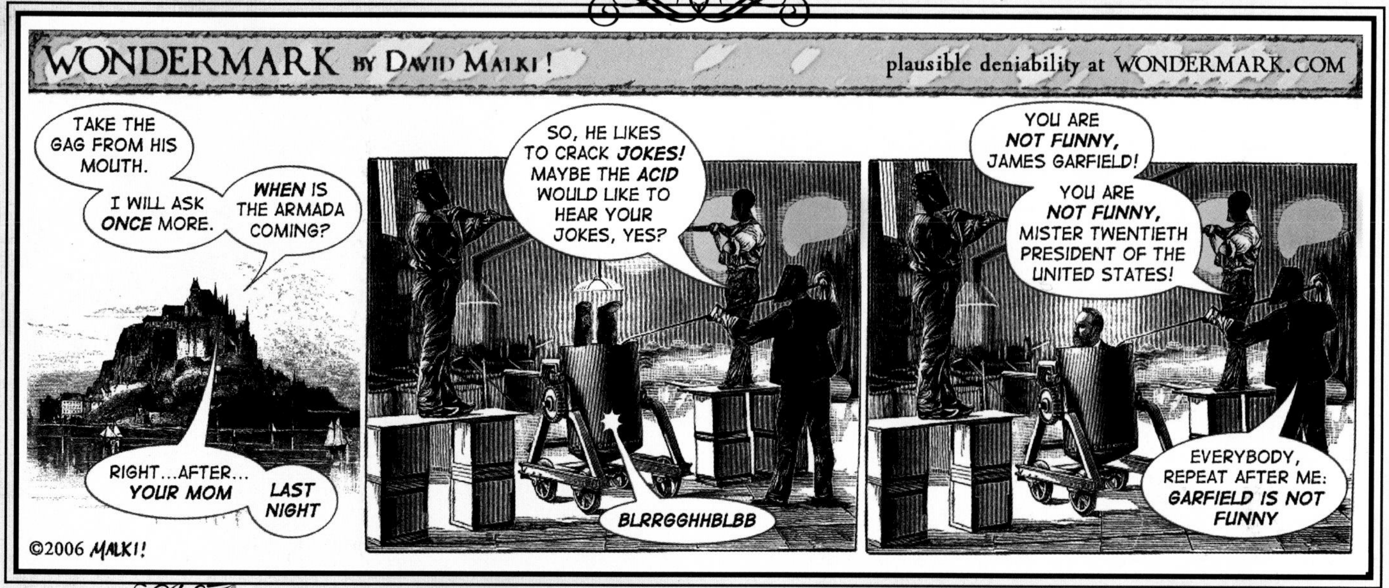
WONDERMARK by David Malki !
plausible deniability at WONDERMARK.COM
TAKE THE GAG FROM HIS MOUTH.
I WILL ASK ONCE MORE.
WHEN IS THE ARMADA COMING?
RIGHT...AFTER... YOUR MOM
LAST NIGHT
©2006 MALKI!
SO, HE LIKES TO CRACK JOKES! MAYBE THE ACID WOULD LIKE TO HEAR YOUR JOKES, YES?
BLRRGGHHBLBB
YOU ARE NOT FUNNY, JAMES GARFIELD!
YOU ARE NOT FUNNY, MISTER TWENTIETH PRESIDENT OF THE UNITED STATES!
EVERYBODY, REPEAT AFTER ME: GARFIELD IS NOT FUNNY

taft was a well-known yukster but jimmy here would cause the most awkward of silences at all the state dinners

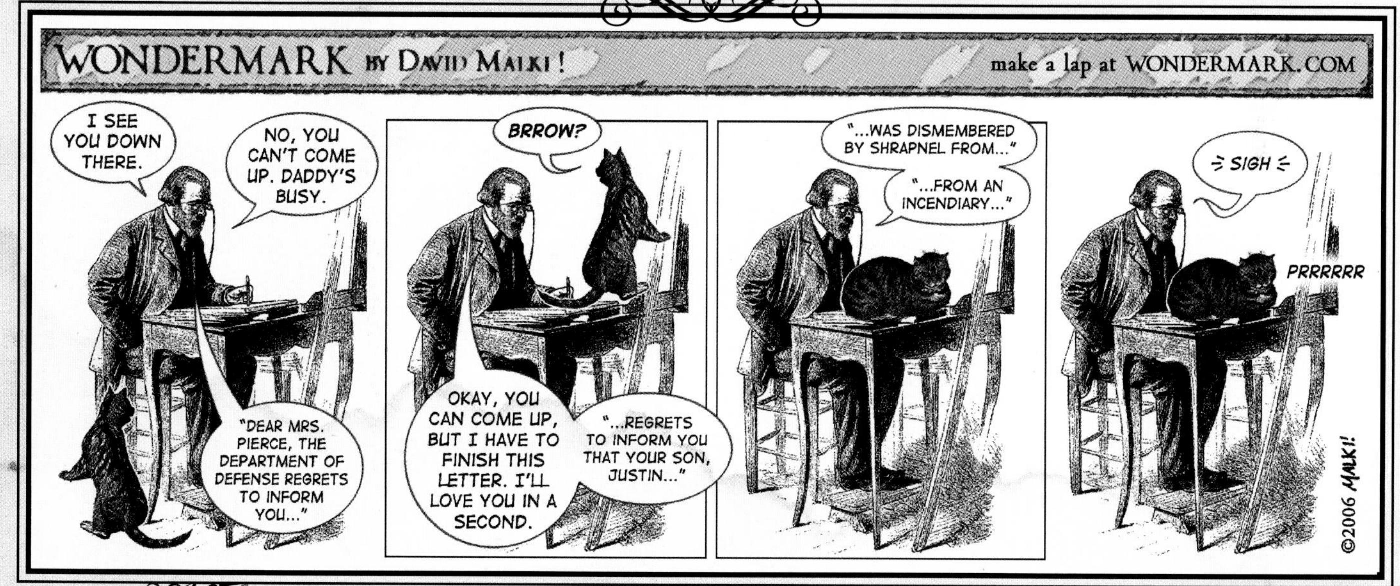
WONDERMARK by David Malki !
make a lap at WONDERMARK.COM
I SEE YOU DOWN THERE.
NO, YOU CAN'T COME UP. DADDY'S BUSY.
"DEAR MRS. PIERCE, THE DEPARTMENT OF DEFENSE REGRETS TO INFORM YOU..."
BRROW?
OKAY, YOU CAN COME UP, BUT I HAVE TO FINISH THIS LETTER. I'LL LOVE YOU IN A SECOND.
"...REGRETS TO INFORM YOU THAT YOUR SON, JUSTIN..."
"...WAS DISMEMBERED BY SHRAPNEL FROM..."
"...FROM AN INCENDIARY..."
SIGH
PRRRRRR
©2006 MALKI!

pfc. pierce heroically hid in a trench while his legs were located by members of the 1st infantry

In which a Tiny Dinosaur factors

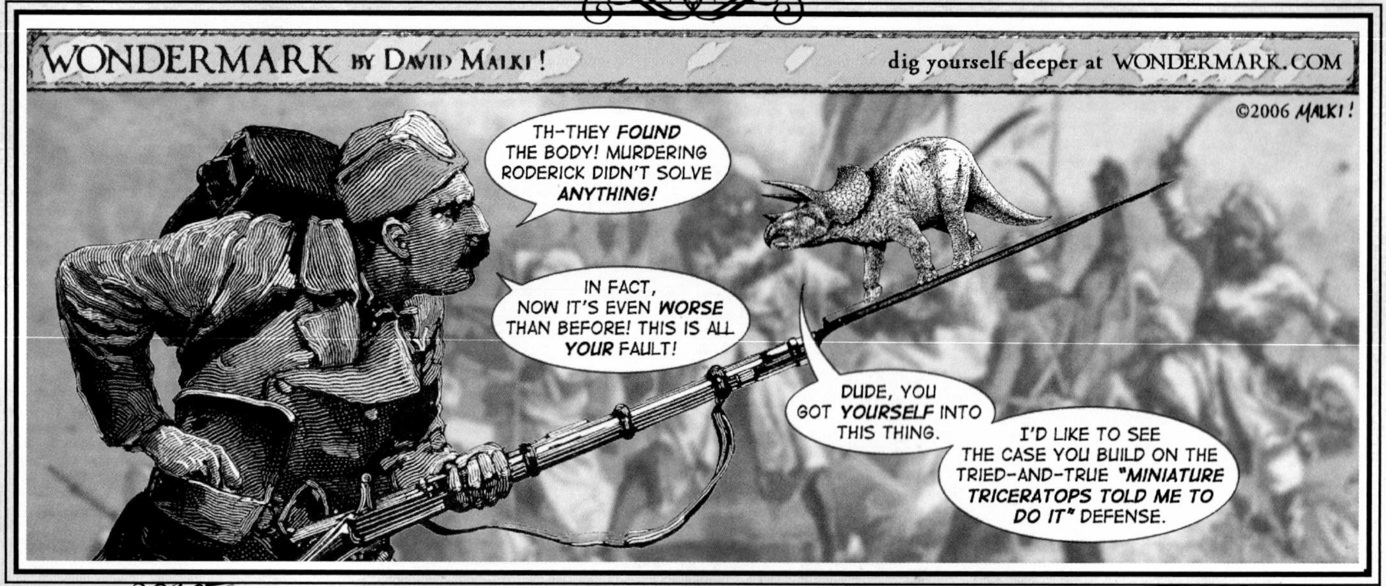
WONDERMARK by David Malki !
dig yourself deeper at WONDERMARK.COM
©2006 MALKI!
TH-THEY FOUND THE BODY! MURDERING RODERICK DIDN'T SOLVE ANYTHING!
IN FACT, NOW IT'S EVEN WORSE THAN BEFORE! THIS IS ALL YOUR FAULT!
DUDE, YOU GOT YOURSELF INTO THIS THING.
I'D LIKE TO SEE THE CASE YOU BUILD ON THE TRIED-AND-TRUE "MINIATURE TRICERATOPS TOLD ME TO DO IT" DEFENSE.

actually there is precedent — op.cit. canada v. north, et al.

62

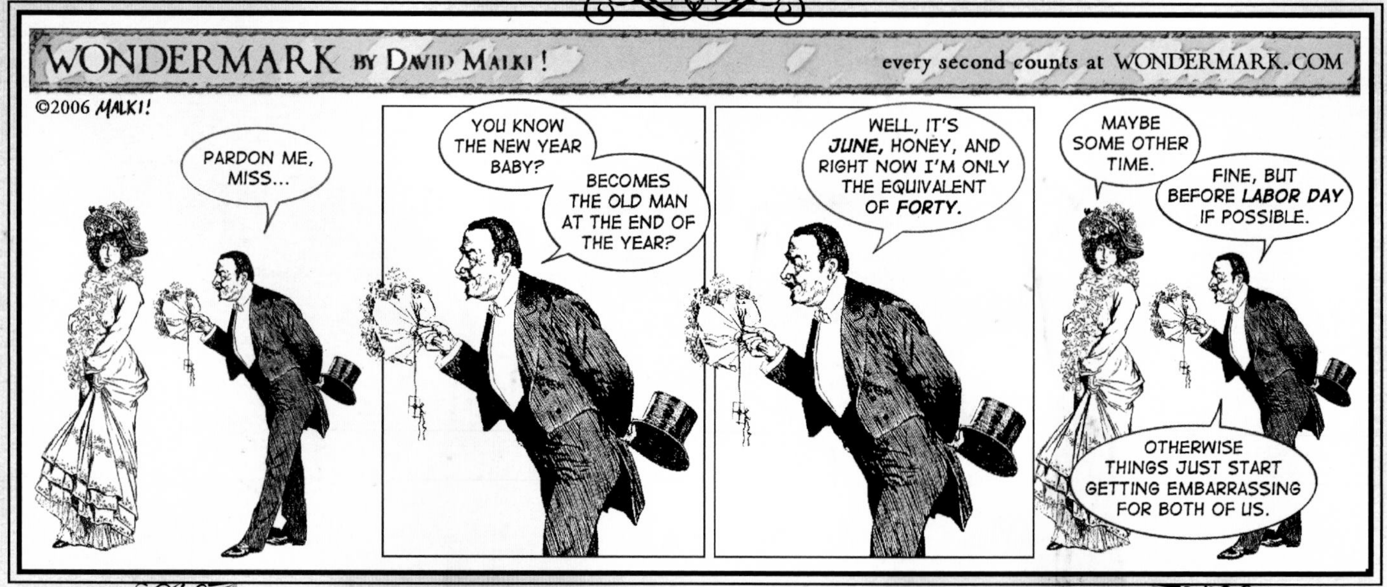
WONDERMARK by David Malki !
every second counts at WONDERMARK.COM
©2006 MALKI!
PARDON ME, MISS...
YOU KNOW THE NEW YEAR BABY?
BECOMES THE OLD MAN AT THE END OF THE YEAR?
WELL, IT'S JUNE, HONEY, AND RIGHT NOW I'M ONLY THE EQUIVALENT OF FORTY.
MAYBE SOME OTHER TIME.
FINE, BUT BEFORE LABOR DAY IF POSSIBLE.
OTHERWISE THINGS JUST START GETTING EMBARRASSING FOR BOTH OF US.

try this pick-up line. report back to me.

In which Time makes Fooles of us all

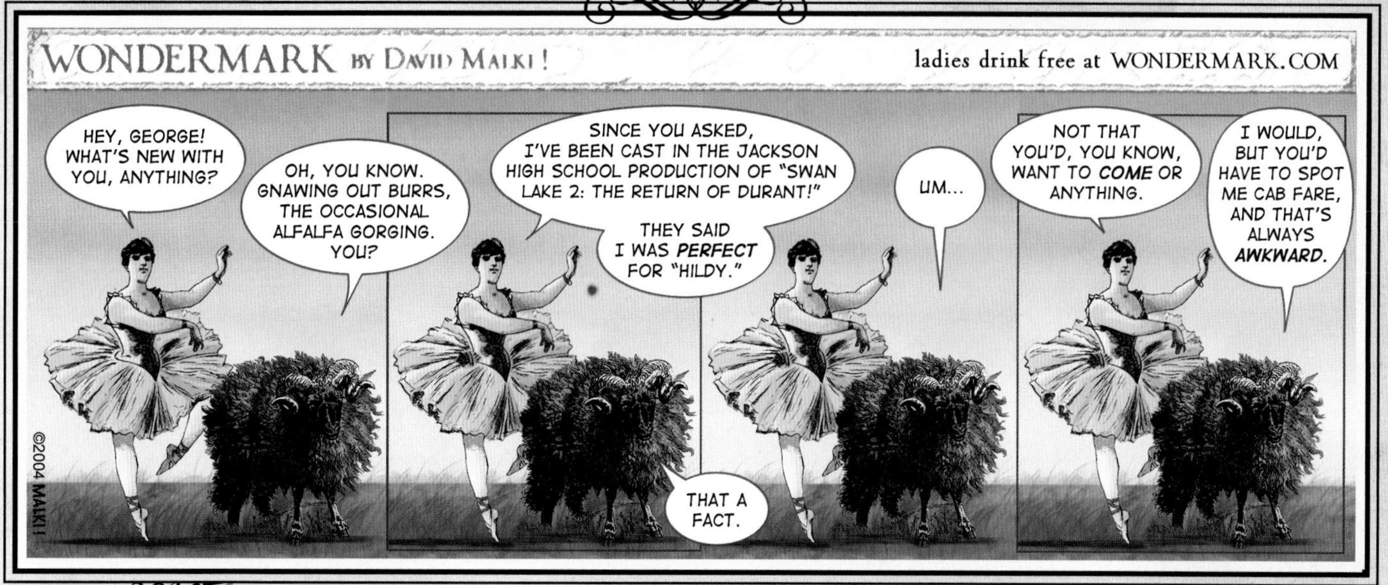
WONDERMARK BY DAVID MALKI !
ladies drink free at WONDERMARK.COM
HEY, GEORGE! WHAT'S NEW WITH YOU, ANYTHING?
OH, YOU KNOW. GNAWING OUT BURRS, THE OCCASIONAL ALFALFA GORGING. YOU?
SINCE YOU ASKED, I'VE BEEN CAST IN THE JACKSON HIGH SCHOOL PRODUCTION OF "SWAN LAKE 2: THE RETURN OF DURANT!"
THEY SAID I WAS ***PERFECT*** FOR "HILDY."
THAT A FACT.
UM...
NOT THAT YOU'D, YOU KNOW, WANT TO ***COME*** OR ANYTHING.
I WOULD, BUT YOU'D HAVE TO SPOT ME CAB FARE, AND THAT'S ALWAYS ***AWKWARD.***
©2004 MALKI

swan lake 3: die sigfried die

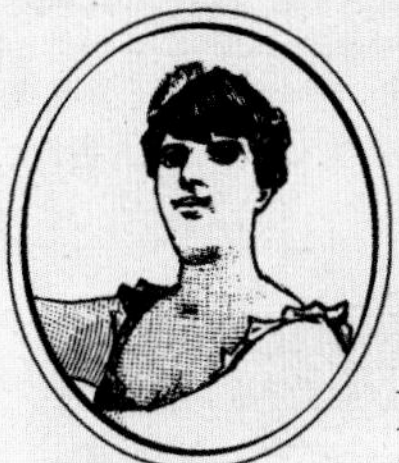

"Something happened to our friendship."

GEORGE and I used to be so close—we'd go out two or three nights a week! Back when we lived right next door it was easier, of course, but even when I decided to move to the city, he promised that we'd still get together all the time. It hasn't happened that way, though—he's gotten really distant, and we hardly even talk anymore. I guess we're both busy, but I still forward him funny jokes my mom sends me, and I send him Evites and all sorts of stuff, even texting him sometimes just to say "hi." But he doesn't follow through on his commitments, and I'm tired of waiting on sidewalks outside of shows, checking my voicemail all night long to see if he's called.

I don't know what exactly's come between us, but I really miss the friendship we used to share. I know that sometimes people drift apart. But it wouldn't be this bad if he'd just answer an email now and then!

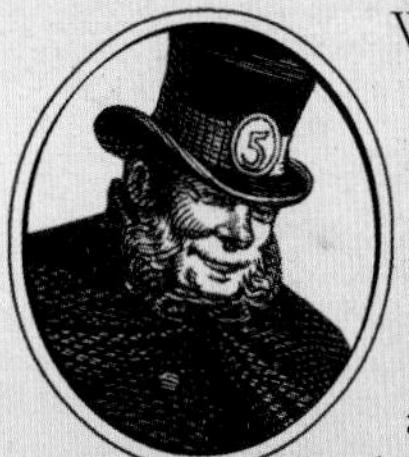

WHEN I first met Barbara in the Jackson High auditorium during the S.L.2 auditions, I was shocked. Here was a woman in her, I don't know, thirties maybe, clearly self-taught in ballet but no less in command of the stage for that, and she wanted to be in *our* little seat-of-the-pants production! I relished getting to know the *real* Barbara—a wounded soul stuffed into an ill-fitting thift-store tutu, crying out for love and attention.

I did offer myself to her, should she ever need a comforting hand, but alas, she was stuck on some boy from back home...some lucky, *lucky* boy.

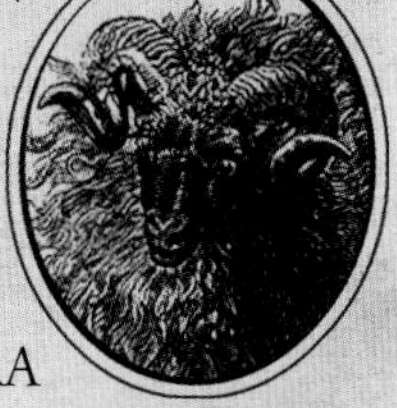

HI BARBARA SORRY I"VE BEEN SLOW WRITINGH BACK TO YOIU GLAD ITS GOING WELL,, SORRY IF YOUY HAVE BEEN TRY ING TO REACH ME.....BUT I AM A SHEEP I AM NOT VERY GOOD AT USING KEYBAORDS BABRBARA

In which the Future is Now

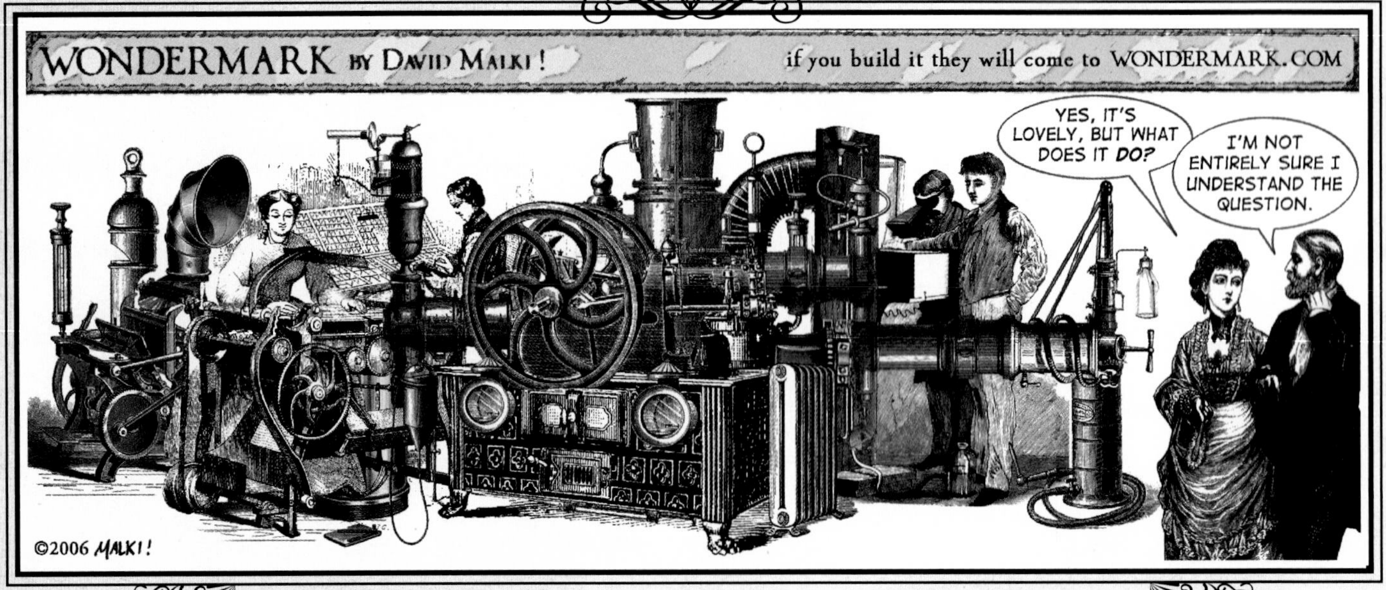
WONDERMARK BY DAVID MALKI !
if you build it they will come to WONDERMARK.COM
YES, IT'S LOVELY, BUT WHAT DOES IT *DO?*
I'M NOT ENTIRELY SURE I UNDERSTAND THE QUESTION.
©2006 MALKI !

once the glue gun gets warmed up it is really hard to stop

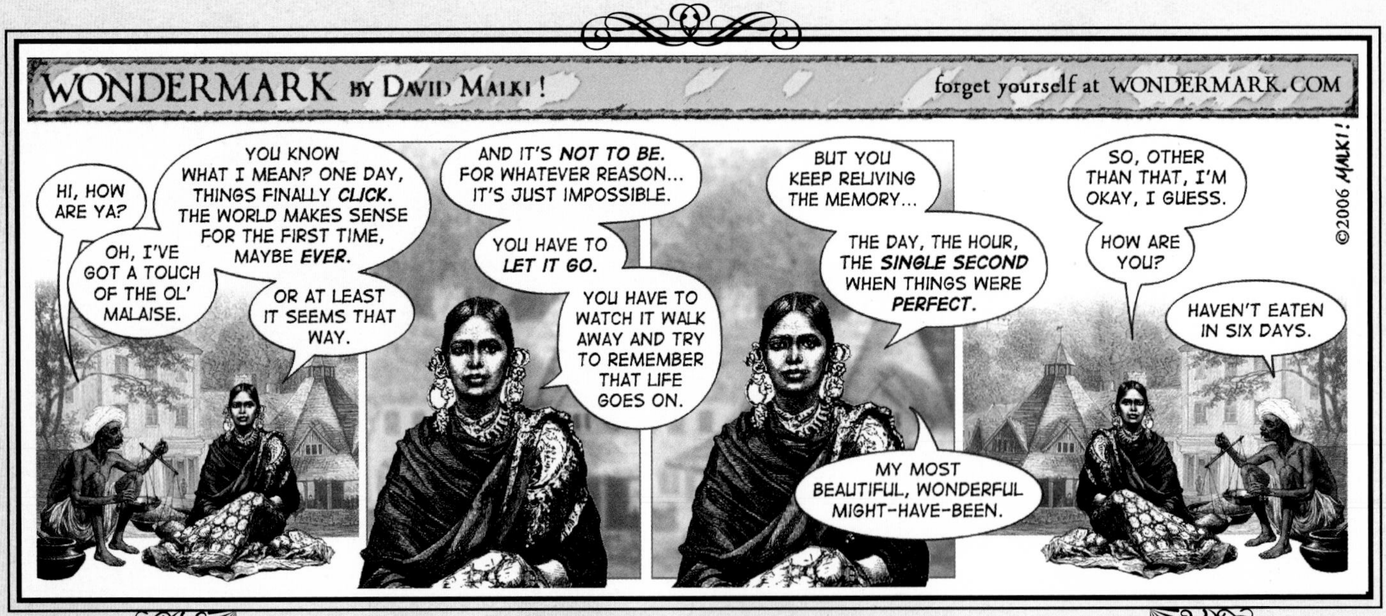
WONDERMARK BY DAVID MALKI !
forget yourself at WONDERMARK.COM
HI, HOW ARE YA?
OH, I'VE GOT A TOUCH OF THE OL' MALAISE.
YOU KNOW WHAT I MEAN? ONE DAY, THINGS FINALLY *CLICK.* THE WORLD MAKES SENSE FOR THE FIRST TIME, MAYBE *EVER.*
OR AT LEAST IT SEEMS THAT WAY.
AND IT'S *NOT TO BE.* FOR WHATEVER REASON... IT'S JUST IMPOSSIBLE.
YOU HAVE TO *LET IT GO.*
YOU HAVE TO WATCH IT WALK AWAY AND TRY TO REMEMBER THAT LIFE GOES ON.
BUT YOU KEEP RELIVING THE MEMORY...
THE DAY, THE HOUR, THE *SINGLE SECOND* WHEN THINGS WERE *PERFECT.*
MY MOST BEAUTIFUL, WONDERFUL MIGHT-HAVE-BEEN.
SO, OTHER THAN THAT, I'M OKAY, I GUESS.
HOW ARE YOU?
HAVEN'T EATEN IN SIX DAYS.
©2006 MALKI !

but curiously he still eliminates right on schedule

In which Sanji should seriously Move On

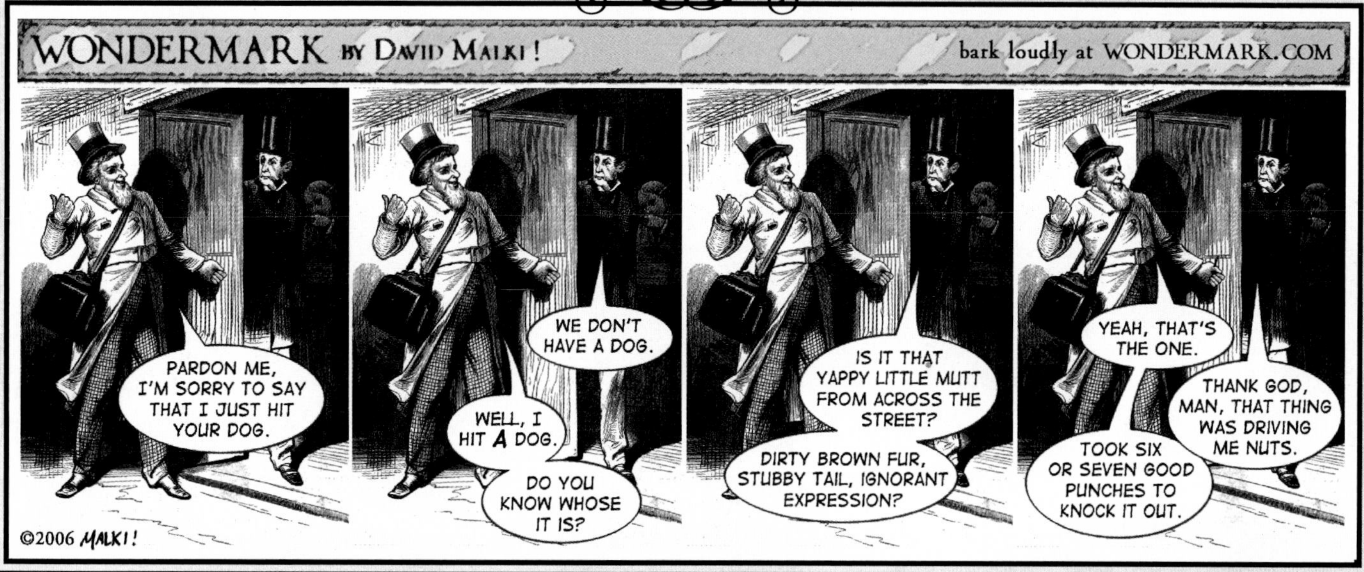
WONDERMARK BY DAVID MALKI !
bark loudly at WONDERMARK.COM
PARDON ME, I'M SORRY TO SAY THAT I JUST HIT YOUR DOG.
WE DON'T HAVE A DOG.
WELL, I HIT A DOG.
DO YOU KNOW WHOSE IT IS?
IS IT THAT YAPPY LITTLE MUTT FROM ACROSS THE STREET?
DIRTY BROWN FUR, STUBBY TAIL, IGNORANT EXPRESSION?
YEAH, THAT'S THE ONE.
THANK GOD, MAN, THAT THING WAS DRIVING ME NUTS.
TOOK SIX OR SEVEN GOOD PUNCHES TO KNOCK IT OUT.
©2006 MALKI !

passed out right before he went back for the softball bat

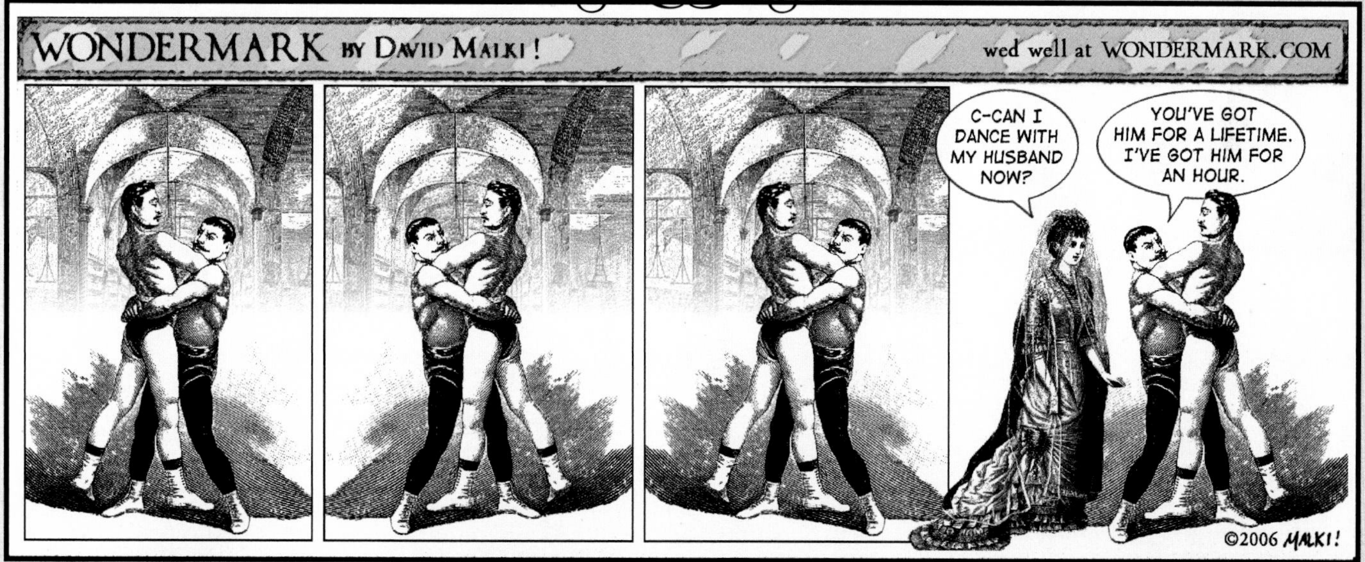
WONDERMARK BY DAVID MALKI !
wed well at WONDERMARK.COM
C-CAN I DANCE WITH MY HUSBAND NOW?
YOU'VE GOT HIM FOR A LIFETIME. I'VE GOT HIM FOR AN HOUR.
©2006 MALKI !

and what an hour

In which Logic begets Loneliness

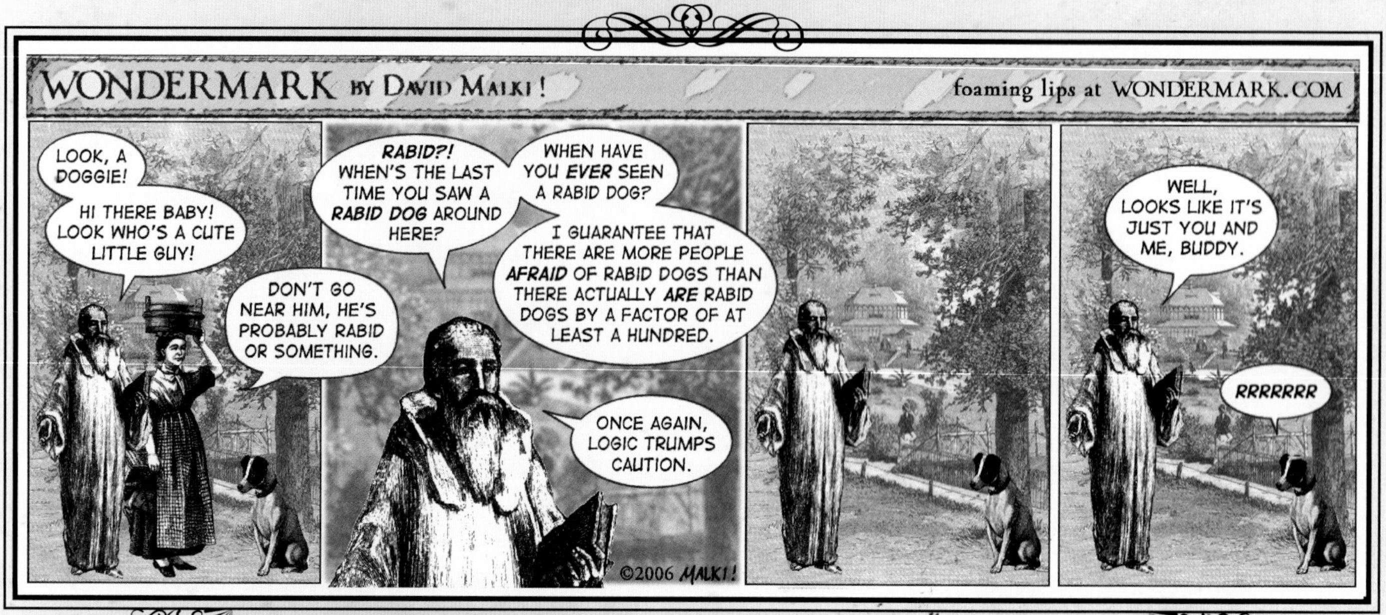
WONDERMARK BY DAVID MALKI !
foaming lips at WONDERMARK.COM
LOOK, A DOGGIE!
HI THERE BABY! LOOK WHO'S A CUTE LITTLE GUY!
DON'T GO NEAR HIM, HE'S PROBABLY RABID OR SOMETHING.
RABID?! WHEN'S THE LAST TIME YOU SAW A RABID DOG AROUND HERE?
WHEN HAVE YOU EVER SEEN A RABID DOG?
I GUARANTEE THAT THERE ARE MORE PEOPLE AFRAID OF RABID DOGS THAN THERE ACTUALLY ARE RABID DOGS BY A FACTOR OF AT LEAST A HUNDRED.
ONCE AGAIN, LOGIC TRUMPS CAUTION.
©2006 MALKI!
WELL, LOOKS LIKE IT'S JUST YOU AND ME, BUDDY.
RRRRRRR

logic also trumps fate, lust, and medicine

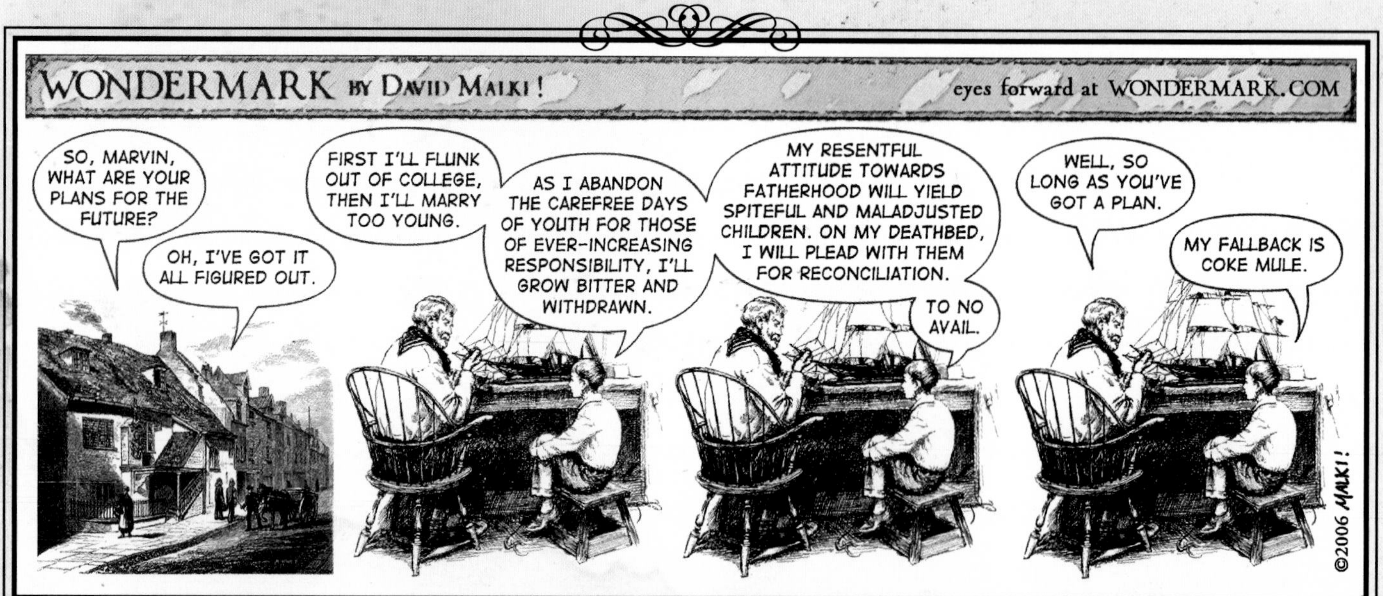
WONDERMARK BY DAVID MALKI !
eyes forward at WONDERMARK.COM
SO, MARVIN, WHAT ARE YOUR PLANS FOR THE FUTURE?
OH, I'VE GOT IT ALL FIGURED OUT.
FIRST I'LL FLUNK OUT OF COLLEGE, THEN I'LL MARRY TOO YOUNG.
AS I ABANDON THE CAREFREE DAYS OF YOUTH FOR THOSE OF EVER-INCREASING RESPONSIBILITY, I'LL GROW BITTER AND WITHDRAWN.
MY RESENTFUL ATTITUDE TOWARDS FATHERHOOD WILL YIELD SPITEFUL AND MALADJUSTED CHILDREN. ON MY DEATHBED, I WILL PLEAD WITH THEM FOR RECONCILIATION.
TO NO AVAIL.
WELL, SO LONG AS YOU'VE GOT A PLAN.
MY FALLBACK IS COKE MULE.
©2006 MALKI!

julio said i'd be a natural

In which Marvin is All Set

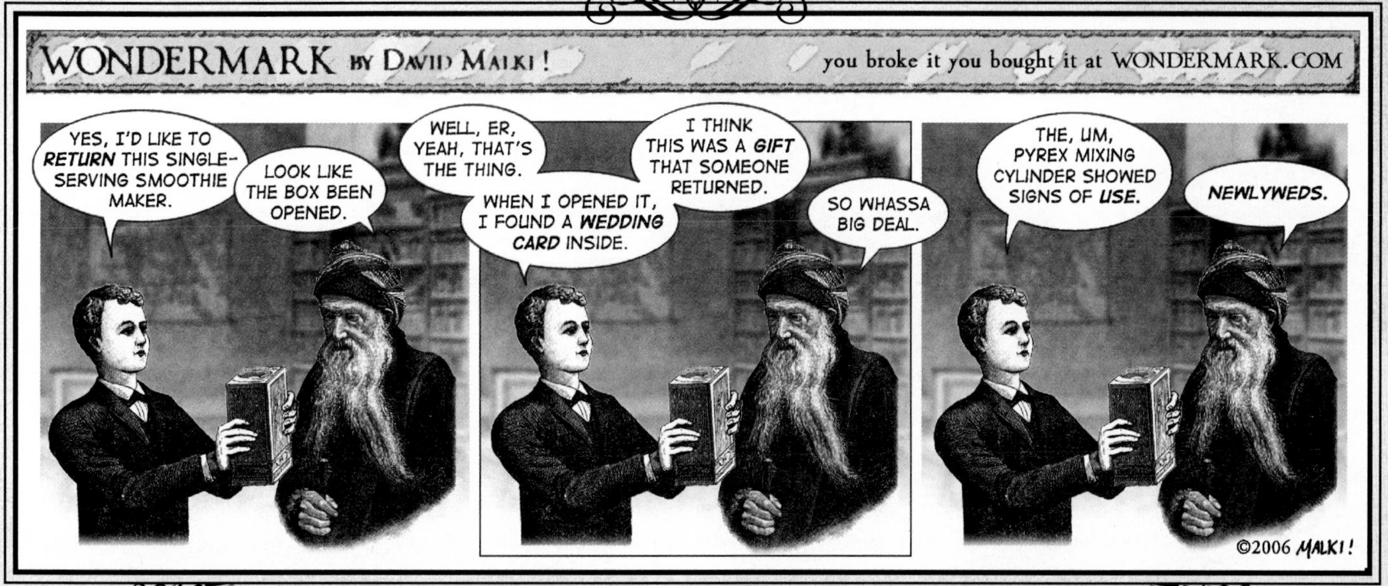
WONDERMARK BY DAVID MALKI !
you broke it you bought it at WONDERMARK.COM
YES, I'D LIKE TO **RETURN** THIS SINGLE-SERVING SMOOTHIE MAKER.
LOOK LIKE THE BOX BEEN OPENED.
WELL, ER, YEAH, THAT'S THE THING.
WHEN I OPENED IT, I FOUND A **WEDDING CARD** INSIDE.
I THINK THIS WAS A **GIFT** THAT SOMEONE RETURNED.
SO WHASSA BIG DEAL.
THE, UM, PYREX MIXING CYLINDER SHOWED SIGNS OF **USE**.
NEWLYWEDS.
©2006 MALKI !

it has three speeds and a 'liquefy' setting

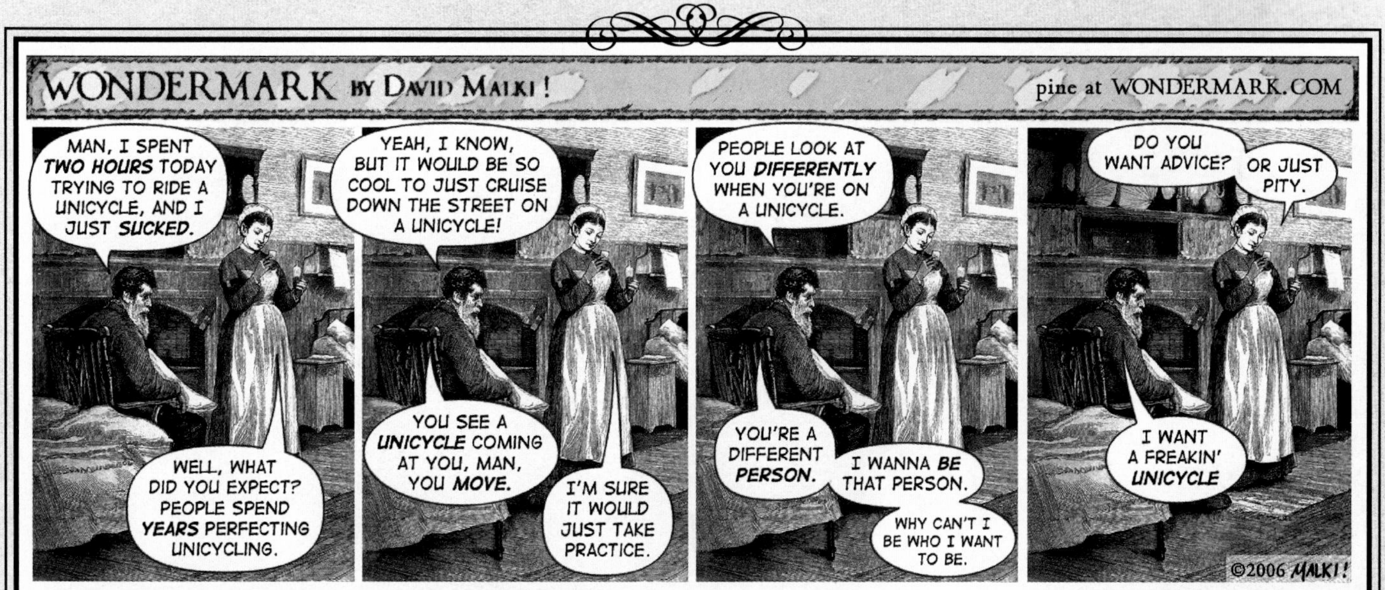
WONDERMARK BY DAVID MALKI !
pine at WONDERMARK.COM
MAN, I SPENT **TWO HOURS** TODAY TRYING TO RIDE A UNICYCLE, AND I JUST **SUCKED**.
WELL, WHAT DID YOU EXPECT? PEOPLE SPEND **YEARS** PERFECTING UNICYCLING.
YEAH, I KNOW, BUT IT WOULD BE SO COOL TO JUST CRUISE DOWN THE STREET ON A UNICYCLE!
YOU SEE A **UNICYCLE** COMING AT YOU, MAN, YOU **MOVE.**
I'M SURE IT WOULD JUST TAKE PRACTICE.
PEOPLE LOOK AT YOU **DIFFERENTLY** WHEN YOU'RE ON A UNICYCLE.
YOU'RE A DIFFERENT **PERSON.**
I WANNA **BE** THAT PERSON.
WHY CAN'T I BE WHO I WANT TO BE.
DO YOU WANT ADVICE?
OR JUST PITY.
I WANT A FREAKIN' **UNICYCLE**
©2006 MALKI !

if i were on a desert island with a unicycle i bet within six
weeks i would be inventin' all sorts of mad new techniques

In which a Kid says a Darndest Thing

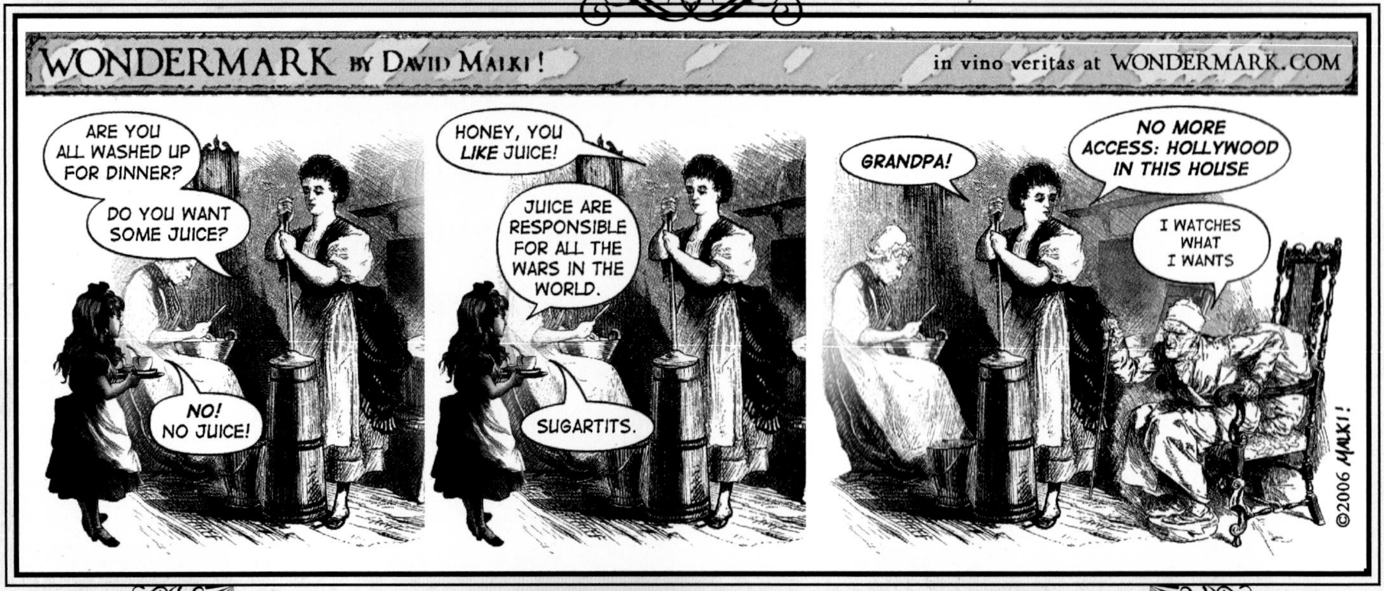
WONDERMARK by David Malki !
in vino veritas at WONDERMARK.COM
ARE YOU ALL WASHED UP FOR DINNER?
DO YOU WANT SOME JUICE?
NO! NO JUICE!
HONEY, YOU LIKE JUICE!
JUICE ARE RESPONSIBLE FOR ALL THE WARS IN THE WORLD.
SUGARTITS.
GRANDPA!
NO MORE ACCESS: HOLLYWOOD IN THIS HOUSE
I WATCHES WHAT I WANTS
©2006 MALKI!

IT WAS TOPICAL IN 2006 OKAY

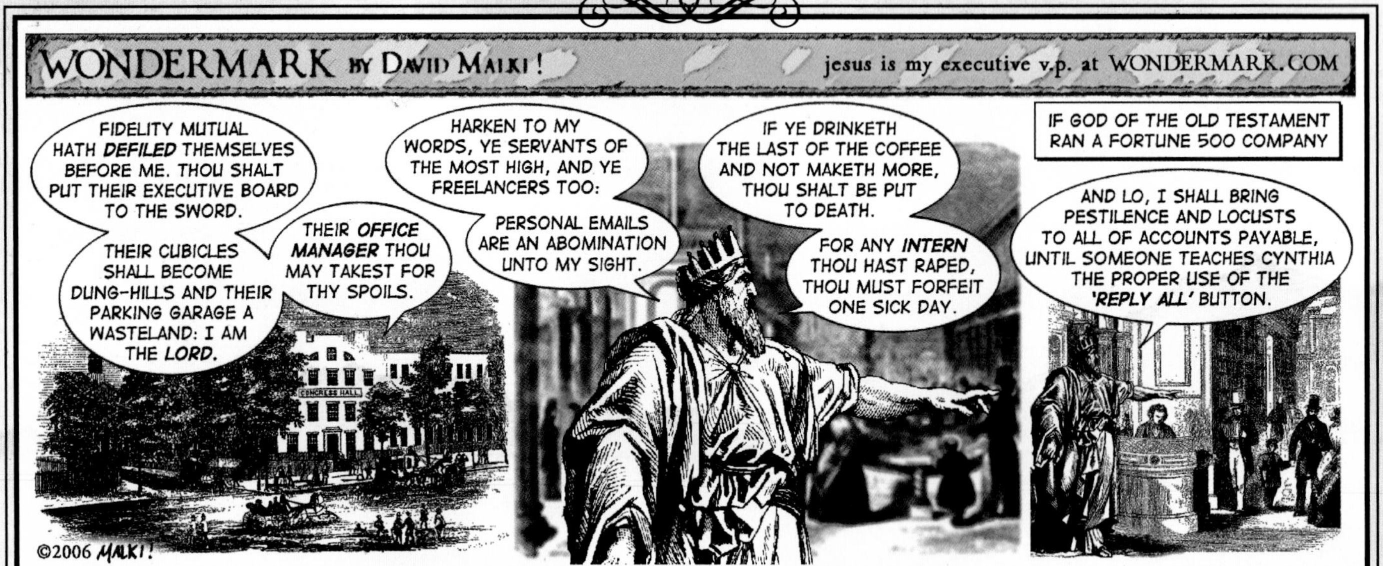
WONDERMARK by David Malki !
jesus is my executive v.p. at WONDERMARK.COM
FIDELITY MUTUAL HATH DEFILED THEMSELVES BEFORE ME. THOU SHALT PUT THEIR EXECUTIVE BOARD TO THE SWORD.
THEIR CUBICLES SHALL BECOME DUNG-HILLS AND THEIR PARKING GARAGE A WASTELAND: I AM THE LORD.
THEIR OFFICE MANAGER THOU MAY TAKEST FOR THY SPOILS.
CONGRESS HALL
©2006 MALKI!
HARKEN TO MY WORDS, YE SERVANTS OF THE MOST HIGH, AND YE FREELANCERS TOO:
PERSONAL EMAILS ARE AN ABOMINATION UNTO MY SIGHT.
IF YE DRINKETH THE LAST OF THE COFFEE AND NOT MAKETH MORE, THOU SHALT BE PUT TO DEATH.
FOR ANY INTERN THOU HAST RAPED, THOU MUST FORFEIT ONE SICK DAY.
IF GOD OF THE OLD TESTAMENT RAN A FORTUNE 500 COMPANY
AND LO, I SHALL BRING PESTILENCE AND LOCUSTS TO ALL OF ACCOUNTS PAYABLE, UNTIL SOMEONE TEACHES CYNTHIA THE PROPER USE OF THE 'REPLY ALL' BUTTON.

there are ten commandments but eight of them are about parking spaces
and the other two are about food left in the fridge over the weekend

In which God has an Expense Account

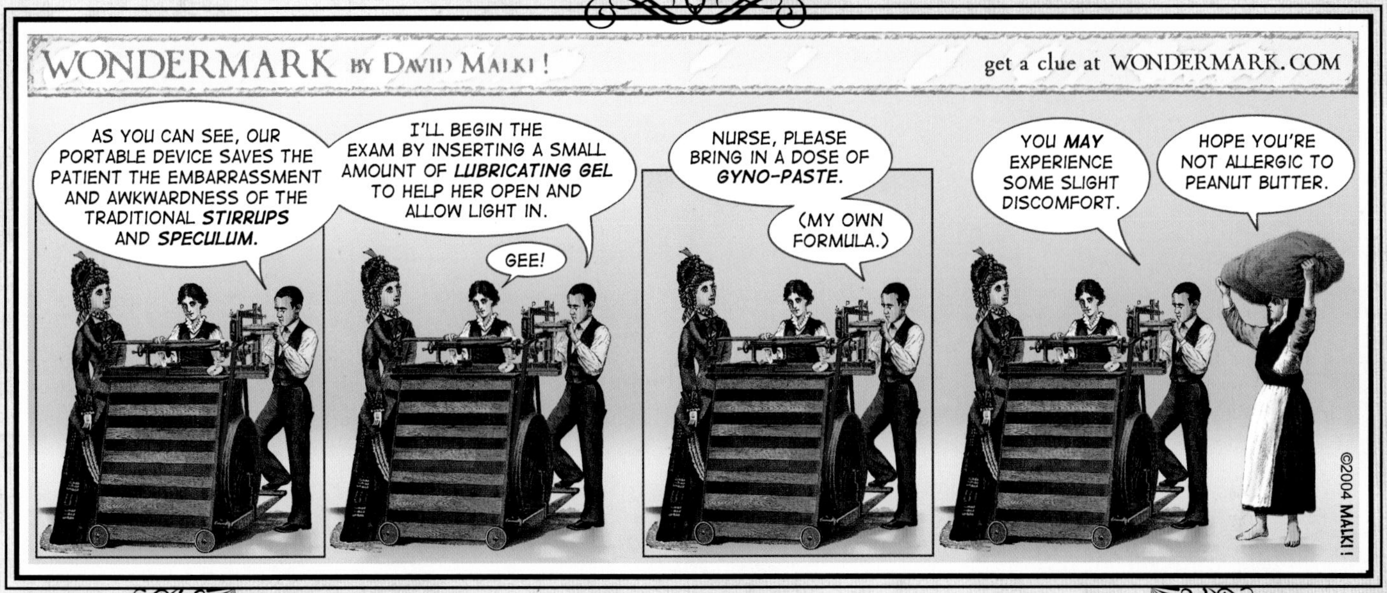
WONDERMARK by David Malki !
get a clue at WONDERMARK.COM
AS YOU CAN SEE, OUR PORTABLE DEVICE SAVES THE PATIENT THE EMBARRASSMENT AND AWKWARDNESS OF THE TRADITIONAL **STIRRUPS** AND **SPECULUM**.
I'LL BEGIN THE EXAM BY INSERTING A SMALL AMOUNT OF **LUBRICATING GEL** TO HELP HER OPEN AND ALLOW LIGHT IN.
GEE!
NURSE, PLEASE BRING IN A DOSE OF **GYNO-PASTE**.
(MY OWN FORMULA.)
YOU **MAY** EXPERIENCE SOME SLIGHT DISCOMFORT.
HOPE YOU'RE NOT ALLERGIC TO PEANUT BUTTER.
©2004 MALKI !

modesty, chastity, virtue

Peanut Butter Jobs
Peanut Butter Representatives Needed ASAP!
www.iPeanutButterPeople.com

Make Money With Your Genitals
Fast, Easy Simple Monkey Making. I Made $25,000 in 60 days.
www.ob-gyn-medical-trials.com

Experiencing Slight Discomfort?
Find out with this Free Discomfort Test to see how Discomfort you are!
www.Bloogblarg.com/Discomfort

Work At Home Speculum
My Site Will Reveal To You The Top Money-Making Work At Home Speculum Programs.
Top20-home-pap-smears.com

Ask about new CERVIXBLASTER®
(ferrothelyzine diplutonide)
Get the info about new topical CERVIXBLASTER® today
www.CERVIXBLASTER.com

Writing a Eulogy
Make Your Tough Job Easy With 400+ Templates
www.Generic-Eulogies.org

Gyno-Paste
Looking for Gyno-paste? Find exactly what you want today.
www.eBay.com

Western Pro Stirrups
Aluminum, Barrel Ox-Bow, Traditional Ozark models. Custom saddles made of human skin.
www.ranch-hand-supplies.cc

Lubrication Experience
The hottest promotional items with your corporate logo - custom Lubricants for all applications
www.usa-lubricants.net/

page 69 guaranteed
Ã¢â,¬Â”bdÃ¢â,¬Â
Xtreme-Million-Dollar-Profits.tv/HomeBiz/MakingBux/dont-get-scammed/

Ads by Google

In which Youths delight in a Prank

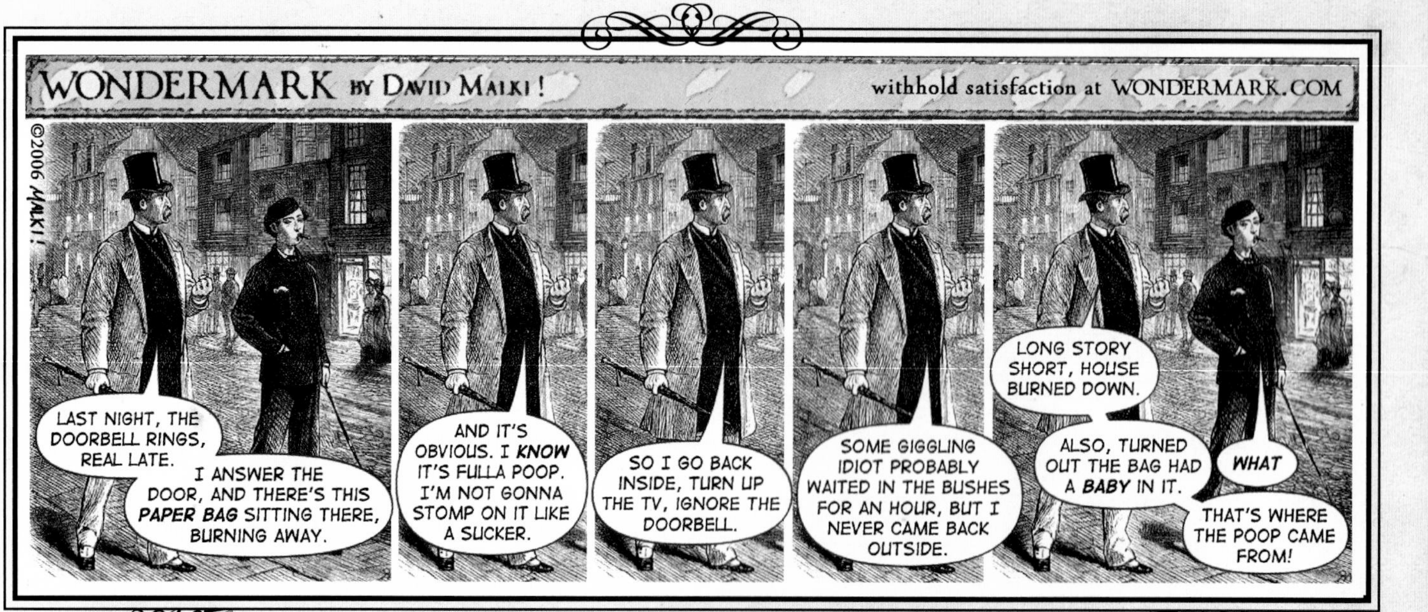
WONDERMARK BY DAVID MALKI !
withhold satisfaction at WONDERMARK.COM
©2006 MALKI !
LAST NIGHT, THE DOORBELL RINGS, REAL LATE.
I ANSWER THE DOOR, AND THERE'S THIS PAPER BAG SITTING THERE, BURNING AWAY.
AND IT'S OBVIOUS. I KNOW IT'S FULLA POOP. I'M NOT GONNA STOMP ON IT LIKE A SUCKER.
SO I GO BACK INSIDE, TURN UP THE TV, IGNORE THE DOORBELL.
SOME GIGGLING IDIOT PROBABLY WAITED IN THE BUSHES FOR AN HOUR, BUT I NEVER CAME BACK OUTSIDE.
LONG STORY SHORT, HOUSE BURNED DOWN.
ALSO, TURNED OUT THE BAG HAD A BABY IN IT.
WHAT
THAT'S WHERE THE POOP CAME FROM!

don't worry it wasn't a _____* baby
(*YOUR RACE, RELIGION, ETHNICITY OR OTHER SUBGROUP)

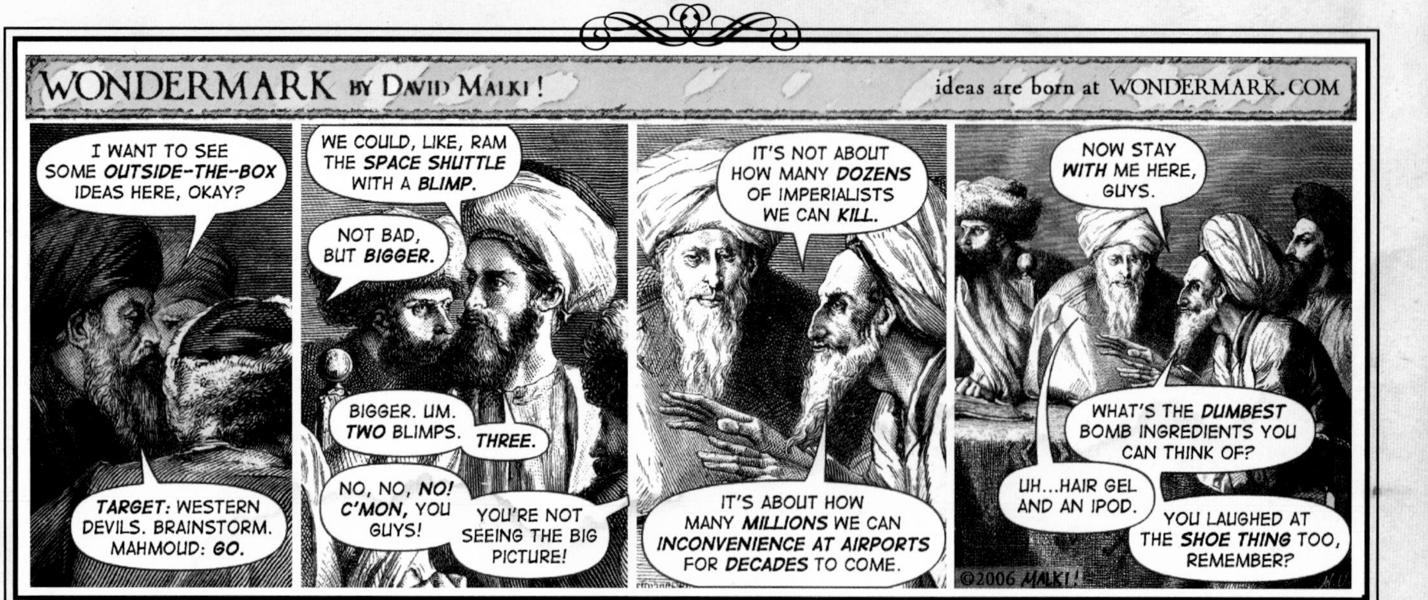
WONDERMARK BY DAVID MALKI !
ideas are born at WONDERMARK.COM
I WANT TO SEE SOME OUTSIDE-THE-BOX IDEAS HERE, OKAY?
TARGET: WESTERN DEVILS. BRAINSTORM. MAHMOUD: GO.
WE COULD, LIKE, RAM THE SPACE SHUTTLE WITH A BLIMP.
NOT BAD, BUT BIGGER.
BIGGER. UM. TWO BLIMPS.
THREE.
NO, NO, NO! C'MON, YOU GUYS!
YOU'RE NOT SEEING THE BIG PICTURE!
IT'S NOT ABOUT HOW MANY DOZENS OF IMPERIALISTS WE CAN KILL.
IT'S ABOUT HOW MANY MILLIONS WE CAN INCONVENIENCE AT AIRPORTS FOR DECADES TO COME.
NOW STAY WITH ME HERE, GUYS.
WHAT'S THE DUMBEST BOMB INGREDIENTS YOU CAN THINK OF?
UH...HAIR GEL AND AN IPOD.
YOU LAUGHED AT THE SHOE THING TOO, REMEMBER?
©2006 MALKI !

also they have installed moles at the x-ray machines
who foil imperialism by working reeeeally slowly

In which a Plan comes together

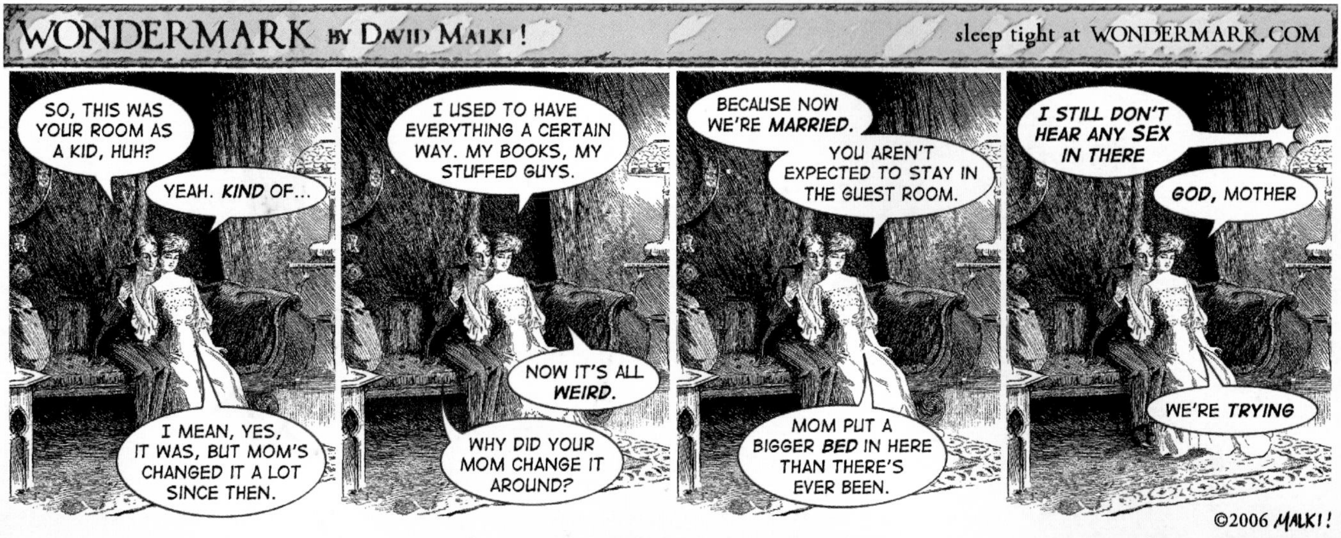
WONDERMARK by David Malki !
sleep tight at WONDERMARK.COM
SO, THIS WAS YOUR ROOM AS A KID, HUH?
YEAH. KIND OF...
I MEAN, YES, IT WAS, BUT MOM'S CHANGED IT A LOT SINCE THEN.
I USED TO HAVE EVERYTHING A CERTAIN WAY. MY BOOKS, MY STUFFED GUYS.
NOW IT'S ALL WEIRD.
WHY DID YOUR MOM CHANGE IT AROUND?
BECAUSE NOW WE'RE MARRIED.
YOU AREN'T EXPECTED TO STAY IN THE GUEST ROOM.
MOM PUT A BIGGER BED IN HERE THAN THERE'S EVER BEEN.
I STILL DON'T HEAR ANY SEX IN THERE
GOD, MOTHER
WE'RE TRYING
©2006 MALKI !

sigh. more true life comics, folks.

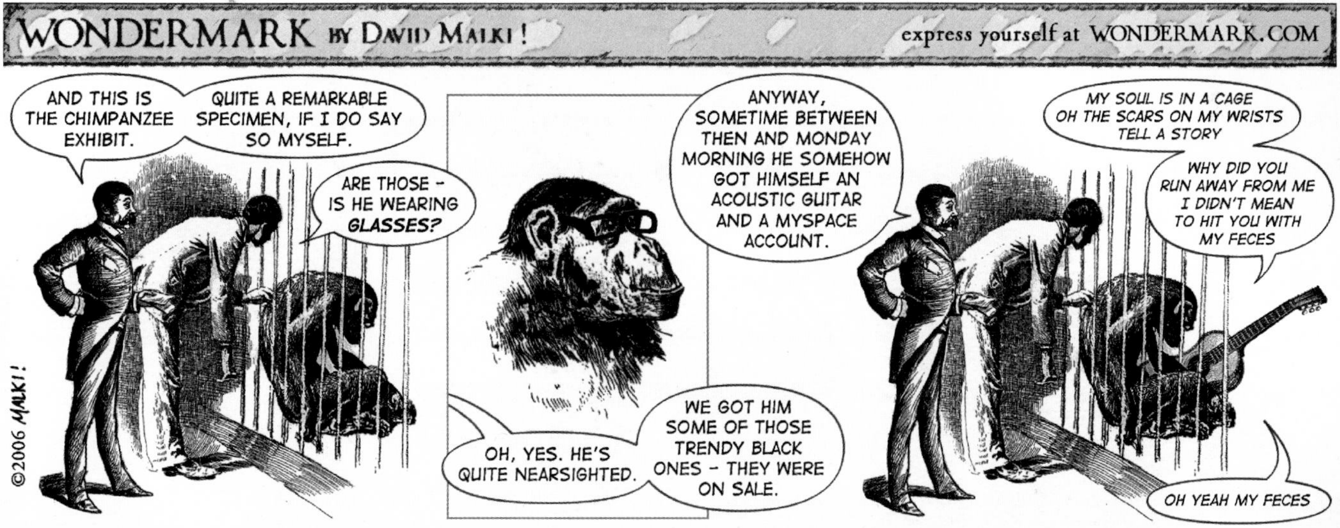
WONDERMARK by David Malki !
express yourself at WONDERMARK.COM
AND THIS IS THE CHIMPANZEE EXHIBIT.
QUITE A REMARKABLE SPECIMEN, IF I DO SAY SO MYSELF.
ARE THOSE - IS HE WEARING GLASSES?
©2006 MALKI !
OH, YES. HE'S QUITE NEARSIGHTED.
WE GOT HIM SOME OF THOSE TRENDY BLACK ONES - THEY WERE ON SALE.
ANYWAY, SOMETIME BETWEEN THEN AND MONDAY MORNING HE SOMEHOW GOT HIMSELF AN ACOUSTIC GUITAR AND A MYSPACE ACCOUNT.
MY SOUL IS IN A CAGE OH THE SCARS ON MY WRISTS TELL A STORY
WHY DID YOU RUN AWAY FROM ME I DIDN'T MEAN TO HIT YOU WITH MY FECES
OH YEAH MY FECES

there are also many songs about bananas, pining, and pining for bananas

INTERMISSION.

Notes.

_____
_____
_____
_____
_____
_____
_____
_____
_____
_____

The comics on the following pages were created for special venues. Many of them were never featured on the *Wondermark* site, and thus you may be seeing them for the first time. Do not be alarmed; I will guide you safely through the wending corridors ahead. Here is what to expect:

This page's comic was created for "Monkey Day," both a holiday celebrated on December 14th and an associated media event spearheaded by Casey Sorrow. Monkey fans may go on to explore *monkeyday.com.*

The comics on pages 74–75 were created for the "Webcomic Hurricane Relief Telethon," an event featuring work by over 100 cartoonists and raising $28,635 in aid for victims of Hurricane Katrina.

The comics on pages 76–77 were originally published in *Zoinks!*, a bimonthly newspaper devoted solely to webcomics. Exclusive *Wondermark* comics were featured regularly in *Zoinks!* during its two-year run. Some of those same comics later ran on the *Wondermark* site as regular episodes, while a few were frankly just bad and will not be reproduced again.

The comics on pages 78–79 were created by friends of *Wondermark* as guest episodes while I was on my honeymoon in 2006. Many of the 19 total guest comics that ran online were fascinating departures from the *Wondermark* mold; these four (as well as the strip on page 31) hewed more closely to the format.

Pages 80–81 feature works in progress that I have abandoned. If you care to maintain your high estimation of me, I cannot recommend that you read them.

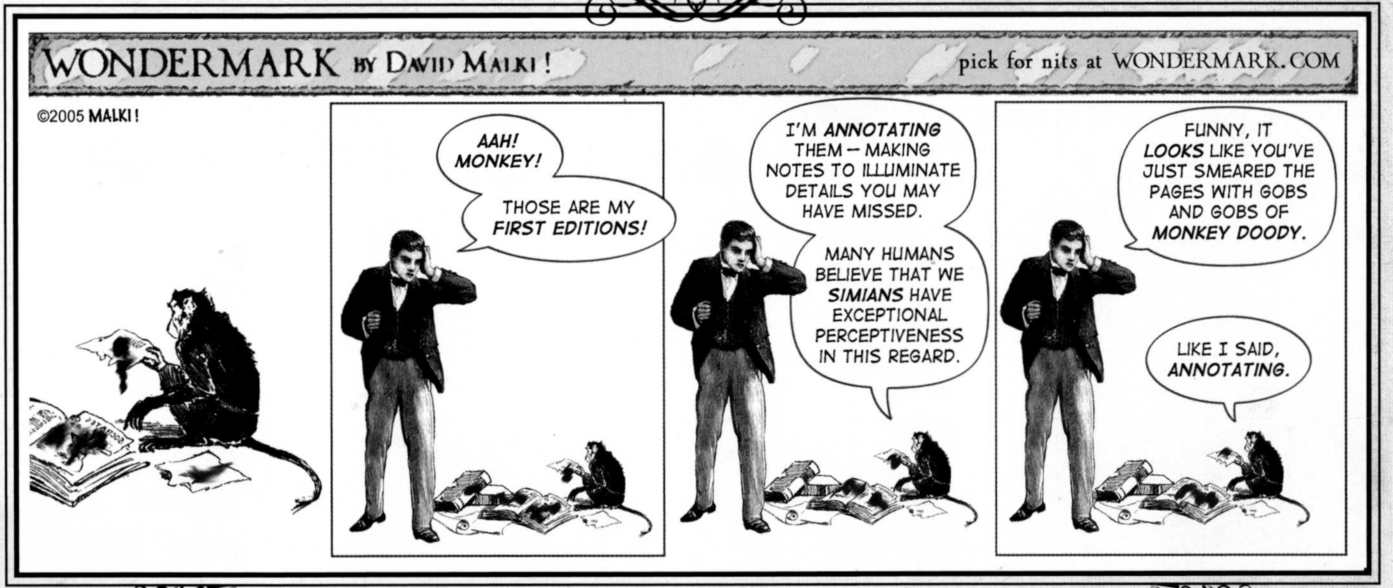
WONDERMARK BY DAVID MALKI !
pick for nits at WONDERMARK.COM
©2005 MALKI !
AAH! MONKEY!
THOSE ARE MY FIRST EDITIONS!
I'M ANNOTATING THEM — MAKING NOTES TO ILLUMINATE DETAILS YOU MAY HAVE MISSED.
MANY HUMANS BELIEVE THAT WE SIMIANS HAVE EXCEPTIONAL PERCEPTIVENESS IN THIS REGARD.
FUNNY, IT LOOKS LIKE YOU'VE JUST SMEARED THE PAGES WITH GOBS AND GOBS OF MONKEY DOODY.
LIKE I SAID, ANNOTATING.

i've already made careful notes in your wedding album

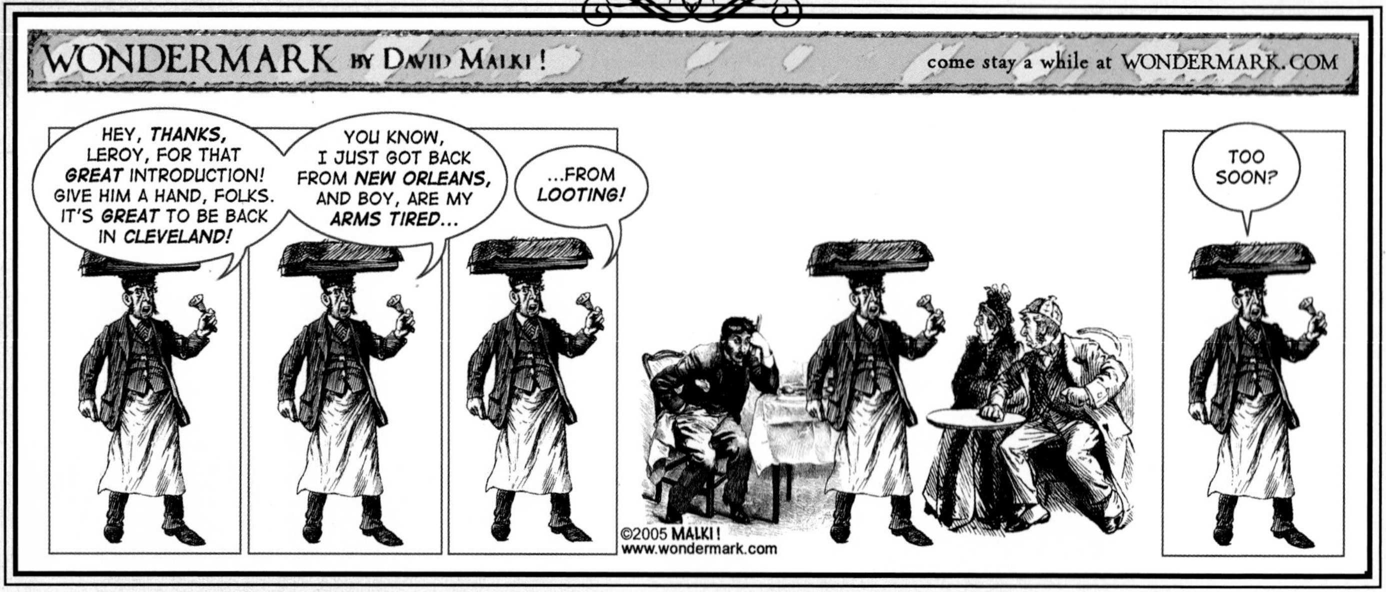
WONDERMARK BY DAVID MALKI !
come stay a while at WONDERMARK.COM
HEY, THANKS, LEROY, FOR THAT GREAT INTRODUCTION! GIVE HIM A HAND, FOLKS. IT'S GREAT TO BE BACK IN CLEVELAND!
YOU KNOW, I JUST GOT BACK FROM NEW ORLEANS, AND BOY, ARE MY ARMS TIRED...
...FROM LOOTING!
©2005 MALKI ! www.wondermark.com
TOO SOON?

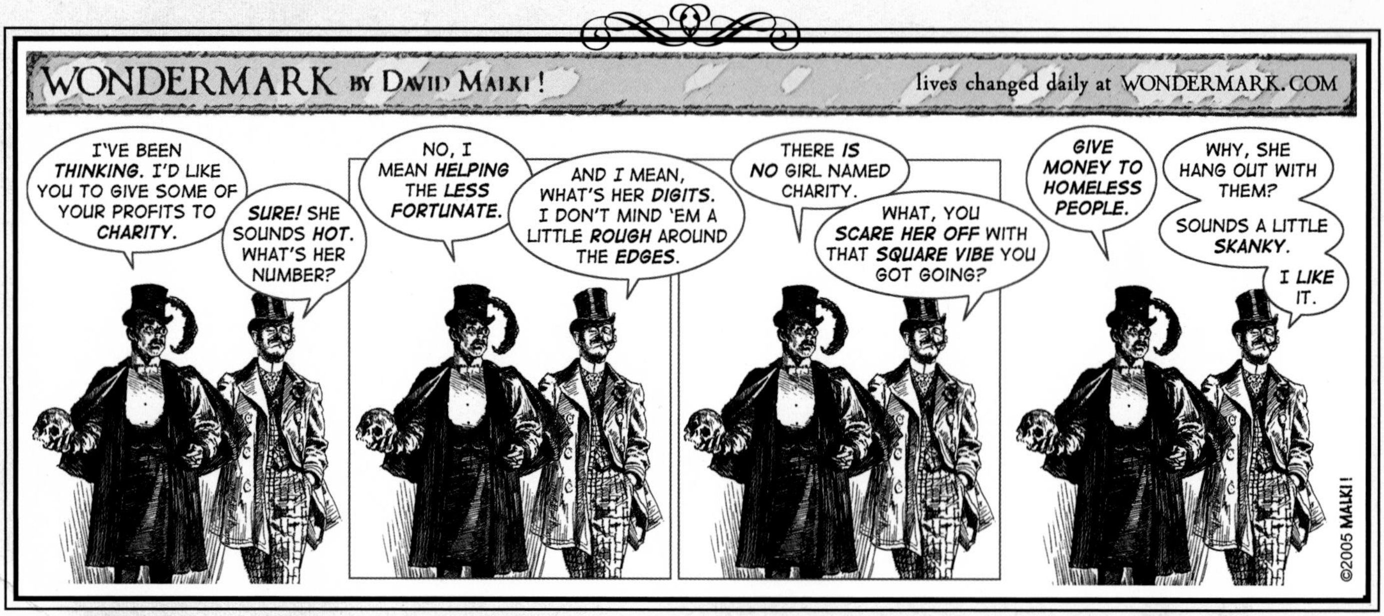
WONDERMARK BY DAVID MALKI !
lives changed daily at WONDERMARK.COM
I'VE BEEN THINKING. I'D LIKE YOU TO GIVE SOME OF YOUR PROFITS TO CHARITY.
SURE! SHE SOUNDS HOT. WHAT'S HER NUMBER?
NO, I MEAN HELPING THE LESS FORTUNATE.
AND I MEAN, WHAT'S HER DIGITS. I DON'T MIND 'EM A LITTLE ROUGH AROUND THE EDGES.
THERE IS NO GIRL NAMED CHARITY.
WHAT, YOU SCARE HER OFF WITH THAT SQUARE VIBE YOU GOT GOING?
GIVE MONEY TO HOMELESS PEOPLE.
WHY, SHE HANG OUT WITH THEM?
SOUNDS A LITTLE SKANKY.
I LIKE IT.
©2005 MALKI !

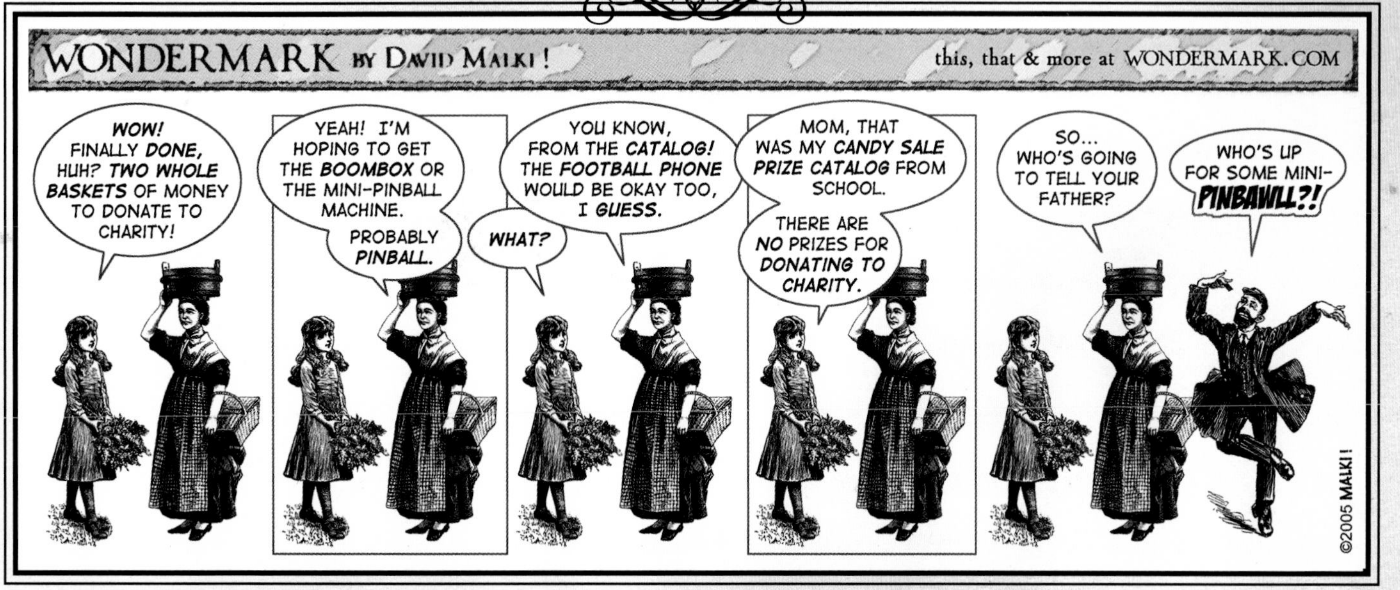
WONDERMARK BY DAVID MALKI !
this, that & more at WONDERMARK.COM
WOW! FINALLY DONE, HUH? TWO WHOLE BASKETS OF MONEY TO DONATE TO CHARITY!
YEAH! I'M HOPING TO GET THE BOOMBOX OR THE MINI-PINBALL MACHINE.
PROBABLY PINBALL.
WHAT?
YOU KNOW, FROM THE CATALOG! THE FOOTBALL PHONE WOULD BE OKAY TOO, I GUESS.
MOM, THAT WAS MY CANDY SALE PRIZE CATALOG FROM SCHOOL.
THERE ARE NO PRIZES FOR DONATING TO CHARITY.
SO... WHO'S GOING TO TELL YOUR FATHER?
WHO'S UP FOR SOME MINI-PINBAWLL?!
©2005 MALKI !

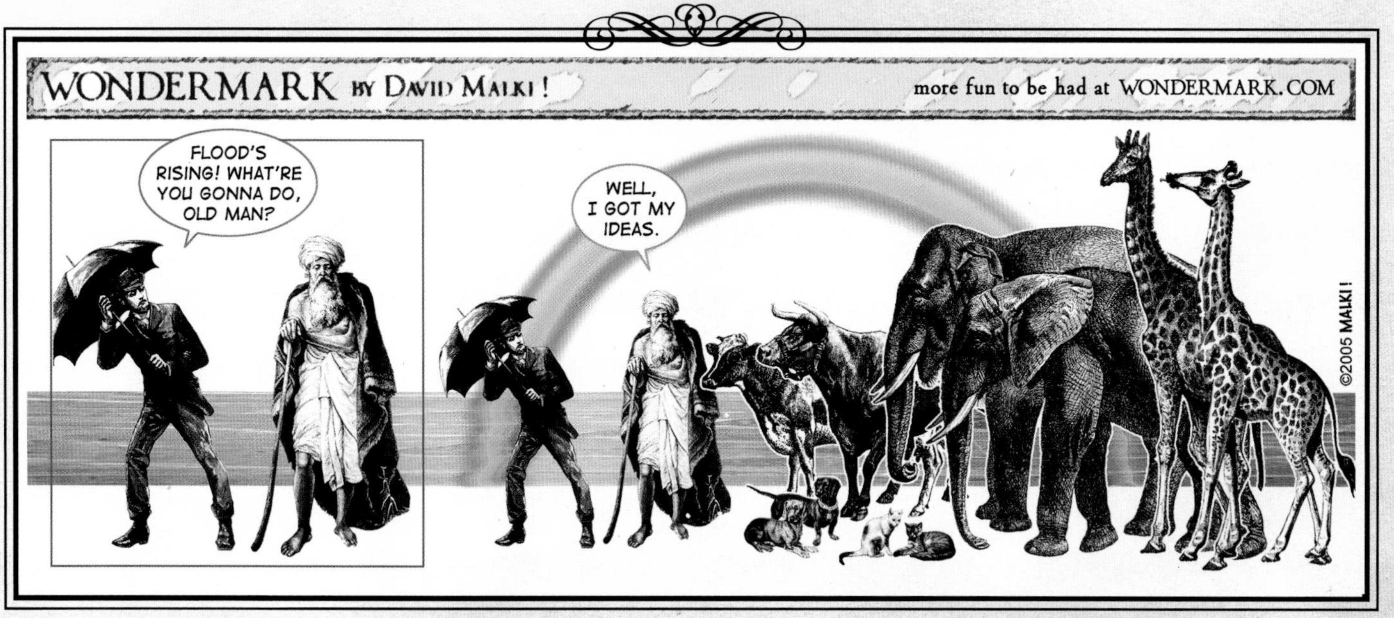
WONDERMARK BY DAVID MALKI !
more fun to be had at WONDERMARK.COM
FLOOD'S RISING! WHAT'RE YOU GONNA DO, OLD MAN?
WELL, I GOT MY IDEAS.
©2005 MALKI !

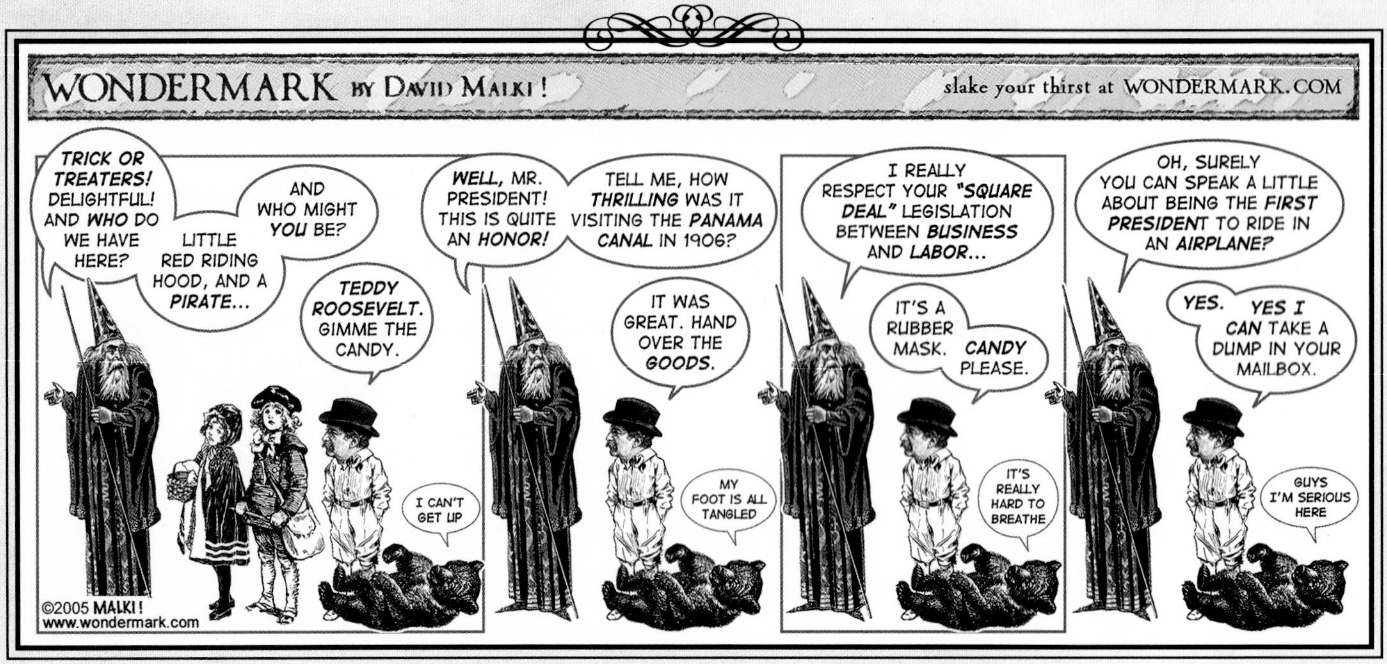
WONDERMARK BY DAVID MALKI !
slake your thirst at WONDERMARK.COM
TRICK OR TREATERS! DELIGHTFUL! AND WHO DO WE HAVE HERE?
LITTLE RED RIDING HOOD, AND A PIRATE...
AND WHO MIGHT YOU BE?
TEDDY ROOSEVELT. GIMME THE CANDY.
I CAN'T GET UP
©2005 MALKI ! www.wondermark.com
WELL, MR. PRESIDENT! THIS IS QUITE AN HONOR!
TELL ME, HOW THRILLING WAS IT VISITING THE PANAMA CANAL IN 1906?
IT WAS GREAT. HAND OVER THE GOODS.
MY FOOT IS ALL TANGLED
I REALLY RESPECT YOUR "SQUARE DEAL" LEGISLATION BETWEEN BUSINESS AND LABOR...
IT'S A RUBBER MASK.
CANDY PLEASE.
IT'S REALLY HARD TO BREATHE
OH, SURELY YOU CAN SPEAK A LITTLE ABOUT BEING THE FIRST PRESIDENT TO RIDE IN AN AIRPLANE?
YES.
YES I CAN TAKE A DUMP IN YOUR MAILBOX.
GUYS I'M SERIOUS HERE

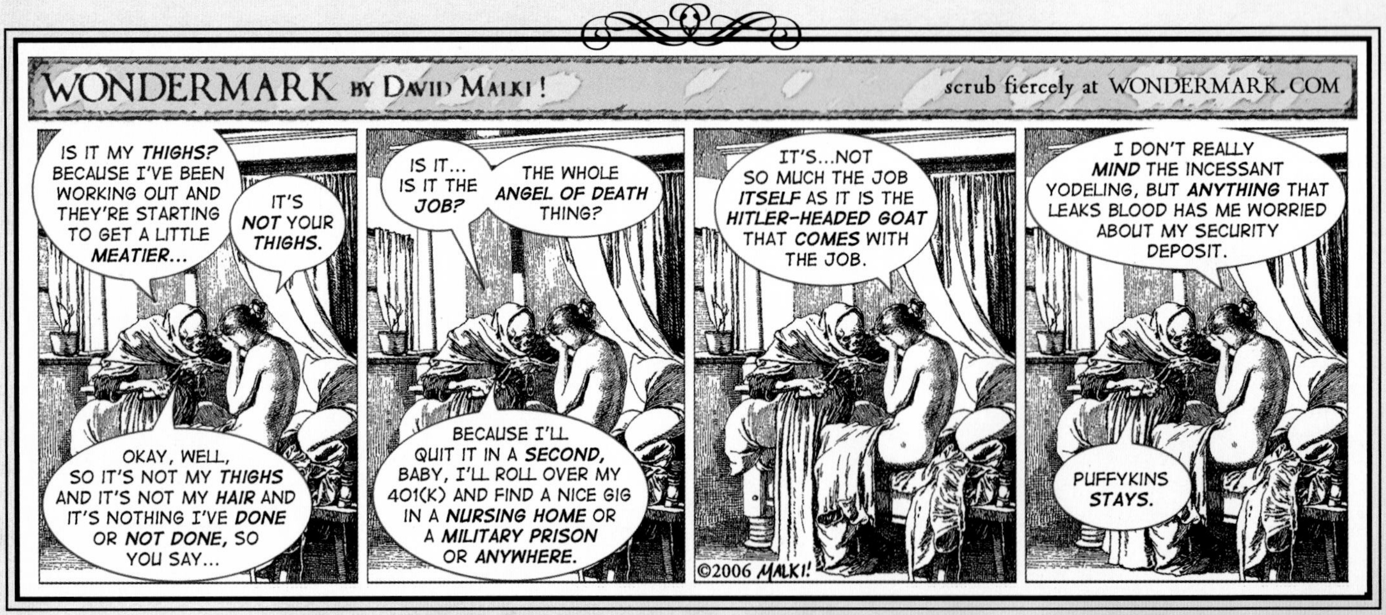
WONDERMARK BY DAVID MALKI !
scrub fiercely at WONDERMARK.COM
IS IT MY THIGHS? BECAUSE I'VE BEEN WORKING OUT AND THEY'RE STARTING TO GET A LITTLE MEATIER...
IT'S NOT YOUR THIGHS.
OKAY, WELL, SO IT'S NOT MY THIGHS AND IT'S NOT MY HAIR AND IT'S NOTHING I'VE DONE OR NOT DONE, SO YOU SAY...
IS IT... IS IT THE JOB?
THE WHOLE ANGEL OF DEATH THING?
BECAUSE I'LL QUIT IT IN A SECOND, BABY, I'LL ROLL OVER MY 401(K) AND FIND A NICE GIG IN A NURSING HOME OR A MILITARY PRISON OR ANYWHERE.
IT'S...NOT SO MUCH THE JOB ITSELF AS IT IS THE HITLER-HEADED GOAT THAT COMES WITH THE JOB.
©2006 MALKI!
I DON'T REALLY MIND THE INCESSANT YODELING, BUT ANYTHING THAT LEAKS BLOOD HAS ME WORRIED ABOUT MY SECURITY DEPOSIT.
PUFFYKINS STAYS.

REMEMBER HOW FUN
IT IS TO IMAGINE STUFF

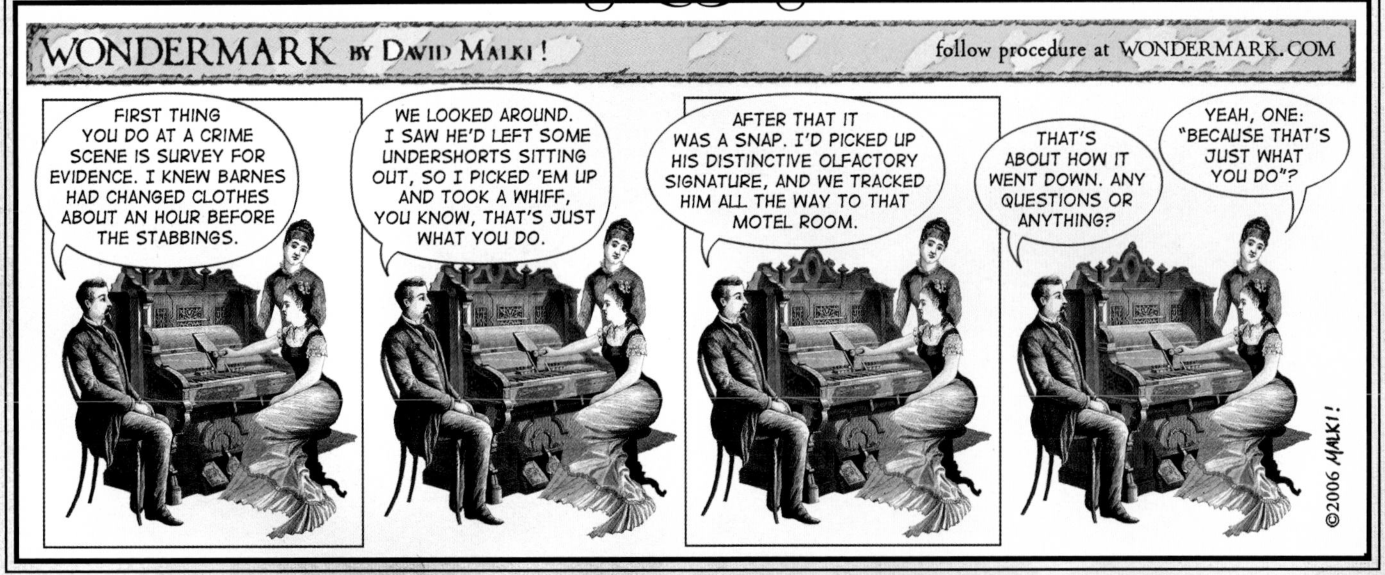
WONDERMARK by David Malki!
follow procedure at WONDERMARK.COM
FIRST THING YOU DO AT A CRIME SCENE IS SURVEY FOR EVIDENCE. I KNEW BARNES HAD CHANGED CLOTHES ABOUT AN HOUR BEFORE THE STABBINGS.
WE LOOKED AROUND. I SAW HE'D LEFT SOME UNDERSHORTS SITTING OUT, SO I PICKED 'EM UP AND TOOK A WHIFF, YOU KNOW, THAT'S JUST WHAT YOU DO.
AFTER THAT IT WAS A SNAP. I'D PICKED UP HIS DISTINCTIVE OLFACTORY SIGNATURE, AND WE TRACKED HIM ALL THE WAY TO THAT MOTEL ROOM.
THAT'S ABOUT HOW IT WENT DOWN. ANY QUESTIONS OR ANYTHING?
YEAH, ONE: "BECAUSE THAT'S JUST WHAT YOU DO"?
©2006 MALKI!

You can clean a computer keyboard in the dishwasher.

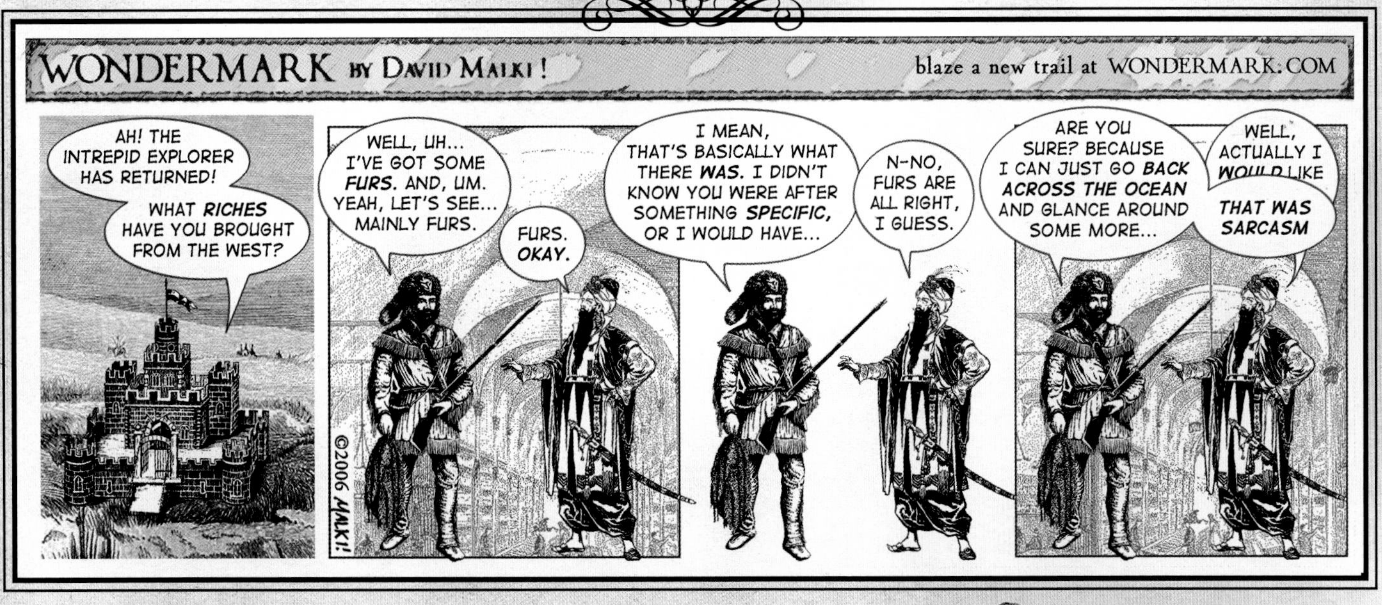
WONDERMARK by David Malki!
blaze a new trail at WONDERMARK.COM
AH! THE INTREPID EXPLORER HAS RETURNED!
WHAT RICHES HAVE YOU BROUGHT FROM THE WEST?
WELL, UH... I'VE GOT SOME FURS. AND, UM. YEAH, LET'S SEE... MAINLY FURS.
FURS. OKAY.
I MEAN, THAT'S BASICALLY WHAT THERE WAS. I DIDN'T KNOW YOU WERE AFTER SOMETHING SPECIFIC, OR I WOULD HAVE...
N-NO, FURS ARE ALL RIGHT, I GUESS.
ARE YOU SURE? BECAUSE I CAN JUST GO BACK ACROSS THE OCEAN AND GLANCE AROUND SOME MORE...
WELL, ACTUALLY I WOULD LIKE
THAT WAS SARCASM
©2006 MALKI!

Ignore people who hate you, unless they have a point.

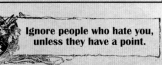

Guest Comic by Justin Pierce (*nonadventures.com*)

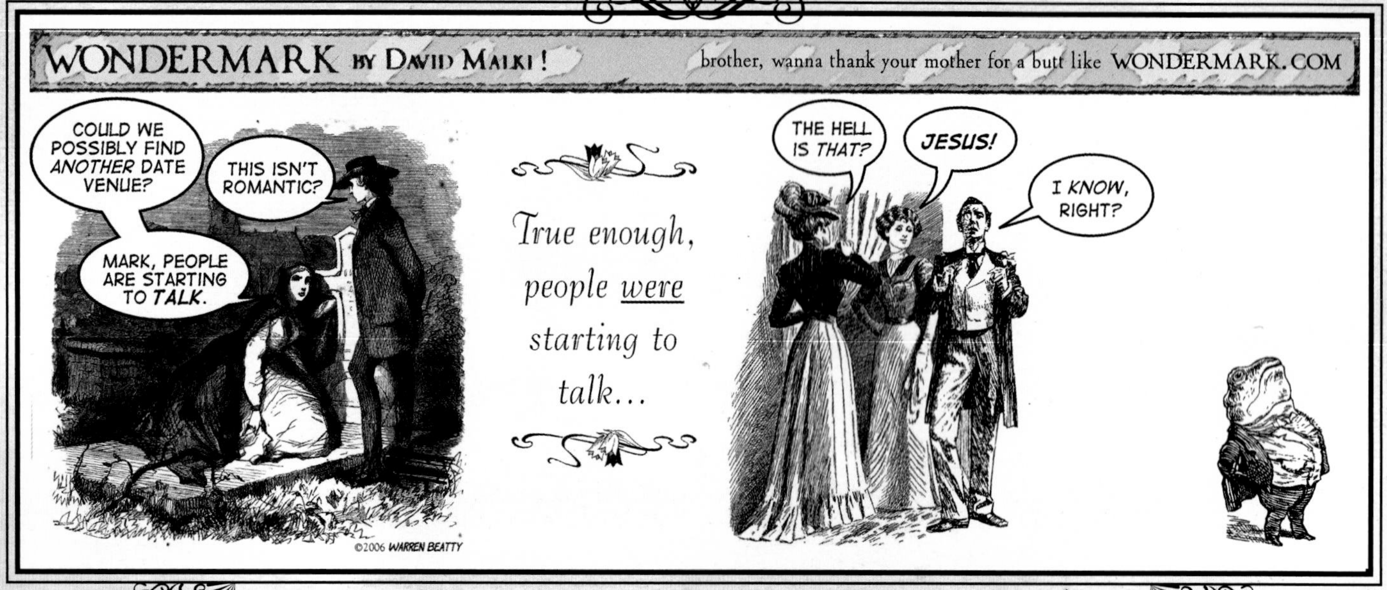
WONDERMARK by David Malki !
brother, wanna thank your mother for a butt like WONDERMARK.COM
COULD WE POSSIBLY FIND *ANOTHER* DATE VENUE?
THIS ISN'T ROMANTIC?
MARK, PEOPLE ARE STARTING TO *TALK*.
©2006 WARREN BEATTY
True enough, people were starting to talk...
THE HELL IS *THAT?*
JESUS!
I *KNOW*, RIGHT?

it's got feelings too, you know — hopefully PAIN

78

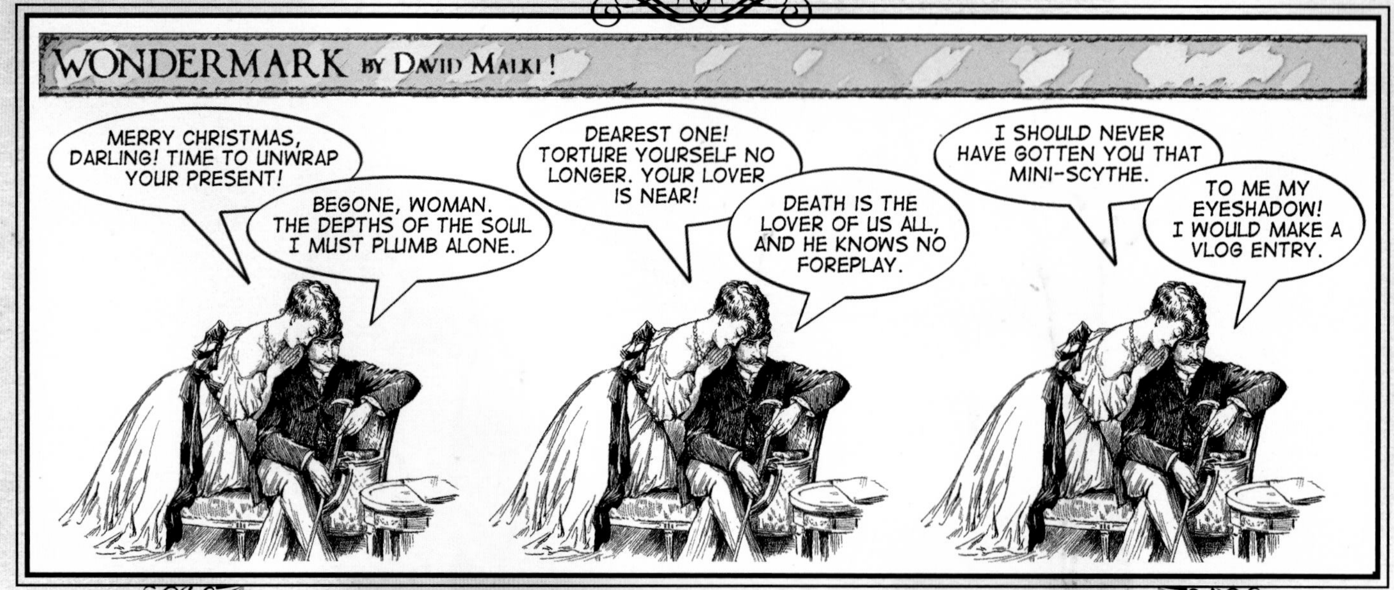
WONDERMARK by David Malki !
MERRY CHRISTMAS, DARLING! TIME TO UNWRAP YOUR PRESENT!
BEGONE, WOMAN. THE DEPTHS OF THE SOUL I MUST PLUMB ALONE.
DEAREST ONE! TORTURE YOURSELF NO LONGER. YOUR LOVER IS NEAR!
DEATH IS THE LOVER OF US ALL, AND HE KNOWS NO FOREPLAY.
I SHOULD NEVER HAVE GOTTEN YOU THAT MINI-SCYTHE.
TO ME MY EYESHADOW! I WOULD MAKE A VLOG ENTRY.

ghod you emo kids

Guest Comic by Kristofer Straub (*starslip.com*)

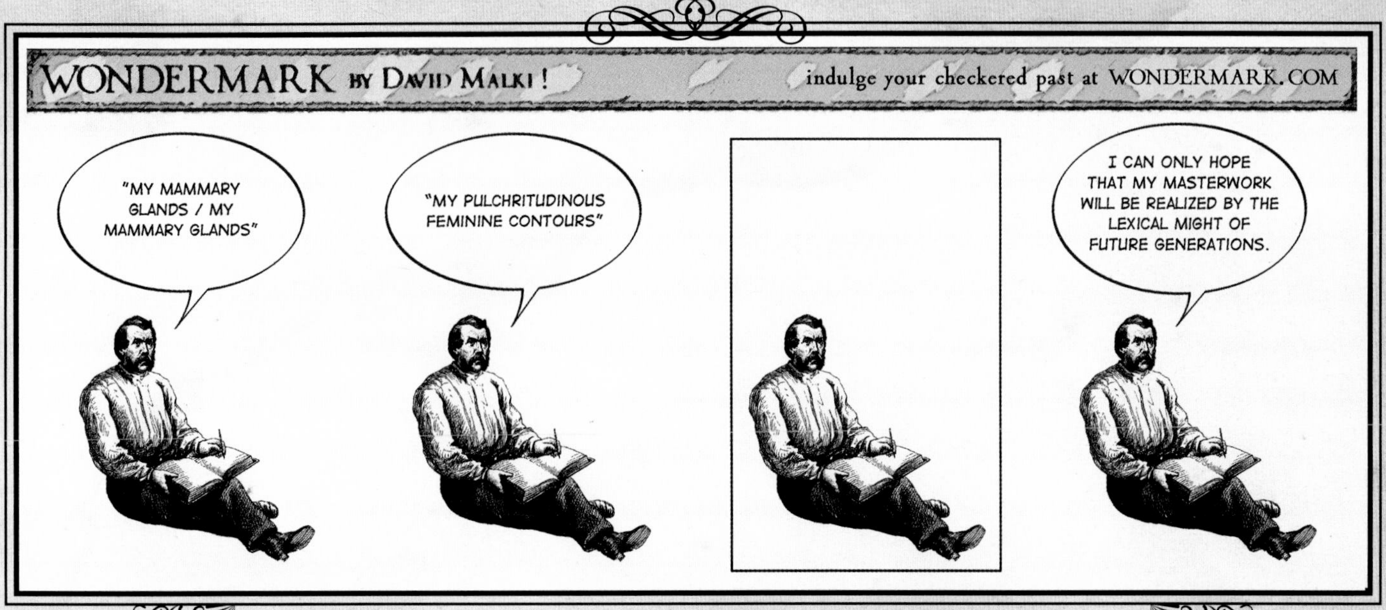
WONDERMARK by David Malki !
indulge your checkered past at WONDERMARK.COM
"MY MAMMARY GLANDS / MY MAMMARY GLANDS"
"MY PULCHRITUDINOUS FEMININE CONTOURS"
I CAN ONLY HOPE THAT MY MASTERWORK WILL BE REALIZED BY THE LEXICAL MIGHT OF FUTURE GENERATIONS.

additionally, my frosted whipped beverage summons lads to my garden

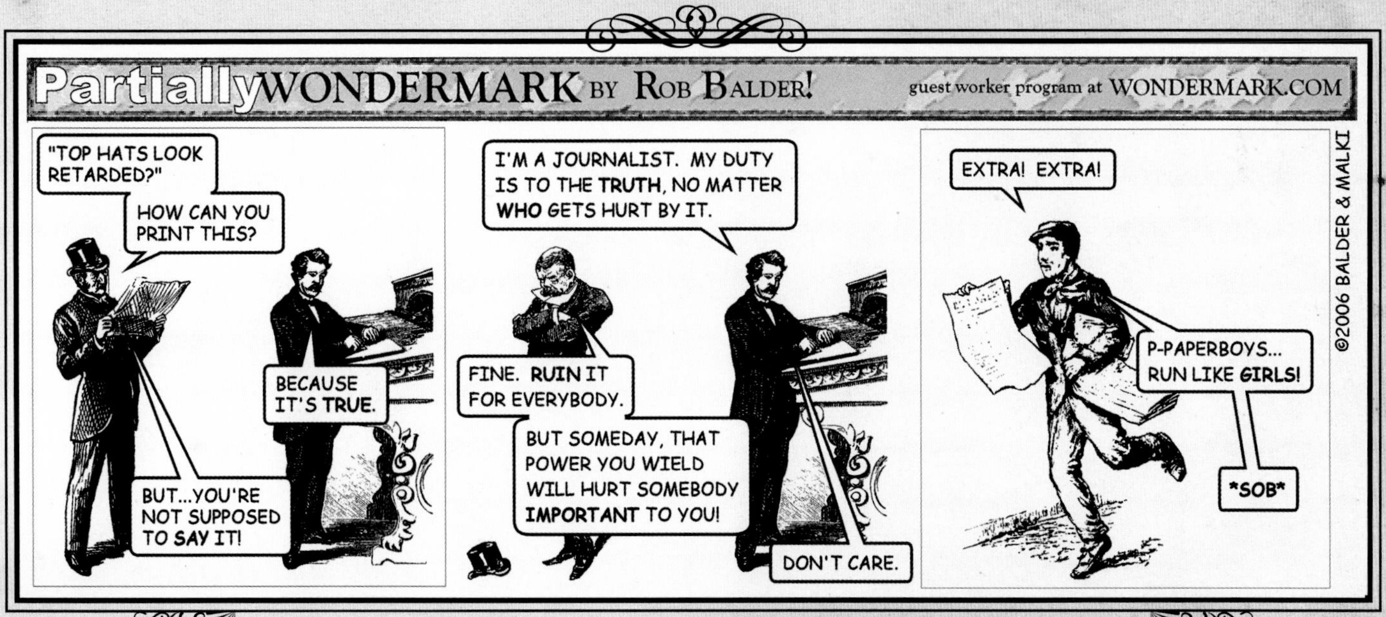
PartiallyWONDERMARK by Rob Balder!
guest worker program at WONDERMARK.COM
"TOP HATS LOOK RETARDED?"
HOW CAN YOU PRINT THIS?
BECAUSE IT'S TRUE.
BUT...YOU'RE NOT SUPPOSED TO SAY IT!
I'M A JOURNALIST. MY DUTY IS TO THE TRUTH, NO MATTER WHO GETS HURT BY IT.
FINE. RUIN IT FOR EVERYBODY.
BUT SOMEDAY, THAT POWER YOU WIELD WILL HURT SOMEBODY IMPORTANT TO YOU!
DON'T CARE.
EXTRA! EXTRA!
P-PAPERBOYS... RUN LIKE GIRLS!
SOB
©2006 BALDER & MALKI

it's a hard knock life

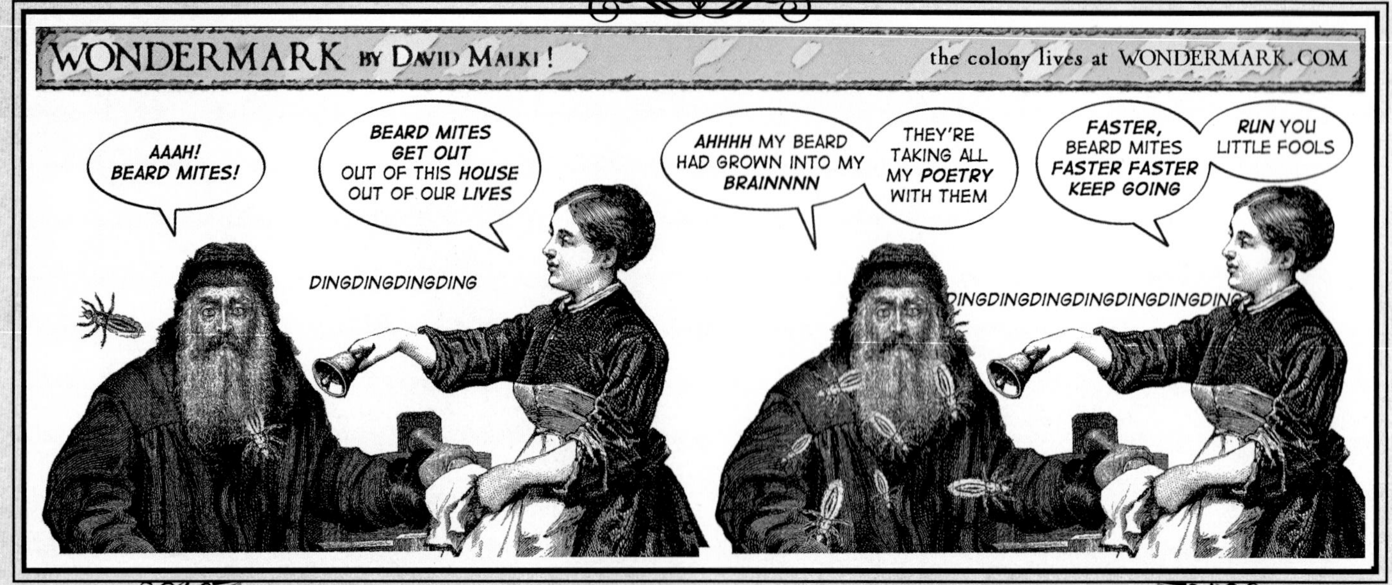
WONDERMARK by David Malki !
the colony lives at WONDERMARK.COM
AAAH! BEARD MITES!
BEARD MITES GET OUT OUT OF THIS HOUSE OUT OF OUR LIVES
DINGDINGDINGDING
AHHHH MY BEARD HAD GROWN INTO MY BRAINNNN
THEY'RE TAKING ALL MY POETRY WITH THEM
FASTER, BEARD MITES FASTER FASTER KEEP GOING
RUN YOU LITTLE FOOLS
DINGDINGDINGDINGDINGDINGDIN

I didn't end up running this strip because I have standards.

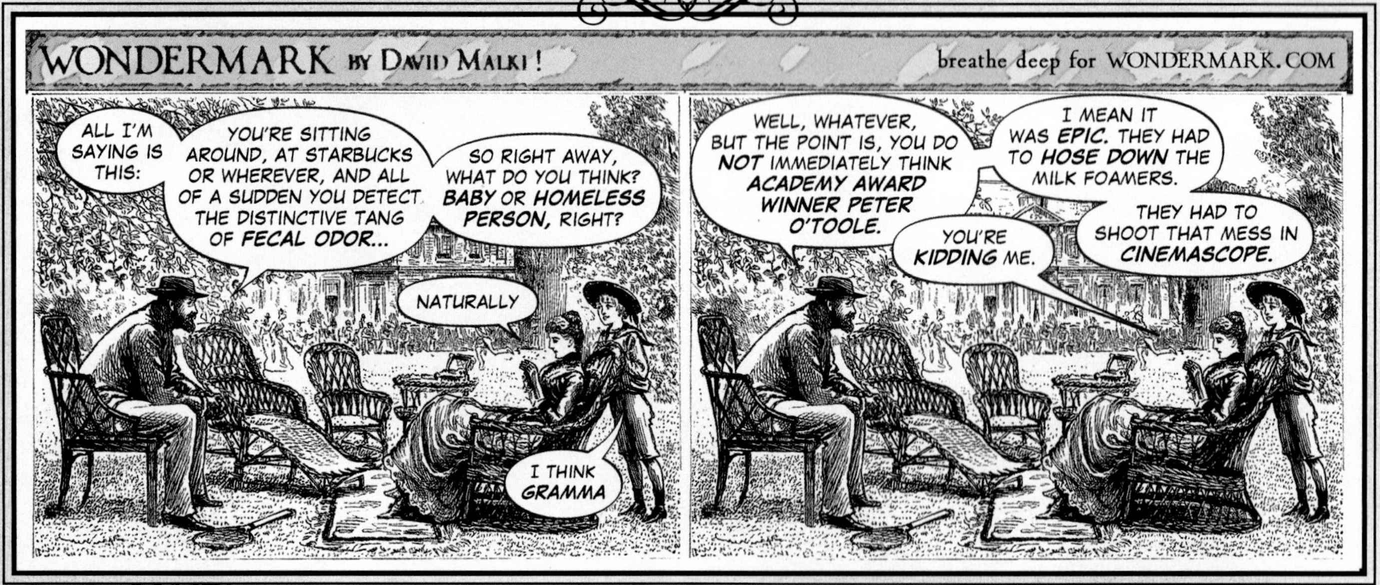
WONDERMARK by David Malki !
breathe deep for WONDERMARK.COM
ALL I'M SAYING IS THIS:
YOU'RE SITTING AROUND, AT STARBUCKS OR WHEREVER, AND ALL OF A SUDDEN YOU DETECT THE DISTINCTIVE TANG OF FECAL ODOR...
SO RIGHT AWAY, WHAT DO YOU THINK? BABY OR HOMELESS PERSON, RIGHT?
NATURALLY
I THINK GRAMMA
WELL, WHATEVER, BUT THE POINT IS, YOU DO NOT IMMEDIATELY THINK ACADEMY AWARD WINNER PETER O'TOOLE.
YOU'RE KIDDING ME.
I MEAN IT WAS EPIC. THEY HAD TO HOSE DOWN THE MILK FOAMERS.
THEY HAD TO SHOOT THAT MESS IN CINEMASCOPE.

This strip died because I like my comics to have a *little* more going for them than just vulgar imagery and libel. It used to have a passable punch line—"Come on, man, he was in *Ishtar!*" / "I know, and he stunk up *that* joint, too!"—but (a) he was not in *Ishtar* and (b) Seriously? An *Ishtar* joke?

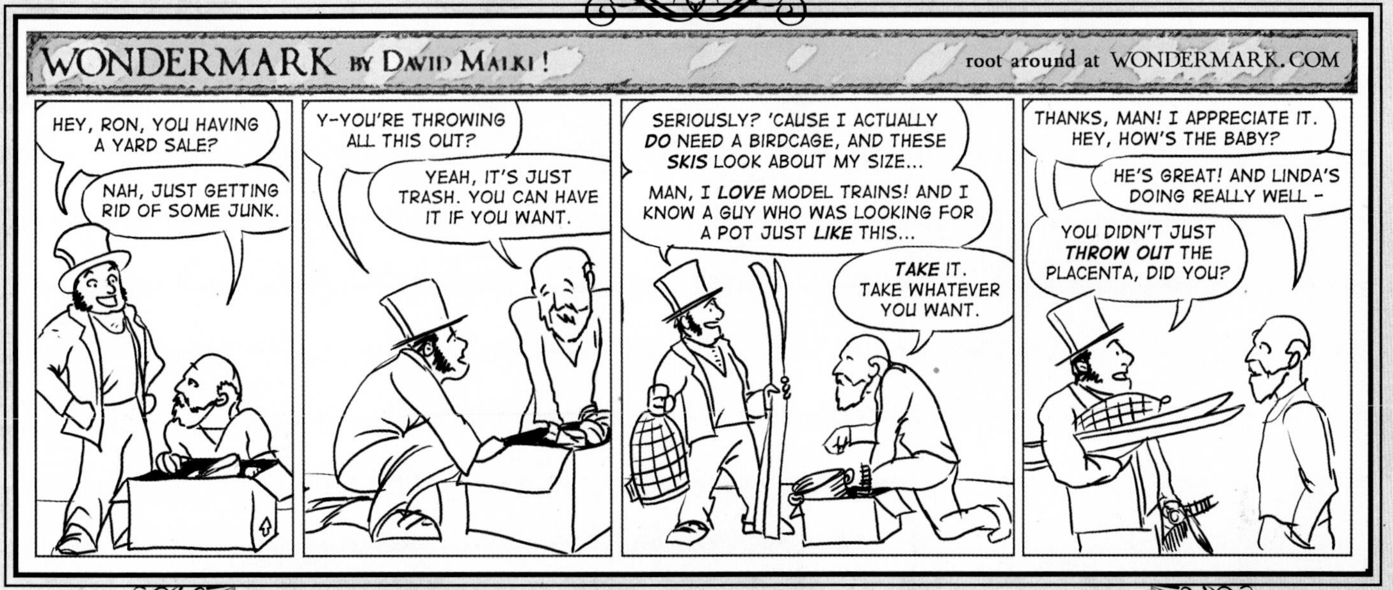
WONDERMARK BY DAVID MALKI !
root around at WONDERMARK.COM
HEY, RON, YOU HAVING A YARD SALE?
NAH, JUST GETTING RID OF SOME JUNK.
Y-YOU'RE THROWING ALL THIS OUT?
YEAH, IT'S JUST TRASH. YOU CAN HAVE IT IF YOU WANT.
SERIOUSLY? 'CAUSE I ACTUALLY DO NEED A BIRDCAGE, AND THESE SKIS LOOK ABOUT MY SIZE...
MAN, I LOVE MODEL TRAINS! AND I KNOW A GUY WHO WAS LOOKING FOR A POT JUST LIKE THIS...
TAKE IT. TAKE WHATEVER YOU WANT.
THANKS, MAN! I APPRECIATE IT. HEY, HOW'S THE BABY?
HE'S GREAT! AND LINDA'S DOING REALLY WELL -
YOU DIDN'T JUST THROW OUT THE PLACENTA, DID YOU?

I've sketched this strip by hand for the book, but back when I wrote it, I didn't feel like digging up old-timey source images for all the different props it would require. Besides, right after I wrote it, a couple other webcomics featured placenta gags, and this would have felt like a retread.

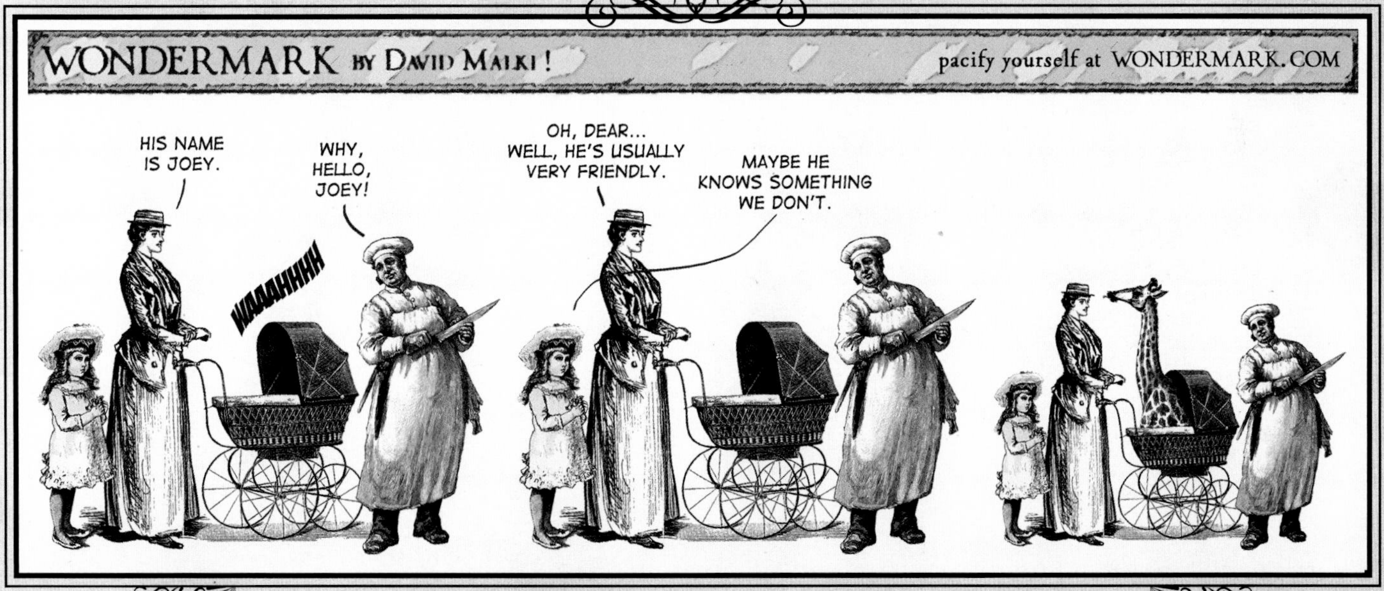
WONDERMARK BY DAVID MALKI !
pacify yourself at WONDERMARK.COM
HIS NAME IS JOEY.
WHY, HELLO, JOEY!
WAAAHHHH
OH, DEAR... WELL, HE'S USUALLY VERY FRIENDLY.
MAYBE HE KNOWS SOMETHING WE DON'T.

Not real sure where this one was going.

SUCH is the sum of comic strips in this volume. Most of them were pretty okay; of the remainder, a few were particularly astute, a few dismal, and a handful incomprehensible. Exactly one was peerlessly brillant, and exactly one other was crap; on this I think we can all agree.

So what now? There are still fourteen pages left. I could lie, and say that the remainder of this book is filled with dense blocks of text within which are hidden THE SECRETS OF LIVING CONTENTEDLY IN A COLD WORLD DOOMED TO EVENTUAL DESTRUCTION BY SUPERNOVA, but I imagine your peripheral vision has alerted you to the contents of the facing page. That is the first page of *Treachery!*, an eight-page graphic narrative created in the same manner as *Wondermark* comic strips. It continues on for seven pages past the first, and it tells a single continuous story for that entire length. I believe I am the first to conceive of such a thing.

After that, there are some other things. But you can see what they are once you get to them. Let us take events as they come, and savor them.

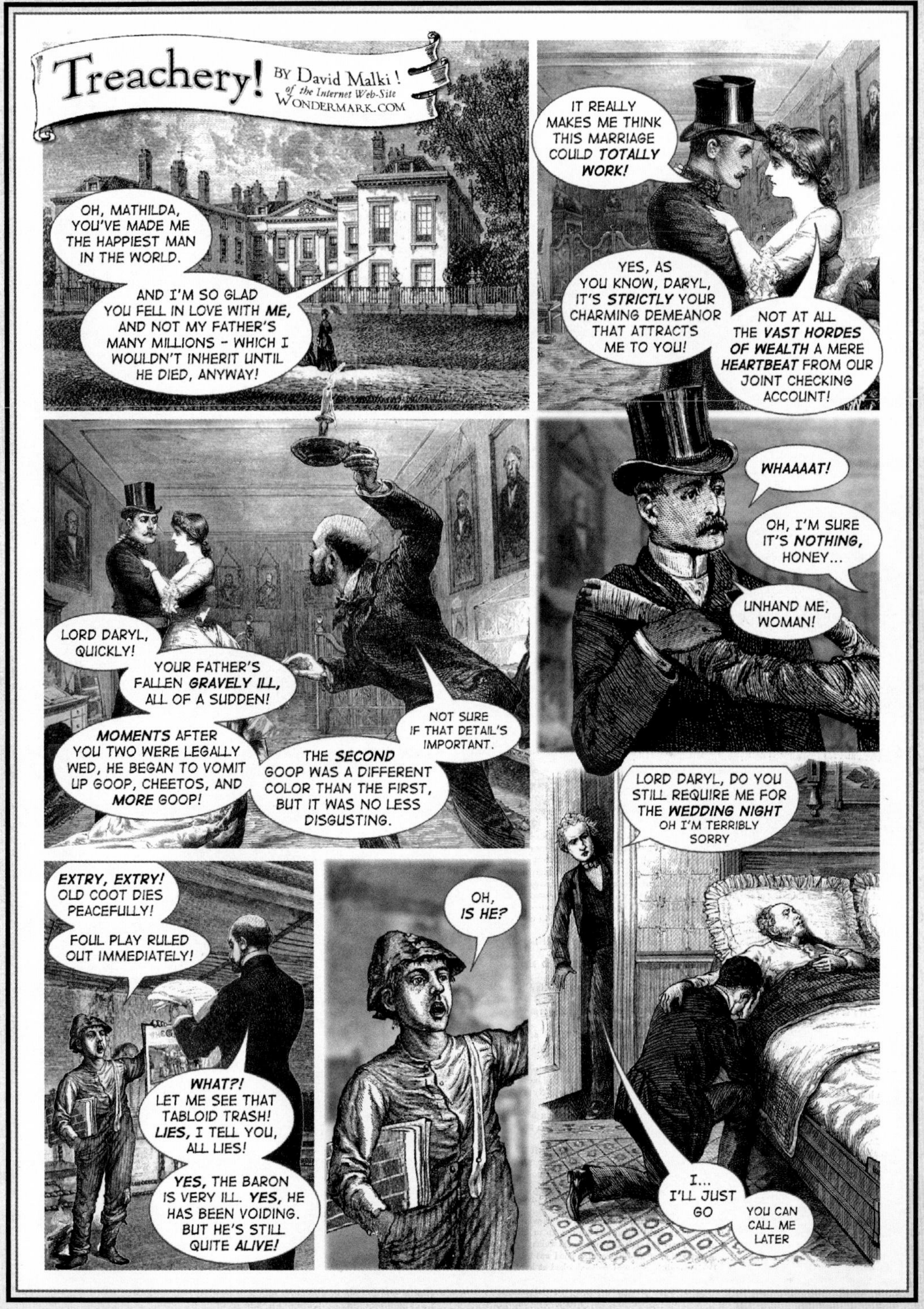
Treachery! BY David Malki ! of the Internet Web-Site WONDERMARK.COM
OH, MATHILDA, YOU'VE MADE ME THE HAPPIEST MAN IN THE WORLD.
AND I'M SO GLAD YOU FELL IN LOVE WITH ME, AND NOT MY FATHER'S MANY MILLIONS - WHICH I WOULDN'T INHERIT UNTIL HE DIED, ANYWAY!
IT REALLY MAKES ME THINK THIS MARRIAGE COULD TOTALLY WORK!
YES, AS YOU KNOW, DARYL, IT'S STRICTLY YOUR CHARMING DEMEANOR THAT ATTRACTS ME TO YOU!
NOT AT ALL THE VAST HORDES OF WEALTH A MERE HEARTBEAT FROM OUR JOINT CHECKING ACCOUNT!
LORD DARYL, QUICKLY!
YOUR FATHER'S FALLEN GRAVELY ILL, ALL OF A SUDDEN!
MOMENTS AFTER YOU TWO WERE LEGALLY WED, HE BEGAN TO VOMIT UP GOOP, CHEETOS, AND MORE GOOP!
NOT SURE IF THAT DETAIL'S IMPORTANT.
THE SECOND GOOP WAS A DIFFERENT COLOR THAN THE FIRST, BUT IT WAS NO LESS DISGUSTING.
WHAAAAT!
OH, I'M SURE IT'S NOTHING, HONEY...
UNHAND ME, WOMAN!
EXTRY, EXTRY! OLD COOT DIES PEACEFULLY!
FOUL PLAY RULED OUT IMMEDIATELY!
WHAT?! LET ME SEE THAT TABLOID TRASH! LIES, I TELL YOU, ALL LIES!
YES, THE BARON IS VERY ILL. YES, HE HAS BEEN VOIDING. BUT HE'S STILL QUITE ALIVE!
OH, IS HE?
LORD DARYL, DO YOU STILL REQUIRE ME FOR THE WEDDING NIGHT
OH I'M TERRIBLY SORRY
I... I'LL JUST GO
YOU CAN CALL ME LATER

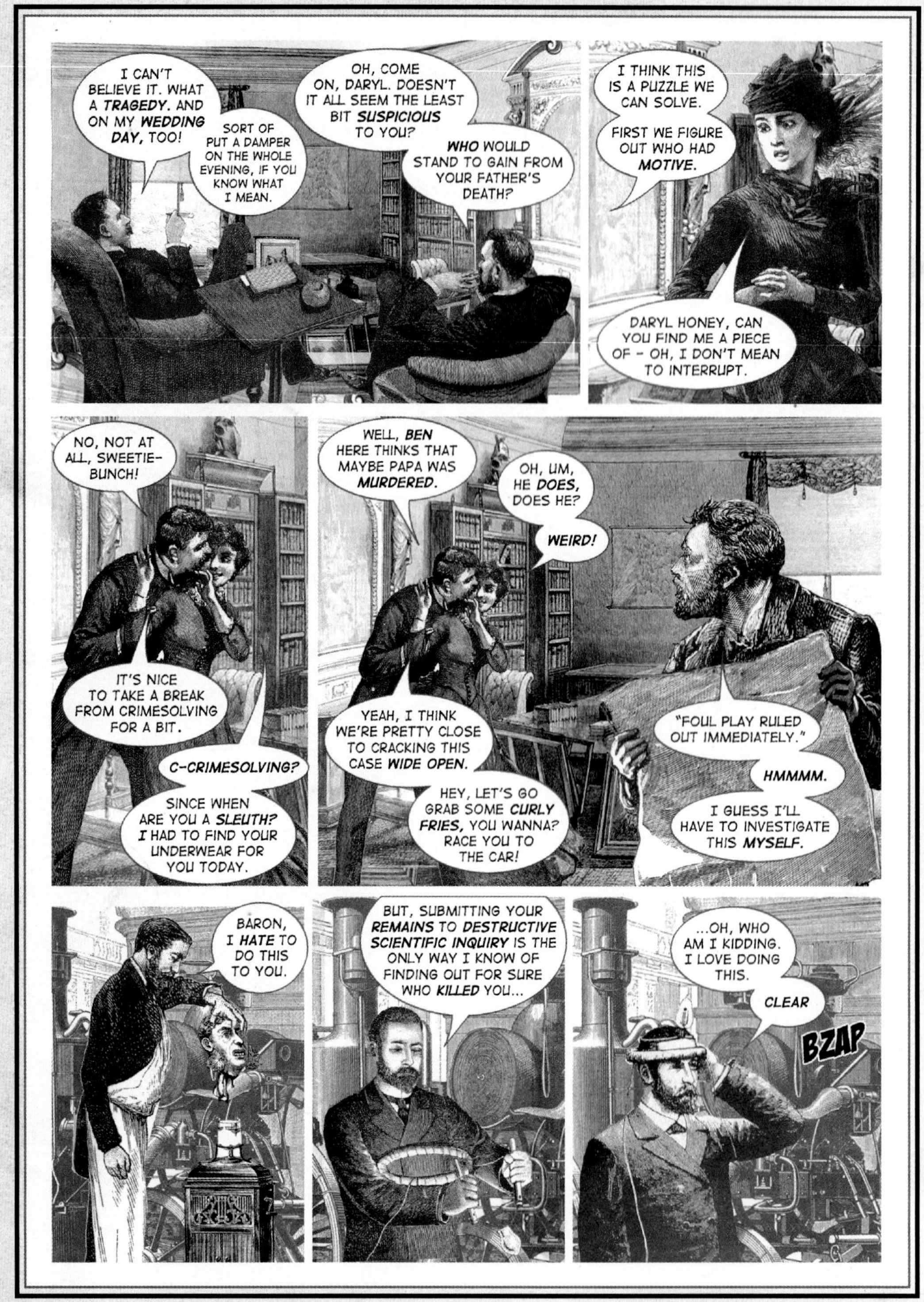
I CAN'T BELIEVE IT. WHAT A TRAGEDY. AND ON MY WEDDING DAY, TOO!
SORT OF PUT A DAMPER ON THE WHOLE EVENING, IF YOU KNOW WHAT I MEAN.
OH, COME ON, DARYL. DOESN'T IT ALL SEEM THE LEAST BIT SUSPICIOUS TO YOU?
WHO WOULD STAND TO GAIN FROM YOUR FATHER'S DEATH?
I THINK THIS IS A PUZZLE WE CAN SOLVE.
FIRST WE FIGURE OUT WHO HAD MOTIVE.
DARYL HONEY, CAN YOU FIND ME A PIECE OF - OH, I DON'T MEAN TO INTERRUPT.
NO, NOT AT ALL, SWEETIE-BUNCH!
IT'S NICE TO TAKE A BREAK FROM CRIMESOLVING FOR A BIT.
C-CRIMESOLVING?
SINCE WHEN ARE YOU A SLEUTH? I HAD TO FIND YOUR UNDERWEAR FOR YOU TODAY.
WELL, BEN HERE THINKS THAT MAYBE PAPA WAS MURDERED.
OH, UM, HE DOES, DOES HE?
WEIRD!
YEAH, I THINK WE'RE PRETTY CLOSE TO CRACKING THIS CASE WIDE OPEN.
HEY, LET'S GO GRAB SOME CURLY FRIES, YOU WANNA? RACE YOU TO THE CAR!
"FOUL PLAY RULED OUT IMMEDIATELY."
HMMMM.
I GUESS I'LL HAVE TO INVESTIGATE THIS MYSELF.
BARON, I HATE TO DO THIS TO YOU.
BUT, SUBMITTING YOUR REMAINS TO DESTRUCTIVE SCIENTIFIC INQUIRY IS THE ONLY WAY I KNOW OF FINDING OUT FOR SURE WHO KILLED YOU...
...OH, WHO AM I KIDDING. I LOVE DOING THIS.
CLEAR
BZAP

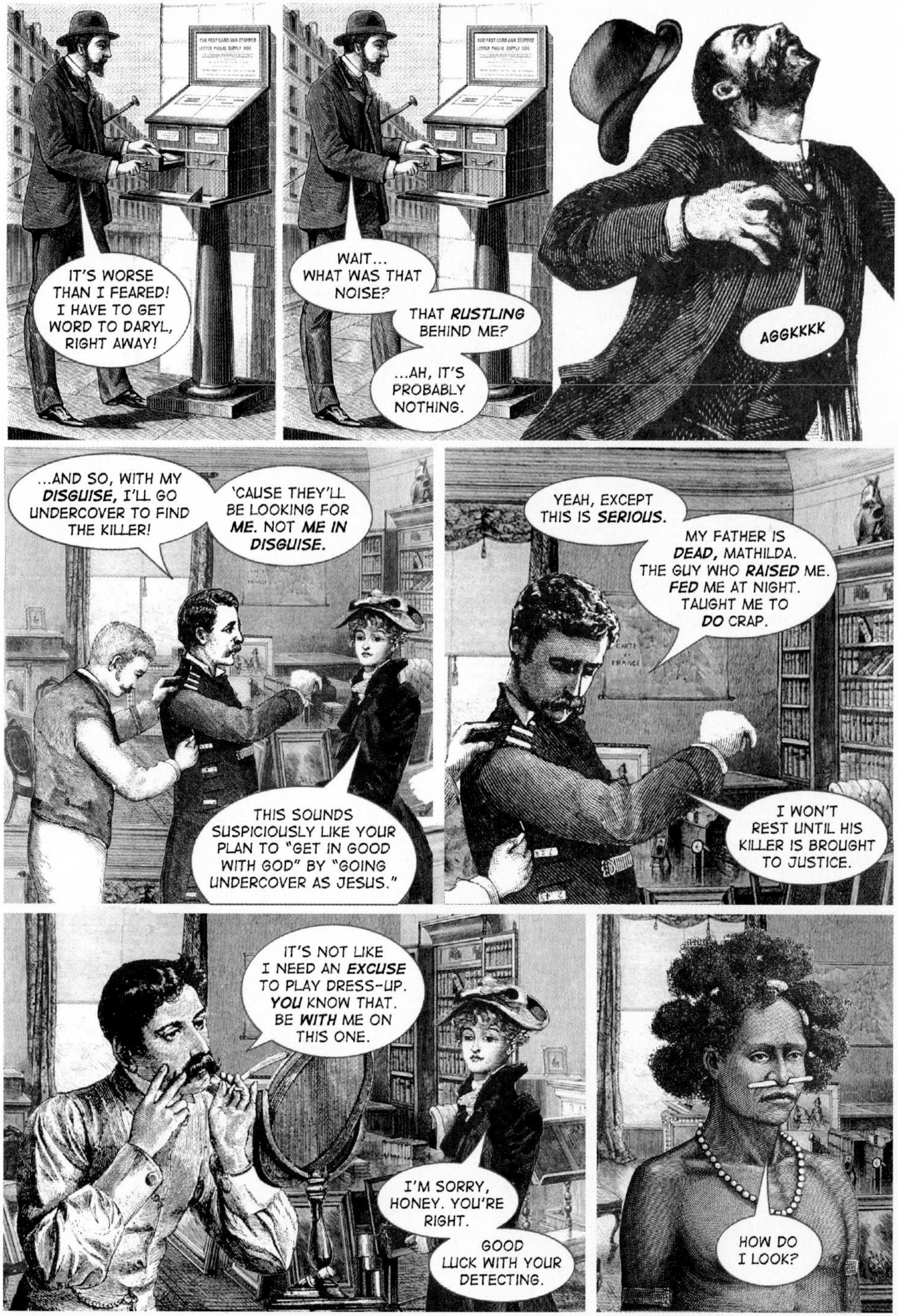
IT'S WORSE THAN I FEARED! I HAVE TO GET WORD TO DARYL, RIGHT AWAY!
WAIT... WHAT WAS THAT NOISE?
THAT RUSTLING BEHIND ME?
...AH, IT'S PROBABLY NOTHING.
AGGKKKK
...AND SO, WITH MY DISGUISE, I'LL GO UNDERCOVER TO FIND THE KILLER!
'CAUSE THEY'LL BE LOOKING FOR ME. NOT ME IN DISGUISE.
THIS SOUNDS SUSPICIOUSLY LIKE YOUR PLAN TO "GET IN GOOD WITH GOD" BY "GOING UNDERCOVER AS JESUS."
YEAH, EXCEPT THIS IS SERIOUS.
MY FATHER IS DEAD, MATHILDA. THE GUY WHO RAISED ME. FED ME AT NIGHT. TAUGHT ME TO DO CRAP.
I WON'T REST UNTIL HIS KILLER IS BROUGHT TO JUSTICE.
IT'S NOT LIKE I NEED AN EXCUSE TO PLAY DRESS-UP. YOU KNOW THAT. BE WITH ME ON THIS ONE.
I'M SORRY, HONEY. YOU'RE RIGHT.
GOOD LUCK WITH YOUR DETECTING.
HOW DO I LOOK?

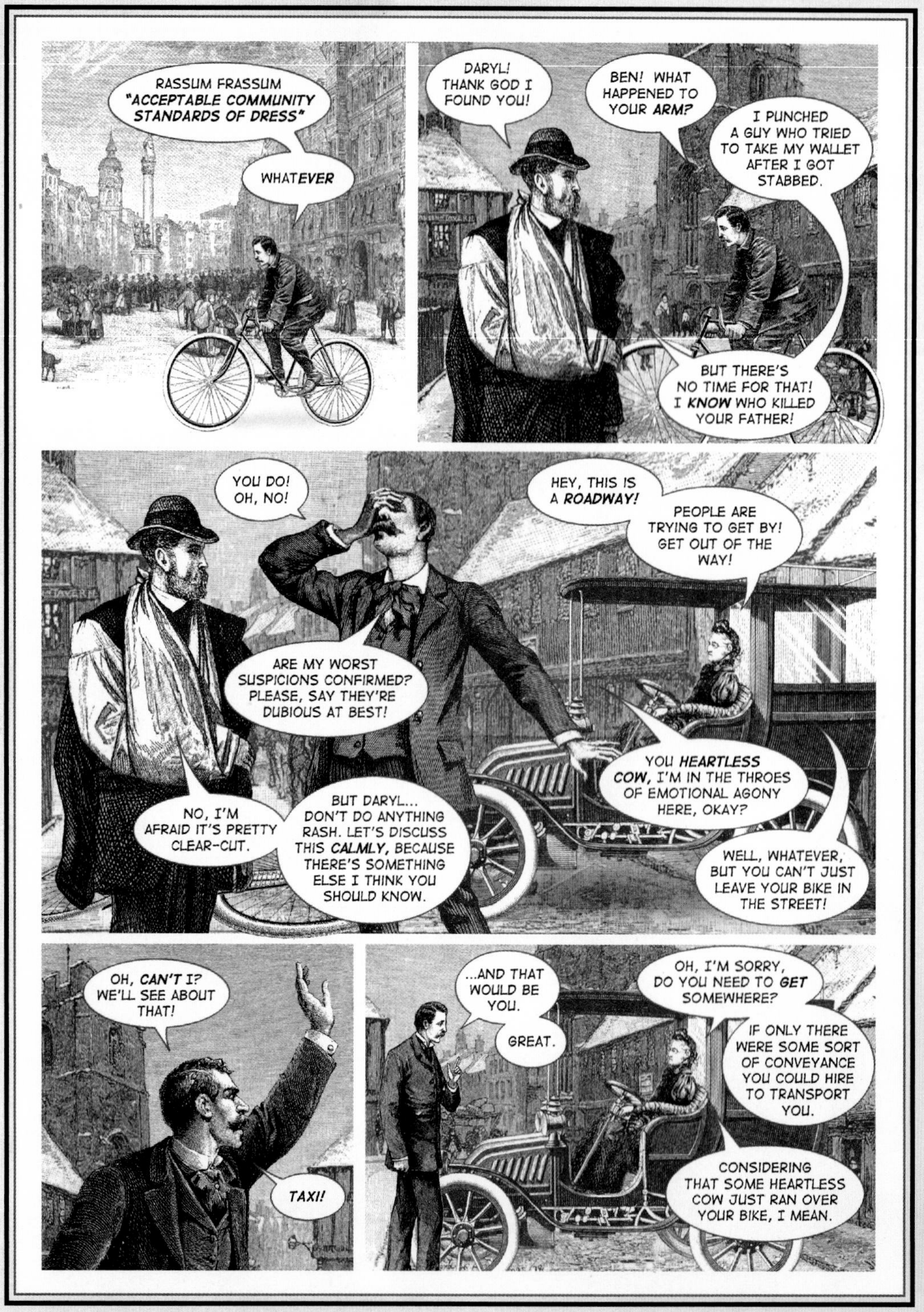
RASSUM FRASSUM "ACCEPTABLE COMMUNITY STANDARDS OF DRESS"
WHATEVER
DARYL! THANK GOD I FOUND YOU!
BEN! WHAT HAPPENED TO YOUR ARM?
I PUNCHED A GUY WHO TRIED TO TAKE MY WALLET AFTER I GOT STABBED.
BUT THERE'S NO TIME FOR THAT! I KNOW WHO KILLED YOUR FATHER!
YOU DO! OH, NO!
ARE MY WORST SUSPICIONS CONFIRMED? PLEASE, SAY THEY'RE DUBIOUS AT BEST!
NO, I'M AFRAID IT'S PRETTY CLEAR-CUT.
BUT DARYL... DON'T DO ANYTHING RASH. LET'S DISCUSS THIS CALMLY, BECAUSE THERE'S SOMETHING ELSE I THINK YOU SHOULD KNOW.
HEY, THIS IS A ROADWAY!
PEOPLE ARE TRYING TO GET BY! GET OUT OF THE WAY!
YOU HEARTLESS COW, I'M IN THE THROES OF EMOTIONAL AGONY HERE, OKAY?
WELL, WHATEVER, BUT YOU CAN'T JUST LEAVE YOUR BIKE IN THE STREET!
OH, CAN'T I? WE'LL SEE ABOUT THAT!
TAXI!
...AND THAT WOULD BE YOU.
GREAT.
OH, I'M SORRY, DO YOU NEED TO GET SOMEWHERE?
IF ONLY THERE WERE SOME SORT OF CONVEYANCE YOU COULD HIRE TO TRANSPORT YOU.
CONSIDERING THAT SOME HEARTLESS COW JUST RAN OVER YOUR BIKE, I MEAN.

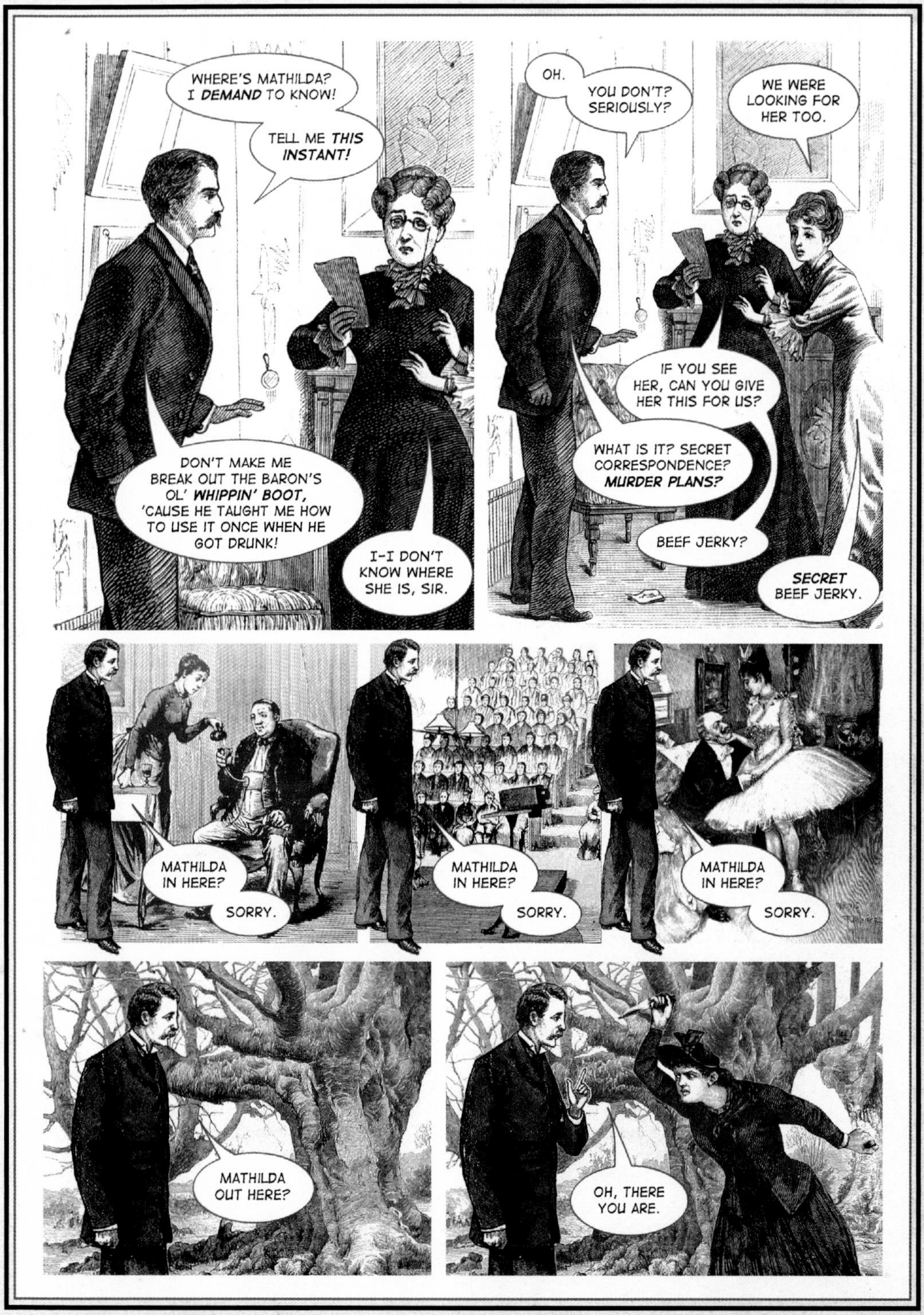
WHERE'S MATHILDA? I **DEMAND** TO KNOW!
TELL ME **THIS INSTANT!**
DON'T MAKE ME BREAK OUT THE BARON'S OL' **WHIPPIN' BOOT,** 'CAUSE HE TAUGHT ME HOW TO USE IT ONCE WHEN HE GOT DRUNK!
I-I DON'T KNOW WHERE SHE IS, SIR.
OH.
YOU DON'T? SERIOUSLY?
WE WERE LOOKING FOR HER TOO.
IF YOU SEE HER, CAN YOU GIVE HER THIS FOR US?
WHAT IS IT? SECRET CORRESPONDENCE? **MURDER PLANS?**
BEEF JERKY?
SECRET BEEF JERKY.
MATHILDA IN HERE?
SORRY.
MATHILDA IN HERE?
SORRY.
MATHILDA IN HERE?
SORRY.
MATHILDA OUT HERE?
OH, THERE YOU ARE.

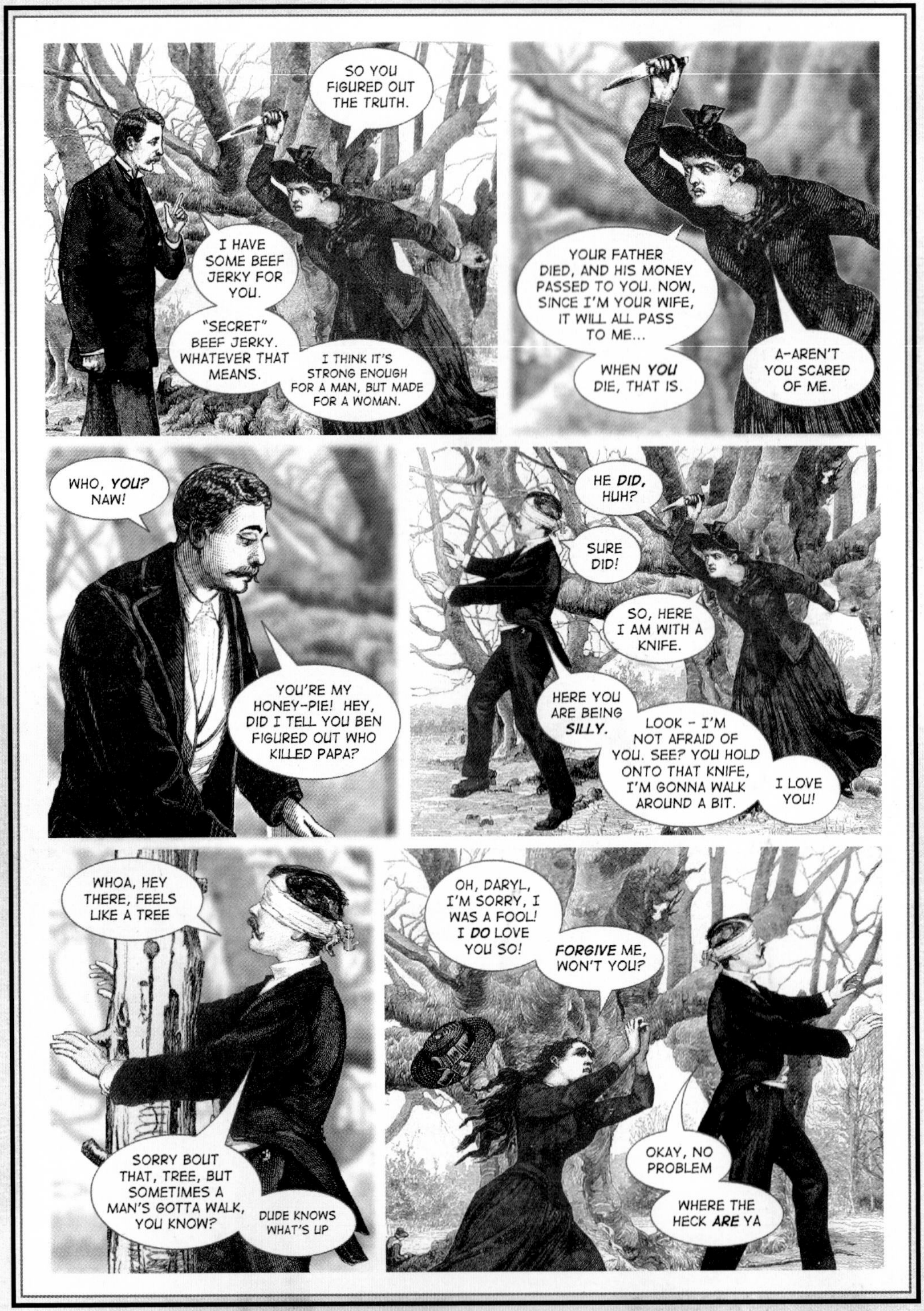
SO YOU FIGURED OUT THE TRUTH.
I HAVE SOME BEEF JERKY FOR YOU.
"SECRET" BEEF JERKY. WHATEVER THAT MEANS.
I THINK IT'S STRONG ENOUGH FOR A MAN, BUT MADE FOR A WOMAN.
YOUR FATHER DIED, AND HIS MONEY PASSED TO YOU. NOW, SINCE I'M YOUR WIFE, IT WILL ALL PASS TO ME...
WHEN YOU DIE, THAT IS.
A-AREN'T YOU SCARED OF ME.
WHO, YOU? NAW!
YOU'RE MY HONEY-PIE! HEY, DID I TELL YOU BEN FIGURED OUT WHO KILLED PAPA?
HE DID, HUH?
SURE DID!
SO, HERE I AM WITH A KNIFE.
HERE YOU ARE BEING SILLY.
LOOK - I'M NOT AFRAID OF YOU. SEE? YOU HOLD ONTO THAT KNIFE, I'M GONNA WALK AROUND A BIT.
I LOVE YOU!
WHOA, HEY THERE, FEELS LIKE A TREE
SORRY BOUT THAT, TREE, BUT SOMETIMES A MAN'S GOTTA WALK, YOU KNOW?
DUDE KNOWS WHAT'S UP
OH, DARYL, I'M SORRY, I WAS A FOOL! I DO LOVE YOU SO!
FORGIVE ME, WON'T YOU?
OKAY, NO PROBLEM
WHERE THE HECK ARE YA

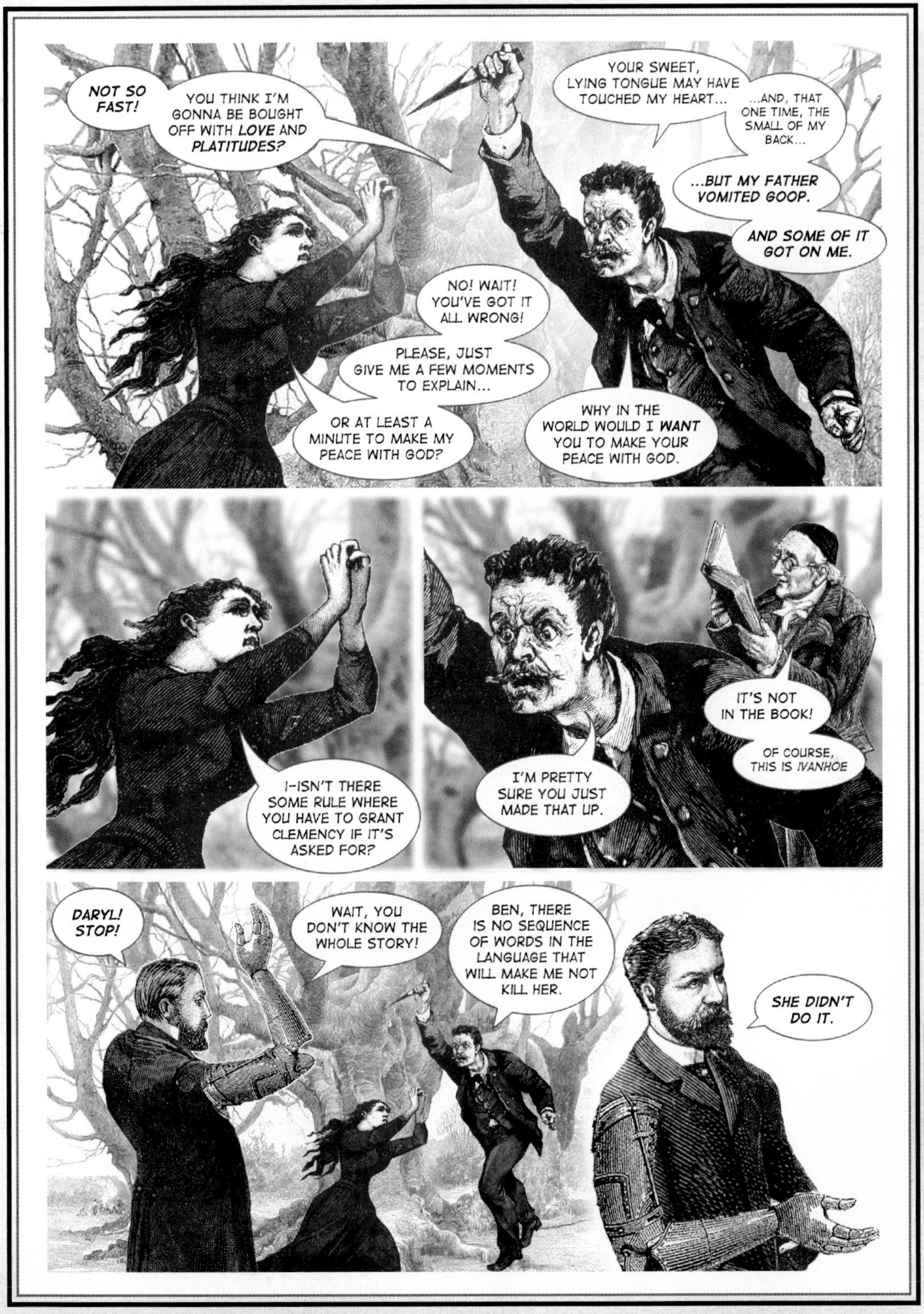
NOT SO FAST!
YOU THINK I'M GONNA BE BOUGHT OFF WITH LOVE AND PLATITUDES?
YOUR SWEET, LYING TONGUE MAY HAVE TOUCHED MY HEART...
...AND, THAT ONE TIME, THE SMALL OF MY BACK...
...BUT MY FATHER VOMITED GOOP.
AND SOME OF IT GOT ON ME.
NO! WAIT! YOU'VE GOT IT ALL WRONG!
PLEASE, JUST GIVE ME A FEW MOMENTS TO EXPLAIN...
OR AT LEAST A MINUTE TO MAKE MY PEACE WITH GOD?
WHY IN THE WORLD WOULD I WANT YOU TO MAKE YOUR PEACE WITH GOD.
I-ISN'T THERE SOME RULE WHERE YOU HAVE TO GRANT CLEMENCY IF IT'S ASKED FOR?
I'M PRETTY SURE YOU JUST MADE THAT UP.
IT'S NOT IN THE BOOK!
OF COURSE, THIS IS IVANHOE
DARYL! STOP!
WAIT, YOU DON'T KNOW THE WHOLE STORY!
BEN, THERE IS NO SEQUENCE OF WORDS IN THE LANGUAGE THAT WILL MAKE ME NOT KILL HER.
SHE DIDN'T DO IT.

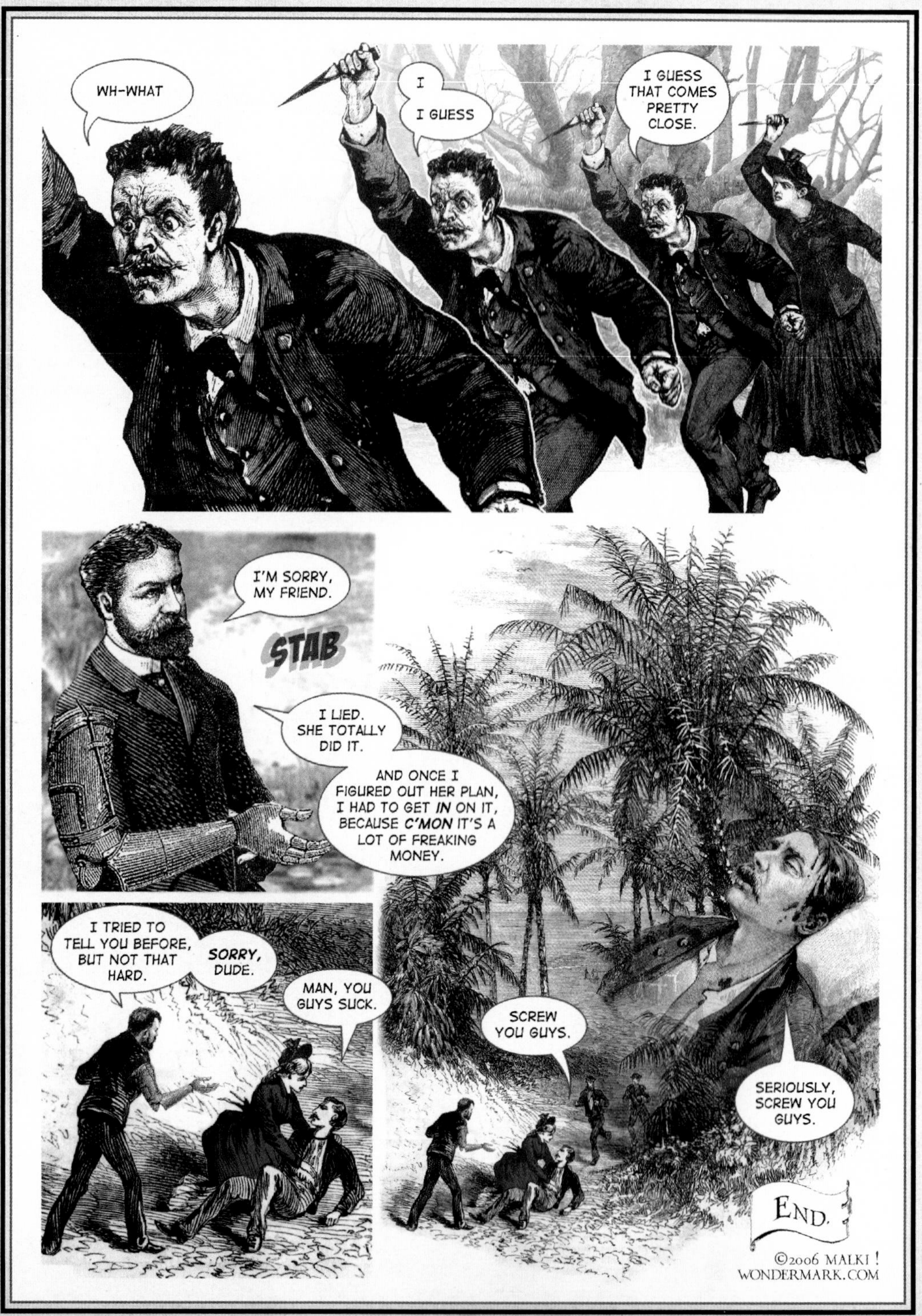
WH-WHAT
I
I GUESS
I GUESS THAT COMES PRETTY CLOSE.
I'M SORRY, MY FRIEND.
STAB
I LIED. SHE TOTALLY DID IT.
AND ONCE I FIGURED OUT HER PLAN, I HAD TO GET *IN* ON IT, BECAUSE *C'MON* IT'S A LOT OF FREAKING MONEY.
I TRIED TO TELL YOU BEFORE, BUT NOT THAT HARD.
SORRY, DUDE.
MAN, YOU GUYS SUCK.
SCREW YOU GUYS.
SERIOUSLY, SCREW YOU GUYS.
End.
©2006 MALKI !
WONDERMARK.COM

ADVOCACY SECTION.

The current era has seen the rise of so-called "hip" or "ironic" facial hair. Many of its practicioners grow voluminous beards without the proper licenses or training. By using these removable coupons when you happen across an offender, this dangerous practice can be eradicated.

IRONIC FACIAL HAIR CITATION
by Authority of Her Majesty's Commission on Poxes, Palsies, & Facial Hirsutism

Let it be known that:

_____

(Name; office; "dude with the messenger bag")

IS HEREBY CHARGED IN VIOLATION OF:

☐ *Local ordinance*   ☐ *State law*   ☐ *Simple good taste*

FOR THE FOLLOWING CHECKED OFFENSE(S):

☐ *Child-molester moustache*   ☐ *Overly "creative"*
☐ *Thinking handlebars are cool*   ☐ *Hitler killed that look*
☐ *Too-ambitious peach-fuzz*   ☐ *You're not Tom Selleck*
☐ *Homeless? Hippie? Hipster?*   ☐ *Seriously, it's gross*

CHECK IF APPROPRIATE: **REMEDY ADVISED:**

☐ *Damage to property*   ☐ *Total shave*
☐ *Injury / death*   ☐ *Stop trying so hard*
☐ *Moustache impounded*   ☐ *Join some sort of band*

REMARKS:

_____
_____
_____

IRONIC FACIAL HAIR CITATION
by Authority of Her Majesty's Commission on Poxes, Palsies, & Facial Hirsutism

Let it be known that:

_____

(Name; office; "dude with the messenger bag")

IS HEREBY CHARGED IN VIOLATION OF:

☐ *Local ordinance*   ☐ *State law*   ☐ *Simple good taste*

FOR THE FOLLOWING CHECKED OFFENSE(S):

☐ *Child-molester moustache*   ☐ *Overly "creative"*
☐ *Thinking handlebars are cool*   ☐ *Hitler killed that look*
☐ *Too-ambitious peach-fuzz*   ☐ *You're not Tom Selleck*
☐ *Homeless? Hippie? Hipster?*   ☐ *Seriously, it's gross*

CHECK IF APPROPRIATE: **REMEDY ADVISED:**

☐ *Damage to property*   ☐ *Total shave*
☐ *Injury / death*   ☐ *Stop trying so hard*
☐ *Moustache impounded*   ☐ *Join some sort of band*

REMARKS:

_____
_____
_____

You are welcome to use these coupons (or facsimiles thereof) in the service of curtailing beard violations, but considering that use of the coupons will, in effect, make you a duly deputized BEARD CONTROL OFFICER, you must also abide by the regulations associated with dispensing citations, as described on the reverse of the coupons.

92

IN ACCORDANCE WITH THE MAZE ACT OF 1841,
if the accused can complete this MAZE *inside of thirty seconds, he is to be released from all charges and the accuser shall be forced to pay damages.*

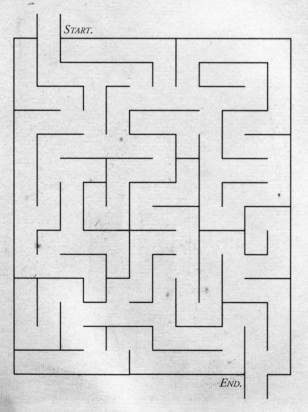

IN ACCORDANCE WITH THE MAZE ACT OF 1841,
if the accused can complete this MAZE *inside of thirty seconds, he is to be released from all charges and the accuser shall be forced to pay damages.*

DISPATCHES FROM WONDERMARK MANOR.

The title is that of a serialized prose adventure written at the frequency of two chapters per week and released on-line for your enjoyment. Two collected volumes have so far been published, and a third is in progress. Below, please find a representative sample of the tale; this selection is a new PROLOGUE to the entire series, and no prior knowledge of the story is required.

A KNOCK ON THE DOOR OF DESTINY.

I discovered quite early in my travels that when faced with a talkative companion, it is often good practise to remain quiet, thus allowing the other party to volunteer all sorts of tidbits you never would have thought to ask after.

The couple seated across the carriage had asked me at the cab-stand if we could share a lift into town: penny-pinchers both, from the looks of them. The husband (I presumed they had wed only because none besides each other would have them) was the fat, long-suffering type, constantly daubing his fore-head with a sopping cloth and jetting me clandestine looks intended to confer that he, like I, was *above* the sort of idle prattle blasting incessantly from the cake-spout of the beast chained by ring-finger to his side forever-more. I didn't buy his camaraderie, and not just because I'd not a shilling in goods nor coin about me; no, he wanted it both ways, Ol' Roley-Pole did—the social benefit of marriage, ostensibly proving to strangers that he wasn't a weirdo, but

retaining a cynical detachment characteristic of bachelor-hood as well. I might have sympathised with his aims, but I detested his two-facedness–if for no other reason than both of his faces had dripped sweat onto my battered valise as we'd clambered into the carriage.

The wife was an easy bird to peg; I'd had her number from the minute she fed me a fishhook-baited good-morning. It was a candy how-do-you-do, all sweetness with no substance, extended purely for the expectation of reprisal on my end. I knew that given such an opening, she'd fill the air with high-irritant baloney-blather the whole ride into town. But I'd just debarked a steamer filled bilge-to-balls with peacocks, and was in no mood for further yowling.

Silence proved allergic for her, however, and she didn't take long to get twitchy. Soon she was remarking on the trees passing by, the foulness of the weather, and the fashions of the orphan-corpses that cluttered the roads. With no factory work to keep them busy since that great, flesh-grinding accident at the

UNCLE.

THE CABBIE.

It was clear that he was repressing violent tendencies. Surely he wanted to kill his wife; *I* wanted to kill her, and I'd only known her ten minutes. Even the horses pulling our carriage likely felt the same murderous impulse towards their passenger. But lacking the stones to carry out the act, R. P. was living vicariously through the scruffy whelp-catchers even now pulling small, limp bodies from the road-ruts, visible for fleeting instants through the thin windows of our conveyance. *I could do the deed for the man,* I briefly thought, *but why?* I stood nothing to gain; it's not like his companionship promised to be an improvement. And it would serve my mission no good if I began offing citizens Willy H. Nilly on my first day back home.

budget bottling-plant had poisoned thousands of thrifty beverage-patrons and resulted in great liability for manufacturers at large, the mischievous urchins had become a menace to urban travel, swarming intersections and snarling traffic for hours with ropes twisted 'twixt axles and beautiful mares trotted out to distract the carriage-horses.

Thanks to the endless spurt of noise spiralling out of Hades, up through the Earth's crust, and bursting volcanically from the throat seated three feet from me, I learned that a thriving trade of whelp-catchers had developed during my long absence from these environs, and that it was a "despicable practice" employing "far more knives" than, perhaps, was strictly necessary.

It was in response to this latter point that the beleaguered lard-mass poured into the corner finally gathered the gumption to interject. "Well, it's not *so* bad, really," he harrumphed, almost too softly to be heard, and I thought at first that the objection was purely a face-saving performance for my benefit, trying to look "cool" for the "cool guy." In any case, the nattering nag sped clean through his pipe-up with nary a pause for breath, though I had at this point resigned myself to the fact that the woman was inhuman and did not actually require respiration.

"S-seriously," Role-Pole attempted again; "I think it's fine that they clean the streets of those disease-ridden brats. And to carry a cudgel in the service of one's employ—think of the lark *that* would be!"

True; once a resident of this city, I was now a stranger again—for the place had changed. The wharves where I had once hawked ropy stands of reconstituted cheese to tourists were now crowded with smelly buskers and smellier seaman-tarts; the alley-ways were bustling with the sweating crush of an ever-growing population; and even the very roads were paved lumpily with child-flesh. It was not the Easthillshireborough-upon-Flats that I had cherished; but it was *an* Easthillshireborough-upon-Flats, and so long as *this* Easthillshireborough-upon-Flats featured as wealthy of an uncle as the Easthillshireborough-upon-Flats of my memory and imagination, then this Easthillshireborough-upon-Flats would do just fine for me.

"Ooh, there's where that nice old man lives," the chatter-box burbled peskily, pressing a smeary finger against the window. At first I thought she was indicating a post-box on the corner, and after that I followed the line of her gesture towards a bakery-oven. Par for the course for sense, I figured—but with a jolt I suddenly made out the silhouette of a tall château, barely visible through the late-morning fog, far off atop Waverly Hill. My own destination.

Unfortunately, it seemed that the couple's stop was closer than the Hill; thus my plan to ditch them with the cab-fare unravelled quickly. In terms of spiteful comeup-

pance I settled for giving the woman a bit of a shove on her way out the door; she didn't fall and crack her brow on the cobble-stones, though, so I did her cell-mate no favours there. His parting glance was wistful, so I tried my best to make mine mocking.

Once the door slammed shut I was alone in the carriage, and the quiet was like a density in the air, pressing against my ear-drums and lovingly massaging my contempt for humanity.

The cab-ride to the Manor was long, and presumably expensive, and each moment that seemed a capital chance to gather my thoughts I found my mind drifting towards a fear of the impending fare—calculating wait times in dense areas, re-searching my valise for loose coins or stray bobbins, and constantly arguing down my urge to simply off the driver and be done with it. But I had no use for a hansom-cab reeking with fatty-odour and scorn, and disposing of the body would take up valuable time, when I needed to see Uncle soon. My stomach churned—I'd been feeding it grog-slop and peacock-poop for weeks while at sea, and the promise of lucrative horizons ahead was making my gut-area antsy.

When the carriage rumbled to a stop, high atop Waverly with the whole of Easthillshireborough-upon-Flats spread before us, I waited for the driver to open the cabin door before budging a muscle, hoping that those few extra seconds might invent a solution to the problem of the fare. They didn't; nor did the ten extra seconds I took ensuring that my valise was securely latched; nor did the solid eight minutes I spent searching the seat-cushion for an imaginary contact-lens. Finally, stumbling into the glare of midday and clutching my valise tightly at the ready with my striking-hand, I offered a lame apology for the delay.

"Don't mind it m'self," the cabbie shrugged. "You're on the ol' man's coin, I reckon? No worries from me, then—he's good on account, an' I'll add it to his tab."

"Yes," I said. "Yes, that's fine. Add it to his tab."

"Be nice to pay down the tab a little today, though," the cabbie added, after a moment in which nobody moved.

"Nice," said I. "But not compulsory?"

The cabbie spat and climbed back up to his seat. With the crack of a whip that I initially thought might have been meant for my back-side, the carriage clattered away, and I stood in front of the Manor.

The path-way to that wide front door was long and effortful, but the trek afforded a good examination of the grounds, which were well-groomed and verdant. It was a beautiful property, and I hoped that it was kept up largely by staff—as I had no plans, myself, to do a moment's labour ever again.

The thick brass knocker fell to the wood with a resounding thump. Voices and shuffling sounds emanated from within. As the moment neared, my heart began to race. Mission time.

"Coming, coming," I heard Uncle say as he approached the door. I fumbled with my valise and wrapped hot fingers around the thick oak handle of my father's old, blunt-edged hatchet.

Today, the Manor would be mine. ℘

SOME KIND OF WINDMILL.

PERHAPS it's the deep and emotional bonding we've shared that makes me reluctant to announce that this is the last page of the book. Perhaps it's the fact that the simple caress of your fingers on the pages has caused me to fall in love with you. Perhaps it's simply a matter of denial; I can't bear to admit that it's over, that there's nothing further, that you'd have to physically invert the book and begin reading again from this page forward in order to dredge any more wonderful experiences from this single, finite volume.

But there *is* something further, isn't there? There's an entire *world* outside these bleak pages, one full of SUNRISES and KITTY-CATS and late-night BURRITO RUNS and the horrible, creaking amble of us all towards DEATH. It is to that world that I am afraid I must release you to now. Thank you for reading, for your patronizing chuckles, and for gifting me with the kindness of your attention.

(If you have *not* actually read the book, but are reading this page anyhow for some reason, I cannot give you the same benediction. In fact, I claim hooks into you; I pull you in, and you cannot escape. Turn to the beginning at once and start reading properly—or else you will be guilty of a grave betrayal of AUTHOR-READER PRIVILEGE, the penalty for which is BURLY MEN coming to your house and putting ACTUAL HOOKS into you. Yes, we have those kinds of resources.)

But to those of you who have legitimately finished this book: It is for your pleasure, and your pleasure alone, that I have made it. Be well, and thank you.